Communication in the Church

Communication in the Church

A Handbook for Healthier Relationships

Thomas G. Kirkpatrick

An Alban Institute Book

ROWMAN & LITTLEFIELD
Lanham • Boulder • New York • London

Published by Rowman & Littlefield
A wholly owned subsidiary of The Rowman & Littlefield Publishing Group, Inc.
4501 Forbes Boulevard, Suite 200, Lanham, Maryland 20706
www.rowman.com

Unit A, Whitacre Mews, 26-34 Stannary Street, London SE11 4AB, United Kingdom

Copyright © 2016 by Rowman & Littlefield

British Library Cataloguing in Publication Information Available

Library of Congress Cataloging-in-Publication Data

Names: Kirkpatrick, Thomas G., author.
Title: Communication in the church : a handbook for healthier relationships /
    Thomas G. Kirkpatrick.
Description: Lanham : Rowman & Littlefield, an Alban Institute book,
[2016] | Includes bibliographical references and index.
Identifiers: LCCN 2016029137 (print) | LCCN 2016033014 (ebook) | ISBN
    9781566997881 (cloth : alk. paper) | ISBN 9781566997898 (pbk. : alk.
    paper) | ISBN 9781566997904 (Electronic)
Subjects: LCSH: Oral communication—Religious aspects—Christianity. |
    Christian leadership.
Classification: LCC BV4597.53.C64 K57 2016 (print) | LCC BV4597.53.C64
    (ebook) | DDC 262.001/4—dc23
LC record available at https://lccn.loc.gov/2016029137

♾™ The paper used in this publication meets the minimum requirements of
American National Standard for Information Sciences—Permanence of Paper
for Printed Library Materials, ANSI/NISO Z39.48-1992.

Printed in the United States of America

~

Contents

~

Acknowledgments

The path to publication can be long and arduous. For direction along the way, I am grateful to:

Rev. Dr. Duncan S. Ferguson, whose mentoring led me to move from a period of "activism" to a period of "writing" at this time in my life.

Dr. John Stewart and Dr. Lyle D. Vanderbroek, for their collegial support.

Rev. Robert Lewis, whose observation that the biggest challenge facing many congregations is communication breakdowns, reenergized my writing.

Kent First Presbyterian Church, who freed me to take a hiatus from responsibilities to concentrate on writing, especially Lois Parkinson, Carole Millam, Aubrey Fredericks, and Andy Ackerman.

Dr. Gordon S. Jackson, for his wise journalistic advice and detailed editorial assistance.

Sarah Stanton and her Rowman & Littlefield editorial team, for appreciating my patient, persistent pursuit of publication and for guiding the publication process.

I am also grateful to members of two support groups, one personal and one professional, for their care and curiosity.

And I am especially grateful to my family, for the openness, acceptance, warmth, and support that create remarkably healthy relationships. It is to them that I dedicate this book:

To my wife, Carol, and my children and their partners, Matt and Lisa, Michele and Joey, Chris and Nicole, and Juliann and Lawrence.

A shorter version of chapter 2, "'Another Committee? You Must Be Crazy!' Eight Guidelines for Leading Meetings," appeared in *Congregations* magazine, issues 3 & 4, 2013, 8–12.

Unless otherwise stated, all scripture quotations are from the New Revised Standard Version of the Bible, copyright © 1989, Division of Christian Education of the National Council of the Churches of Christ in the United States of America. Used by permission. All rights reserved.

The author and Rowman & Littlefield gratefully acknowledge permission to reprint excerpts from:

Death by Meeting: A Leadership Fable. . . About Solving the Most Painful Problem in Business, by Patrick Lencioni. Copyright © 2004 by Patrick Lencioni. Reprinted by permission of John Wiley & Sons, Inc.; permission conveyed through Copyright Clearance Center, Inc.

"How to Deal with Difficult Different," by John Stewart and Tiye Sherrod. Reprinted with the permission of John Stewart.

"Looking Back to 1968 for Riots' Root Causes," by Jerry Large, *The Seattle Times* newspaper, May 7, 2015. © Seattle Times Company. Republished with permission of Seattle Times Company; permission conveyed through Copyright Clearance Center, Inc.

The Powers That Be: Theology for a New Millennium, by Walter Wink. Copyright © 1998 by Augsburg Fortress Publishers. Used by permission.

The Wolf Shall Dwell with the Lamb: A Spirituality for Leadership in a Multicultural Community, by Eric H. F. Law. Copyright © 1993 by Chalice Press. Reprinted by permission of Chalice Press.

"The 75% Rule," by Corey Widmer. Reprinted from *The Presbyterian Outlook* magazine, Outpost Blog, June 19, 2013. © The Presbyterian Outlook. Used by permission.

"3 Reasons Why I Hate Diversity," by Christena Cleveland. Reprinted from *Christianity Today* magazine, Ed Stetzer Blog, February 19, 2015. © Christianity Today. Used by permission of Ed Stetzer and Christena Cleveland.

Introduction

An outreach ministry team seeks council approval to use mission auction monies for an elevator to make the congregation's building more accessible to people with disabilities. During council discussion of this request, the pastor questions the appropriateness of using mission funds for an elevator. After all, she points out, mission monies should be used only for the congregation's outreach ministries. Since no one from the outreach ministry team is present, council refers the request back for clarification.

This referral action seems sensible, except for an important misperception. The outreach ministry team thinks their request is rejected rather than returned for clarification. They also feel that the pastor exerts undue influence in the council's action. Feeling hurt, unappreciated, and ignored, the ministry team members angrily demand a meeting with the pastor. They also send her a feisty memo expressing their frustration, including a sharply worded demand that the council reconsider their request. They argue that people outside the congregation will use the elevator, including a number of organizations that meet at congregation's building (e.g., Alcoholics Anonymous and a preschool). Their rationale acknowledges that an elevator serves the congregation, and presents compelling ways that it also is an outreach ministry.

When the disgruntled outreach ministry team meets with the pastor, she corrects the misperception that the council denied their request. However, rather than talk past one another, play the blame game, let the conflict spiral out of control, further damage trust, or fracture relationships, the pastor listens to ministry team members' feelings of anger and hurt. She also checks her perception of what she heard them say and feel. Moreover, rather than try to convince these members that they no longer have reason to feel angry, the pastor calmly acknowledges their frustration.

This pastor's active listening and perception-checking skills, together with her non-anxious presence, defuse this potentially conflicted situation. It communicates to ministry team members that she takes them seriously. They feel confirmed, understood, and appreciated. It also communicates that the pastor tries to use her power and influence to serve and help rather than cajole and control.

This incident could have had a different, all-too-common outcome. Feelings of neglect, resentment, anger, blame, lack of appreciation, and frustration are often long lasting. Misperceptions, anxiety, passive-aggressive communication styles, power struggles, disconfirming messages, cultural insensitivity, ineffective listening, and destructive conflict often have dire consequences— individually, collectively, and synergistically. In fact, these communication breakdowns can spiral out of control, leading to such disgruntlement, dissension, distrust, and division that people angrily leave the congregation.

This scenario also illustrates how a variety of effectively employed communication behaviors can avert a potentially disastrous situation. Indeed, use of wise, timely, and effective interpersonal, small group, and organizational communication skills can make the difference between destructive, out-of-control, unhealthy relationships and constructive, manageable, healthy ones.

Fortunately, *most congregations are eager to help people create healthier ways of relating to one another.* Wide-ranging topics to consider include communication effectiveness in preaching, leading worship, embracing change, pastoral care and counseling, personnel and staff relations, and church administration. It is not feasible, however, to satisfactorily address all such topics in a single book. So, this book targets six topics that account for the vast majority of communication breakdowns in our congregations:

- *Building Relationships*
- *Leading Meetings*
- *Experiencing Trust*
- *Practicing Forgiveness*
- *Using Power*
- *Bridging Cultures*

It is also possible to offer wide-ranging advice on these topics. Again, discretion is required. So, the *goal of this book is to provide some simple guidelines that can go a long way to help people be more effective in how they build relationships, lead meetings, experience trust, practice forgiveness, use power, and bridge cultures.* Chapters 1 through 5 cover the first five topics. The sixth topic, bridging cultures, is incorporated into these chapters where appropriate. In short, to improve the quality of communication in your congregation and everyday life, you'll find guidelines for creating healthier relationships on each of these six topics.

Overview of This Book

Here's what you'll find in each chapter:

- *All-Too-Common Scenarios*—Real-life contexts
- *Sensible Guidelines*—Good-to-know learning
- *Practical Applications*—Good-to-go applications
- *Suggestions for Further Study*—Good-to-get resources

Further resource materials are at the back of the book, including appendixes, notes, a bibliography, and an index.

You may adapt this book's content and resources to a variety of religious communities, learning audiences, work contexts, educational programs, and training events. While it is geared particularly for clergy, laypersons, continuing educational planners, professors, students and scholars, business and community leaders, nonprofit organizations, consultants, and professional speakers will also find it useful.

Welcome to this exciting journey. I hope you'll find numerous "aha" moments along the way, and even more importantly, some practical skills that will enrich and deepen the relationships in your faith community and everyday life. I think our prospect of making communication work by helping people create healthier ways of relating to each other has promise, indeed!

CHAPTER ONE

Building Relationships

- *"I never know quite how to read Maya."*
- *"What do you mean you don't understand me? I've said it over and over again."*
- *"I wish she didn't get so defensive. It has to be her way or no way."*
- *"I get so irritated listening to him. Nothing I say matters, so I try to avoid talking to him."*
- *"When we have serious differences of opinion, we just talk around and around in circles."*

All-Too-Common Scenario

A worship ministry team gathers for its monthly meeting. Pleasantries and greetings are exchanged. As the group considers new business, results of a recently completed congregational survey reveal considerable interest in diversifying their congregation's style of worship and music. Many members indicate they would prefer more-contemporary worship and music rather than a traditional service.

In the discussion that follows, it becomes clear that the congregation's changing demographics, including growing generational, ethnic, and cultural diversity, are driving this shifting opinion about the congregation's worship and music preferences. Worship ministry team members realize the congregation is not big enough to have two worship services. They also are mindful of the congregation's commitment to being inclusive of all its members. Then someone makes a motion to change the congregation's traditional worship service to a blended one, a service encompassing both traditional and contemporary worship and music.

Immediately, tensions rise and heated discussion ensues. Feelings are hurt as irritation surfaces, and people become ineffective listeners and start engaging in personal attacks. In short, communication and decision-making break down, resulting in injury to relationships—and what could be a long-lasting legacy of unhappy memories.

Careless communication causes needless breakdowns in relational health. Barriers to building healthy relationships include feeling misunderstood, failure to check perceptions, judgmental attitudes, discounting feelings, finding fault, ignoring nonverbal communication, and ineffective listening.

Conversely, careful communication is vital to creating and fostering healthy relationships. For instance, feeling understood, being taken seriously, speaking for ourselves, expressing feelings, problem-solving, taking advantage of nonverbal communication, and listening effectively all play important roles in how we relate to one another.

While people's understanding of the church varies, as does their interpretation of its mission, communication is vital to creating and fostering healthy relationships in our congregations. So, *it pays to be careful with our communication!* Fortunately, most people are eager to become more effective in how they relate to one another. So, here are six sensible, practical guidelines that can go a long way toward helping you and the members of your congregation learn how careful communication builds healthy relationships.

Guidelines for Building Relationships

1. Perception Check.

I find that about 75 percent of careless communication happens when we unconsciously assume that we understand each other. In other words, without even realizing it, we wrongly assume that we understand one another. It's like getting into an argument, and after forty-five minutes of frustrating, spiraling conversation, saying, "Oh, is *that* what you mean?" Supreme Court judge Louis D. Brandeis, who knew a thing or two about conflict, said, "Nine-tenths of the serious controversies which arise in life result from misunderstanding."

Combining research findings from the fields of neuroscience, psychology, and spiritual development, Andrew Newberg and Mark Robert Waldman reach a similar conclusion, particularly when it comes to abstract concepts:

Abstract concepts can also be sources of miscommunication and conflict because we rarely explain to others what these complex terms mean to us. Instead we make the mistake of assuming that other people share the same meanings that we have imposed on our words. They don't.[1]

An example these researchers cite is the word "God." They discovered that 90 percent of people's definitions significantly differ, including among people with the same religious or spiritual background. Moreover, most people aren't aware of these fundamentally unique perceptions.

Newberg and Waldman recommend that we speak slowly and briefly, listen deeply and observe nonverbal cues, and stay in the present moment and express appreciation. They also have this advice:

When an important abstract concept comes up in conversation, take a few minutes to explore what it means to each of you. Don't take your words, or the other person's, for granted. When you take time to converse about important values and beliefs, clarifying terms will help both of you avoid later conflicts and confusion.[2]

Here's a conversation that illustrates the way meaning emerges between people and the value of taking time to check each other's perception in everyday communication:

Maya: Hey, Carole, you're something else.

Carole: You mean I'm strange?

Maya: No, you're unique.

Carole: You mean I'm odd?

Maya: No, you are special.

Carole: You mean I'm different?

Maya: Well, I think you're neat!

Carole: Oh, you like me!

Maya: Yeah, I guess I do!

Unfortunately, when we assume we understand each other's meaning, too often we fail to take the time to listen carefully enough to perceive accurately what another means to say. In his book *Caring Enough to Hear and Be Heard*, David Augsburger offers the helpful notion of *bracketing our judgments*.[3] We can momentarily put our own views on hold—"in brackets"—while we make sure we understand another's meaning. What's needed is the communication skill of *perception checking*: that is, paraphrasing our understanding of each other's meaning.

A useful practice is to say something like, "So the way you see it is . . ." and put in our own words what we understand the other person to mean. We may also ask our conversational partner, "Please tell me what you think I mean." There is one further step we need to take. We need to be sure we wait for each other's response, for often we haven't accurately understood to the other's satisfaction. Maya and Carole are good examples of doing so in their conversation.

So, rather than unconsciously assuming we understand one another, it pays to check our perceptions by paraphrasing one another's meanings. This is especially important when our conversation includes strongly held ideas or below-the-surface feelings. It may well be the case that pausing and taking the time to *check our perception* of what each of us is getting at is the single most important skill we can employ to help us create healthy relationships where we feel understood and taken seriously. Saint Augustine was right when he said, "Hear the other side."

2. Create Meaning.

"What do you mean you don't understand me? I already explained myself three times." Such frustration is common when we try to communicate as if creating understanding were a speaker-centered action in which we attempt to transfer our ideas from one head to the other. It is difficult to understand one another's meaning using this limited, one-way, bow-and-arrow approach. It *oversimplifies* the communication process. It doesn't take feedback into account. And yet, neither should we attempt to communicate as if creating meaning were a message-centered interaction in which we exchange information. This two-way, ping-pong approach *distorts* what normally happens in our communication.

The communication process is more complex than either shooting our ideas to someone or batting ideas back and forth. So, it pays to be careful and approach communication as a dynamic, meaning-centered transaction in which a relationship emerges between people.[4] Effective interpersonal communication is a multidimensional meeting between people.

In *Caring Enough to Hear and Be Heard*, Augsburger puts it this way:

"Experiencing the other side" is, in Martin Buber's words, "the heart of dialogue." Feeling any experience from the side of the other person as well as from one's own side can make the experience twice as rich. Seeing any event through the other's eyes in addition to one's own makes the scene truly three-dimensional.[5]

Augsburger continues:

> The art of dialogue is openness to the other side, a willingness to enter the other's turf and to explore it until it is familiar territory. The heart of dialogue is coming to value a place near the center, on the boundary, where the other person's perspective is valued alongside my own. At this point of meeting, I become as concerned for the clarity of the other's stance as for my own; as willing to contribute an argumentative point to the other side as to assert one on my own; as committed to supporting the other's right to be at his or her position as I am to claim my own.[6]

So remember, how we approach communication affects our ability to understand one another's meaning. The payoff for careful communication is a capacity to connect with people in meaningful, satisfying dialogue. Lucius Annaeus Seneca is on target when he observes, "One of the most beautiful qualities of true friendship is to understand and to be understood."

The conversation between Maya and Carole illustrates the dynamic way meaning evolves between people who have a commitment to dialogue and a healthy, emerging relationship.[7] Notice that their conversation illustrates not only how meaning evolves *between* people, but also how meaning emerges *within* people. Sometimes we aren't sure what we mean when we begin a conversation. Our understanding of our own meaning often emerges as our relationship with another person develops. Indeed, communication between people is relational communication. That's what we see happening between Maya and Carole in their conversation. It takes work and time and patience to experience mutual understanding with your conversational partners. And just think how the complexity of communication between people magnifies in three-way, and small-group, and organizational communication. Complexity is exponential.

3. *Diminish Defensiveness* and *Foster a Supportive Climate.*
In research conducted in problem-solving groups, communication scholar Jack Gibb discovered six sets of supportive and defensive climates[8]:

- Description and evaluation
- Problem-orientation and control
- Spontaneity and strategy
- Empathy and neutrality

- Equality and superiority
- Provisionalism and certainty.

This finding from Gibb remains *the* single most useful insight I've discovered in all my years of study, teaching, and research in the field of interpersonal and small-group communication. Let's briefly examine each pair of supportive and defensive communication climates. Notice how being careful to use supportive communication behaviors creates healthier relationships than carelessly using defensive ones.

Description and Evaluation

In our congregations, as well as in our personal relationships, it helps to diminish defensiveness and foster supportiveness when we communicate with *description* rather than *evaluation*. It helps when people describe their own views rather than tell others what they ought to think. It is the difference between using I-messages ("I think") rather than you-messages ("you ought to" or "you should think").

If failure to paraphrase accounts for a majority of careless communication, then a good portion of the balance comes from being closed-minded or judgmental—attitudes that make it very difficult to experience healthy relationships. It can be helpful to get into the habit of using I-messages, or of owning our own judgments. We can say, for example, "The way I see it is this . . . How do you see it?" If, however, we say, "Here's the way you should see it . . . ," we are in effect speaking not just for ourselves, but for the other person as well. If we speak for someone else and find it is not what she or he believes, then we can expect defensiveness in return. Part of their very being, their views, are denied, misrepresented, or falsified. Others may not, and *often* do not, see things the same way we do. There's hardly anything that pushes our buttons faster than having our selfhood violated. When that happens, relational health is understandably a frequent casualty.

Here is an example that illustrates the value of using I-messages. One time I attended a university student convention during which there was a panel discussion on student-congregation relations. A student from the audience asked this question: "People in my congregation don't care about what we students think. How can you get them to change?" A wise panelist answered, "I suggest when you return home and speak with congregational leaders, that you lead with the indicative rather than the imperative." The panelist was, of course, referring to English grammar. Remember what the indicative mood is? It is used to describe something. The imperative mood, on the other hand, is used for "shoulds" or "oughts"—for commands.

What the panelist suggests the student do is to return home and communicate their concerns without fostering defensiveness. For example, the student could say to congregational leaders back home, "I would like to have a greater voice in our congregation's life and ministry" (a descriptive I-statement). "Is this something that you would welcome?" (a request for inclusion). Rather than being discounted or ignored, the student stands a good chance of being valued and taken seriously. Church leaders and congregations usually listen when someone describes a genuine concern; but they can feel threatened when they feel accused or are told what they ought to do.

Lead with the indicative, rather than the imperative. It helps to use descriptive language, I-messages, rather than evaluative, you-ought-to messages.

Problem-Orientation and Control

The difference here is between taking an open, collaborative approach and working toward a predetermined solution. Problem-orientation involves mutual exploration whereas control involves hidden agendas. Do we work toward a mutually agreeable alternative and thereby foster a supportive problem-solving climate, or do we keep pushing our own views and thereby generate defensiveness? We'll also see the importance of problem solving in handling conflict later in this chapter. And in chapter 2, guideline 7 shows how groups can profit from collaborative leadership for group discussion and decision-making.

Spontaneity and Strategy

Spontaneity involves going with the conversational flow, whereas strategy involves trying to manipulate the conversation. Being willing to consider other viewpoints is a supportive behavior, whereas trying to win our own point with unfair tactics precipitates defensiveness.

Empathy and Neutrality

Empathy involves active listening, whereas neutrality ignores or refuses to consider another's point of view. Refusal to be taken seriously can feel like a vicious slap in the face; it can be hurtful; it can discount and threaten our very being. If our views don't matter, then why continue to talk? Remember, communication requires a *commitment to dialogue*.

Equality and Superiority

The difference here is between believing both sides have valid views and taking a "mine's best" or "mine's right" attitude. It is the way we practice this teaching from Galatians: "In Christ there is no Jew or Greek, slave or citizen, male or female. All are one in Christ Jesus" (Galatians 3:28, The Inclusive Bible). From a Christian perspective, there's simply no place for bias or prejudice or superiority in matters of basic humanness. In reality, Christ came to break down barriers based on class, ethnicity, race, and gender. In such matters, no one is better or worse than anyone else. Claims of superiority often lead to hostility, to defensiveness, to hurt, and to division.

We demonstrate our commitment to equality every time we join together around the Lord's Table. We meet as One in Christ. To do otherwise, to claim a position of privilege, brings dissension. Christ's body becomes divided.

Provisionalism and Certainty

Provisionalism has to do with keeping our ideas tentative and open to change rather than being absolute and closed to change. Certainty brings defensiveness because if we are unable to influence each other, then why talk at all? Communication ends when a "know-it-all" attitude begins.

Our congregations will greatly benefit by paying attention to these six sets of supportive and defensive communication behaviors. Why do people get defensive in our congregations? Because they feel judged, controlled, manipulated, ignored, excluded, and cut off. And what fosters a supportive climate? An atmosphere that is accepting, collaborative, free flowing, attentive, valuing, and inclusive.

4. Use Both Verbal and Nonverbal Communication.

One of our careless communication habits is a tendency to underestimate the power of nonverbal communication in creating healthier relationships. In reality, nonverbal communication is a greater resource for understanding one another than verbal communication. For example, our facial expressions and tone of voice contribute far more to successful communication than words alone.

What percentage do you think words contribute to successful communication? How about facial expressions and tone of voice? In particular, how about communication situations such as the conversation between Maya and Carole wherein Maya's feelings about liking Carole were uncertain? Communication researchers have found that facial expressions can contribute as much as 55 percent to the meaning we create about being liked, tone of voice up to 38 percent, and words as little as 7 percent.[9] This doesn't mean that words are unimportant, or that nonverbal factors are all that matter, or that these percentages are applicable in constructing meaning in all social situations. But it does mean that we need to pay a lot of attention to our nonverbal communication. In short, it is easy to misunderstand the meaning of words without seeing facial expressions and hearing tone of voice.

It also is important to recognize that our nonverbal communication can repeat, contradict, replace, complement, or accent our verbal communication. And when we are unsure about what words mean, we tend to pay more attention to nonverbal cues.

When I quiz people about their understanding of these three factors—facial expressions, tone of voice, and words—most are surprised to learn how important facial expressions and tone of voice are compared with words alone. The discovery that such a huge part of our communication capacity comes from nonverbal factors is an aha moment for most people. Then dawns a new revelation: we underuse this huge nonverbal communication advantage.[10]

Both speakers and listeners can pay a lot more attention to nonverbal factors. Engaged facial expressions show people what our words mean. Remember: *words* don't mean; *people* mean! Variation in our tone of voice, particularly in our pitch, rate, and volume, creates interest and enthusiasm in what we say. Communication research consistently finds that enthusiasm is the number one predictor of credibility and competency.[11] These verbal and nonverbal communication resources work together to establish trust people have in what we say. What we say and how we communicate it matter in establishing our reliability and competency.

It also is important to pay attention to ways cultural differences affect how we communicate and build healthy relationships. Looking someone in the eye is a good example. In some cultures it is a sign of respect and in other cultures it is disrespectful. Tone of voice can convey patience or impatience, receptivity or skepticism differently among cultures. How we regulate time also varies between cultures. Some cultures pay close attention to the clock and adhere closely to a schedule whereas other cultures pay attention to relational time such as completing a conversation rather than keeping to a schedule. How we use silence, touch, personal space, and gestures also varies culturally.

Cultural differences also affect our relationships in how we express emotions. In collectivist cultures, for example, anger and disgust are not expressed in public or in the presence of someone with higher status, whereas in individualistic cultures anger or disgust are expressed alone or in front of others. Moreover, Western individualist cultures tend to rely more on direct, explicit verbal content of what people say whereas Eastern collectivist cultures put more emphasis on indirect, implicit nonverbal context of how people communicate.[12] Likewise, as intercultural communication scholars Stella Ting-Toomey and Leeva Chung point out:

> Some cultural groups (e.g., German and Swiss work teams) may believe that addressing a workplace problem directly and assertively can be stimulating and spark further new ideas. Other cultural groups (e.g., Chinese and Korean work teams) may believe that approaching a conflict issue indirectly and tactfully can facilitate a more harmonious communication process.[13]

They also recommend that we learn to be flexible intercultural communicators by managing cultural differences adaptively and creatively in a wide variety of situations:

> We must be highly imaginative in our assessment of the intercultural contact situation. We also must be behaviorally nimble to decide whether to adapt, to maintain the same posture, or to expect the other person to adapt to our behaviors—depending upon the intentions, process, goals, and people involved in the interactive situation. It takes a flexible mindset to combine the best practices of both cultures to arrive at a creative, synergistic solution.[14]

Later in this chapter we will see how flexible conflict management uses culture-sensitive communication skills to navigate the conflict process adaptively and constructively.

This theme of bridging cultures and the role it plays in creating healthy relationships continues in upcoming chapters. In chapter 2, we will see how cultural sensitivity leads to more inclusive group participation and decision-making in a multicultural community. Then in chapter 3 we will learn how a synthesis of seemingly contradictory value differences builds trust through finding common ground in cross-cultural situations. In chapter 4 we will discover how collectivistic and individualistic worldviews influence people's experience of forgiveness. Finally, we'll examine ethical guidelines for people with similar worldviews as well as transcultural ethics on a global scale in chapter 5. How power differences affect multicultural communication, how we relate to difference, and how to overcome reluctance to welcoming diversity also are covered in chapter 5.

5. Raise Your Listening IQ.

How well do you listen? How well do you think we listen to one another in our congregations, homes, schools, and workplaces?

Consider this helpful perspective from James: "Let everyone be quick to listen, and slow to speak" (James 1:19). Consider also the preferential treatment Jesus gives to listening. Did you know that in the four gospels, Jesus is asked nearly two hundred questions? Guess how many he answers directly? Fewer than ten. Sometimes Jesus answers questions indirectly, sometimes he remains silent, and sometimes he answers a question by asking another question. Jesus prefers to ask questions rather than to provide answers. Asking questions is central in the life and ministry of Jesus. In the four gospels, he asks more than three hundred questions, far more than he is asked.[15] In conversation, questions function to invite and facilitate discussion, gain information, inspire learning, challenge opposing views, prompt reactions, stimulate thinking, reveal motivation, precipitate action, disarm defensiveness, and build closeness.

If Jesus asks so many questions, and he answers so few, then he does a lot of listening in his life and teaching, thus embodying James's counsel to "be quick to listen, and slow to speak."

How much listening goes on in your personal, professional, and social life? Statistically speaking, we do a lot of listening in our daily lives. We actually spend the majority of our waking hours communicating, and of this time, listening accounts for nearly half.[16] As often is the case, however, statistics don't tell the whole story. We can be as listener-challenged as the worship ministry team. Perhaps, then, it is more accurate to say that we spend a lot of time doing something at which we're not very adept.

Fortunately, we congregational leaders and members can learn healthier ways of relating to each another by acquiring the knowledge and skills to improve our listening behavior—*to raise our listening IQ*. We can help people be more careful in how they listen by paying attention to these six topics:

- Listening facts and fallacies
- Listening benefits
- Listening styles
- Listening goals
- Listening process
- Listening power

Listening Facts and Fallacies

Many people learn to listen without formal training. Consequently, we fail to learn our listening ABCs. Often people pick up fallacies about listening that go undetected and result in acquiring poor listening skills. What are some of these listening facts and fallacies?

First, many people confuse hearing and listening. They think that hearing and listening are the same. In reality, hearing is what we do with our ears, while listening is what we do between our ears. We hear with our ears and listen with our minds. Listening is a mental activity while hearing is a physical ability.

Other common listening fallacies include thinking that listening is passive, innate, automatic, simple, and one-way. Let's briefly examine each of these next five common misconceptions.

It is easy to get trapped into thinking that we can just sit back and listen without exerting effort. Listening requires active engagement. A related fallacy is thinking we are born with the ability to listen. In truth, listening is not an innate endowment. Rather, it is a skill to be learned. It is also fallacious to think that listening is an automatic reflex. In reality, listening is an intentional activity requiring a commitment to dialogue by both speakers and listeners. Another common misconception is thinking we can simply pick up what a speaker says without accounting for the complexities involved in human communication. Communication involves more than just words. We've already learned that nonverbal factors such as facial expressions and tone of voice account for a majority of our communication resources. Finally, as we saw in guideline 2, listening requires more than both a one-way transfer of ideas from speaker to listener and a two-way batting of ideas back and forth between speakers and listeners. Frequent perception checking is required as meaning evolves and emerges during a conversation.

Our next two listening fallacies concern how we learn to listen. If listening is a skill to be learned, then how do we develop listening proficiency? Typically, our language arts education concentrates on learning to read and to write. Learning to speak and to listen are frequently ignored, or, at best, undervalued. In our daily lives, we spend nearly three-quarters of our communication time speaking and listening and only about one-quarter reading and writing. Moreover, listening accounts for nearly as much time as speaking, reading, and writing combined. In truth, reading, writing, speaking, and listening are each vitally important skills to be learned. But it also is important to realize that learning to listen does not happen automatically when we learn to read. In fact, we learn to read and listen differently. Just as reading and writing are considered separate language arts skills, so also speaking and listening merit separate consideration.

Another fallacy is the common belief that listening means agreement. Listening demands a willingness to understand ideas different from our own, not necessarily agreement with them. Often we simply see things differently from one another. We need to separate listening to *understand* someone's ideas from listening to *decide* whether or not we agree with them. Listening to *understand* and listening to *decide* are but two purposes of listening. We also listen for our own *enjoyment*, and we listen *empathically* to help others. Not surprisingly, three of these four kinds of listening mirror the three primary purposes of speaking: to *inform*, to *persuade*, and to *entertain*. We'll return to these different types of listening later.

Our final listening fallacy is thinking that the costs of careless listening are minimal. We can miss out on immense benefits that come with effective listening. In *Perceptive Listening*, Florence Wolff and Nadine Marsnik comment: "When we listen perceptively, we learn, grow, and prosper. Listening to learn leads to success in the classroom, the corporate world and as a professional."[17] Whether in our congregations, businesses, social service organizations, or governmental agencies, the consequences of poor listening behaviors are costly in terms of time, productivity, and money. Relationships are broken, conflict is avoided, cultural sensitivity is ignored, and power is abused.

We have now examined ten listening fallacies and facts. Check your own basic knowledge about listening and see if you can raise your listening IQ. Here is a summary of our listening ABCs:

Fallacies	Facts
Hearing and listening are closely related	Hearing is physical; listening is mental
Listening is a passive activity	Listening is an active activity
Listening is innate	Listening is learned
Listening is simple	Listening is complex
Listening is an automatic reflex	Listeners must be trained
Speakers transmit ideas to listeners	Listeners and speakers create meaning
Reading is more important than listening	Listening and reading are both important
We learn to listen when we learn to read	We learn to listen and read differently
Listening means agreement	Listening demands openness
Costs of careless listening are minimal	Benefits of effective listening are immense

Listening Benefits

Listening skills are valuable commodities. They are beneficial in our personal, professional, and social lives. We've just examined the fallacy of thinking that the costs of careless listening are minimal, and the reality that the benefits of effective listening are immense. Florence Wolff, Nadine Marsnik, William Tacey, and Ralph Nichols put it this way:

> Listening is a magnetic, enriching, and rewarding experience. We are drawn magnetically to those who will lend us an ear. We are enriched when we take the time to listen to those who need an ear. We are rewarded and we prosper by learning and personally growing as we use our ears.[18]

Elsewhere, Wolff and Marsnik comment on the importance and value of listening perceptively in our professional lives:

> Educational professionals—both administrators and instructors—must personally learn to listen, as well as to teach the art of listening to other professionals and businesspeople.
>
> Medical and legal professionals will prosper when they learn to view patients and clients as whole human beings rather than as cases. Listening skills ultimately can help avoid loss of life and lawsuits.
>
> As perceptive listeners, religious professionals can reach out with greater spiritual comfort and direction.[19]

Effective listening skills also pay huge dividends in our personal and social relationships, including our congregation-related involvement. They enrich and enhance a whole variety of experiences in our congregational relationships. For example, they help us:

- Develop satisfying interpersonal relationships
- Handle conflict
- Lead and participate in meetings
- Use power appropriately
- Achieve cultural competency.

In short, our personal, professional, and social relationships all benefit when we learn and practice good listening skills.

Listening Styles

Careful listeners pay attention to how we listen and process information. Just as people differ widely in the ways they speak and present information, so too do they have different ways of listening and processing information. Therefore, we need to pay attention to how people listen and adapt to differences in the way people process information.

A majority of people are *visual listeners*. They look directly at a speaker and say, "I see what you mean," or "I get the picture." Other people are *auditory listeners*. They look down or side-to-side in order to concentrate, and often say, "I hear you," and "Does that sound right?" A less common but no less important preference involves *tactile or kinesthetic listening*. People preferring this approach look within to sense what is said: "I grasp what you say," "That feels right," "Let me run this by you," or "That touches me."

Recognition of diverse listening styles affects our ability to communicate in several important ways.

First, we need to pay attention to the way people process information and align our communication accordingly. In other words, we can make our communication behavior congruent with people's listening styles. For example, when we're speaking to a group of people, we can employ diverse, inclusive, and multiple ways to communicate—with words, gestures, handouts, Power-Point presentations, or activities.

Second, when we expect people to come to a meeting prepared to participate, we can offer a variety of ways for them to prepare and make their contributions. As a university faculty professor, I learned to tailor my homework assignments to my students' varied learning preferences. For example, in place of completing written work, I may offer the option of doing a project or watching a movie. I also created a variety of ways for my students to demonstrate their understanding and competency in addition to written exams, such as oral reports, class participation, video presentations, and reflection papers. Likewise, we can offer a variety of ways for people to prepare and contribute work in the congregation such as written reports, handouts, projects, oral presentations, e-mails, and PowerPoints. Such variety increases people's capacity for involvement and offers flexibility in the ways people use their gifts for ministry.

Third, it's important to know why some people do things with their hands when listening to a presentation. It helps me understand why some people bring their knitting to meetings—they are tactile learners. It isn't that they are distracted, or disengaged, or rude, or ignoring the speaker. On the contrary, knitting helps them to concentrate and to process information. The speaker can realize that they are paying attention after all. It also explains why I seldom look at notes I take during presentations afterward—my tactile, note-taking mode helps me process information as I listen. I'm not listening to remember; rather, I'm listening to understand. Here, too, if a speaker understands why I'm taking notes, then she or he realizes I am paying attention to and benefiting from what they have to say.

Listening Goals

Just as speakers must learn to inform, to persuade, and to entertain, so also listeners must learn to understand, to decide, and to appreciate. We need to pay attention to our listening goals. There are different purposes or types of listening that we must learn and master.

Most human communication is purposeful. There are reasons we initiate conversation and there are outcomes we expect. Speakers typically seek to inform, to persuade, or to entertain their listeners. Not surprisingly, listeners typically seek to understand, to decide, or to enjoy what speakers say. For example, notice how Maya and Carole's pursuit of making sense of their relationship requires multiple types or purposes of listening. Their patient, time-consuming work as perceptive listeners enables them to create *understanding* between one another, to *decide* what Maya thinks and feels about Carole, and to *enjoy* their newly defined relationship.

What is surprising, however, is how little attention we pay to purposeful listening. In public-speaking courses, we learn how to prepare and deliver informative speeches, persuasive speeches, and entertaining speeches. But where do we learn how to listen for understanding, for making decisions, and for enjoyment? Dozens of textbooks are available to teach speakers how to inform, persuade, and entertain their listeners. But rare are the textbooks that teach listeners how to understand, decide, and enjoy. And as noted before, most people have no formal training in purposeful listening. Moreover, most listeners are not even aware there are reasons to listen, skills to acquire, or proficiencies to demonstrate. While limited in scope, the skill-building activities at the end of this chapter offer ways to improve our listening practices and behaviors.

Here is a striking paraphrase of I Corinthians 13 by David Augsburger that helps us see from the perspective of both speakers and listeners. Normally, we think of this passage from a speaker's perspective. However, if someone is speaking, then usually other people are listening. Rarely, indeed, do we consider this passage from a listener's perspective. Here is Augsburger's unique and powerful paraphrase in which he juxtaposes the voice of a typical speaker with the mind of an active listener[20]:

I will give to you	I will seek to listen
love that is patient,	with patience,
love that is kind,	with kindness,

love that is not jealous,
love that is not possessive,
love that is not arrogant,
love that is not vain.

without jealousy,
without possessiveness,
without arrogance,
without vanity.

My love for you
will not be insensitive or selfish,
will not be irritable or touchy,
will not be resentful or moody,
will not be thoughtless or rude.

I will hear you
without selfishness and insensitivity,
irritation and touchiness,
resentment and brooding,
inattention or rudeness.

This love I give
will not insist on its own way,
will not keep account of wrongs,
will not remember past failures.
It will rejoice when good prevails.

I will seek
to see your point of view,
to spare you my judgment,
to leave the past behind us,
to rejoice in your possibilities.

There will be
no end to its endurance,
no wavering of its faithfulness,
no conditions to its trust,
no hesitance in its hope,
no limit to its acceptance.

I will be with you
persistently,
faithfully,
trustingly,
hopefully,
acceptantly.

So my hopes for you will be constant.
My faithfulness to you will be sure.
My love for you will be steadfast.
So faith, hope and love will endure,
  but love will be the greatest of all.

So hopeful listening inspires,
faithful listening encourages,
caring listening accepts.
All three are gifts of love.
Caring-listening is the greatest of all.

Listening Process

Listening requires our time and effort. Earlier we learned that listening isn't a simple, automatic process. We create our own meaning of what other people say in a three-part listening process. From what our senses experience, we:

- Select
- Organize
- Interpret

This meaning-making process makes listening a complex, time-consuming, intentional effort. Let's examine this listening process more closely.

In order to "make sense" out of what our senses experience, we must process what we perceive. Otherwise we'd "go crazy," be "spaced-out," and find ourselves "unable to focus." So, first, we *select*, from the myriad sounds, words, noises, feelings, thoughts, and so on that bombard our brains, those relatively few inputs to which we'd like to pay attention. Next, we *organize* the data we've selected into a form that we can handle. Finally, we *interpret* the data on which we've chosen to focus and structure so that it all "makes sense" or "has meaning." This is the same process we use to form concepts: we list, group, and name. It is why, for example, we take the time and effort to listen to one another in "brainstorming" sessions when we create goals or purposes for our mission statement. We list all conceivable options, then group similar items, and finally name or define or identify the categories we've created.

The conversation between Maya and Carole is a case in point. It takes time and patience, effort and intentional listening to define their perception of their relationship. Initially, they are confused. They cannot make sense out of their relationship. So from a myriad of descriptors, they *list* or *select* possible options, e.g., strange, unique, or special. Eventually, they create a *group* of options from which an emerging understanding of what each other means takes shape. Finally, they *organize* or structure the options so as to decide how to *interpret* or *name* their relationship: Maya likes Carole.

Listening Power

Thought speed can mean added listening power. We can think faster than people can speak. Fortunately, we get to decide how best to use our listening power.

Most people speak about 125 words per minute. Most people are capable of listening and computing from *400 to 800 words per minute*. This means that we can think four to six times faster than people speak. This thought-speech differential gives us a powerful listening resource. We must decide, however, how best to use our listening power. Later, in the Practical Applications at the end of this chapter, we will discover a whole set of listening skills and behaviors to help us *raise our listening IQ*. When we begin working to improve our listening skills, we'll learn to wisely use all our listening capabilities.

6. Face and Handle Conflict.

How do you handle your interpersonal conflicts—the strong differences of opinions or disagreements we have with others? How do you feel we handle our dissensions or our difficulties in getting along in the congregation?

Conflicts between people, and conflict in the congregation, are, of course, not new. Early in his first letter to Christians at Corinth, Paul appeals to them to be agreeable and not to allow dissension to emerge. He says, "Be united in the same mind and the same purpose" (I Corinthians 1:10). In other words, Paul says to *keep it together*.

From what he goes on to say, apparently there is quarreling among members of the Corinthian congregation. And, to give credence to their different views, various authorities are claimed: Apollos, Cephas, even Christ. Paul's main concern seems to be that the body of Christ not become divided, and, hence, emptied of its power.

This is a quite typical scenario, isn't it? Disagreements, differences, and dissensions exist. People become polarized, and seek justification for the rightness of their point of view. And, as division widens and settles in, we become immobilized, unable to work together. Rather than *keep it together*, we even part ways and go it alone.

But if our relationships in the body of Christ get fractured or destroyed, so do our common life, witness, and ministry. Much is at stake if conflict gets out of control. Conflict, when not handled skillfully and effectively, can have such hurtful consequences as disunity, dissension, and even the death of relationships. Such painful fracture can block the power of Christ; it can put the presence of Christ at risk. Remember, Christ's work is carried out through the unity of Christ's body in the Church, through our life together, and through our love for one another. As Jesus says, "By this everyone will know that you are my disciples, if you have love for one another" (John 13:35).

Understandably, then, Paul asks his readers to quit their quarreling and come to agreement. The word Paul uses here for quarreling is the Greek word *eris*. As commentators Fred Craddock, John Hayes, Carl Holladay, and Gene Tucker point out in their book, *Preaching the New Common Lectionary*:

> It suggests attitudinal divisions and interpersonal bickering rather than doctrinal or ideological schisms. It is often closely associated with jealousy and petty strife (cf. 3:3; Gal. 5:19–20). His hope, of course, is that these would not develop into full-scale "dissensions" (*schismata*, verse 10), which is always the danger. Petty disagreements become the occasion for more serious doctrinal cleavages, and often the latter become the justification for the former.[21]

We are to handle our differences, and not let our differences divide us. But how shall we do so? *How are we to handle our differences?* Strangely, although Paul tells us to do so, for some reason, he doesn't go on and tell us *how* to go about it.

One of the things I've discovered over the years that I've taught inter-personal communication classes, including courses in managing conflict, is how rare it is for any of us to be schooled in *handling our differences*. Reading, writing, and arithmetic? Yes. But only in recent years have our primary and secondary schools begun to add to the curriculum the teaching of such basic language arts skills as listening and conflict management. Unfortunately, coursework in these areas is not common in most of our undergraduate and graduate schools of higher learning.

People can learn healthier ways of relating to one another and deal with such potential divisive issues as the outreach ministry team described in the introduction faced. Annoying, divisive, fractious interpersonal relationships are preventable. The hurt and pain often accompanying such conflict may be greatly reduced or even completely vanish. While conflict is inevitable, it is how we handle conflict that matters. Clergy and laypersons can learn the principles and skills needed to help groups productively handle their conflicts. We can find ways of *coming to agreement*, of *keeping it together*—of *getting to "yes."*

While there are no magical pathways to pain-free conflict, we can help people be more careful in how they handle their differences by paying atten-tion to these five topics:

- Facing conflict
- Ways to view conflict
- Ways to handle conflict
- Identifying and describing feelings
- Problem solving

Facing Conflict

Many people become tense when conflict arises, and desire to flee from it altogether. *Avoidance* is the most common way people attempt to handle interpersonal conflict. Paul, however, teaches us to *face* our differences and work them through until we reach agreement.

Perhaps we need to remember another of Paul's teachings: few things are bad, in and of themselves.[22] It's what we *do* with them that matters. This truth is especially important when we face conflict.

Conflict isn't inherently bad. Conflict is simply a result of strong differ-ences encountering one another. God made each of us to be unique, to be different from one another. And so, when we get together, we bring our God-given differences. Conflict is natural and inevitable; it is rooted in our human-ness. Conflict, then, in and of itself, isn't bad or even necessarily problematic.

Conflict simply *is*. It need not be avoided; rather, it may be faced. Wherein, then, lies the problem? Our problem comes with *how* we handle our differences. Fortunately, we can learn *how* to disagree without being disagreeable, to become less defensive, and to deal with our feelings of anger and frustration. We can learn *how* to reach sufficient agreement to work together and to keep our interpersonal relationships in harmony.

This seemingly simple observation (that we often experience conflict as bad and try to avoid it) is, I believe, far more important than we realize. For instance, when we feel threatened and avoid conflict, often differences can fester, intensify, and eventually even become divisive. Therefore, before directing attention to how we face our differences, we may need to adjust what we think and feel about conflict.

Ways to View Conflict

There are several ways to view conflict. The most common one, already mentioned, is to think of conflict as bad and to be avoided. But another view of conflict is to see it as good and to be fostered. Conflict can help us not get so staid in our ways that we miss out on fresh ways of seeing things. It can help us be creative rather than get stuck in a rut. Conflict can also energize a relationship or a group, so claim advocates of this positive view of conflict.

There is yet a third option, and that is to see conflict as *neutral* and to be *faced*. Remember: conflict is *neither* inherently bad *nor* good. What matters is what we *do* with our differences. Our conflicts may be handled productively or they may be handled unproductively. So, what matters is *how well* or how *poorly* we face our conflicts.

In short, the reason we need to consider what we think or feel about conflict is that the way we view conflict affects the way we approach and handle it. If we feel conflict is bad, then we'll seek to avoid it. If we feel conflict is good, then we'll seek to foster it. If we feel conflict is neutral, then we're more likely to face it and to handle it productively.

It surely seems that the most appropriate approach to take in order to face our conflicts and work toward agreement is to regard conflict as *neutral*.[23] Neither inherently good nor bad, conflict may be handled well or poorly. Just as good or positive outcomes can come from our conflicts, so also bad or negative results can occur. What matters is *how* we face and manage our differences.

So, if our tendency is to think or feel that conflict is bad or negative, then we'll profit from viewing it as neutral. If we tend to avoid conflict, we can learn how to handle it productively.

Or, if we tend to think or feel that conflict is good or positive, then here too we can profit from viewing it as neutral. There's no need to foster conflict; it will arise naturally. Simply offer fresh, creative, and energizing approaches for people to consider. Such behavior need not precipitate conflict. However, when it does, then we'll need to know how to deal with it productively.

Since it helps to view conflict as neutral and to be faced productively, rather than as bad and to be avoided or good and to be welcomed, let us turn to the really central question: *How can we productively or effectively handle our differences?*

Ways to Handle Conflict

Consider this account of a committee meeting from G. Douglass Lewis in his book, *Resolving Church Conflicts: A Case Study Approach for Local Congregations*:

> The council meeting of Birch Road Baptist Church dragged into its third hour. Everyone was anxious to go home. Still no decision on whether to fire the maintenance man had been made. Two hours earlier Bill Thompson, chairperson of the property committee, made the recommendation to fire him. Bob Barus, the pastor, and several members of the council were hesitant.
> "Maybe we should give him one more chance," said Jane Dillon.
> "Perhaps if I supervised him more closely his performance would improve," said Pastor Barus.
> "Look, we all know he is an alcoholic and has been drinking on the job. As a result, he is totally unreliable," Bill Thompson replied.
> During the two-hour discussion the council ranged over a number of issues. The mention of mowing the lawn led to a discussion of the Christmas crèche, where it should be located next year, and the problems with lighting. The topic of cleanliness of the church school rooms brought a half-hour debate about the day nursery sponsored by the church and whether it should be continued. Even the subject of bathroom maintenance evolved into a proposal for a senior citizens' program and supervision of the maintenance man's work moved into a session on Pastor Barus's responsibilities. At that point, Pastor Barus became defensive and suggested that the setting was inappropriate for an evaluation of his work. And so it went for most of the evening.[24]

Sound familiar? No doubt many of us have been in such conversations, or been in a meeting such as this. What is your *modus operandi*, your process, for effective conflict management? Consider using the image of programming into our mental computers and using three questions to direct the conflict management process:

- What are we differing about?
- What do we each want?
- What other options do we have?

These three sensible, simple questions are useful ways to keep our differences clear and to give direction to the conflict management process. Let's examine how this three-step process for handling conflict works.

First, then, *what are we differing about?* What is the *primary issue* about which we differ? Now, this is quite a different approach to handling conflict than the path many people take. Remember what the council members at Birch Road Baptist Church did. As Lewis points out, "In order to deal with conflict quickly, some people become 'solutionizers,' *pushing an action alternative before the real issue is identified.* Bill Thompson stated the issue incorrectly in the beginning—to fire or not to fire.[25] The real issue was . . . Let's hold it right there for a moment. What do you think is the real issue?

This simple question, when examined, is not always easy to answer. In reality, usually multiple issues are present. Even if conflict begins with a single issue, others quickly emerge, just as they did in our example. Was the real issue alcoholism? Pastoral supervision? Employee competence? Was it the Christmas crèche or nursery school or senior citizens? Or was it something else?

If you say "something else," you are right. Here is the rest of Lewis's statement:

> The real issue was how to provide good maintenance at the congregation. His proposal was an alternative that diverted the group from clarifying the main issue.[26]

Lewis concludes:

> In the church council no one was managing the process very effectively. Consequently, the council spent much unproductive time avoiding the main issue and chasing other concerns that should have been dealt with at another time. When that happens, people become frustrated, angry, and when possible, withdraw. Facing a conflict issue, especially one with a great deal at stake, is difficult but in the long run not nearly as frustrating and debilitating for a group or individual as unproductive wandering and not facing the issue.[27]

So, to help keep our differences clear, the first question we can program into our mental computers and use is: *What are we differing about?* It gives our conflict *direction* by *clarifying the primary issue.*

Here's another illustration. Suppose it's Friday night and my wife, Carol, and I have this conversation:

Carol: I'd like to stay home tonight.

Tom: No, I want to go to a movie.

Carol: Come on, we did that last week. Let's just stay home.

Here, as in the church example, we have jumped right to solutions or alternatives before clarifying the issue. Should we stay home or go to a movie? These are solutions to our difference, aren't they? So, what *are* we differing about? How we'll use our time on Friday night. If we had clarified the issue, then our conversation would have a focus; we could have made progress. Notice how clarifying the issue also gets us working together: how shall *we* spend *our* time, instead of arguing about or trying to win the other over to our position.

After we identify the primary issue about which we differ, we're ready for our second question: *What do we each want?*

This question is fruitful because it gives our conflict *direction* by *clarifying our goals*. It provides additional necessary groundwork for finding a mutually acceptable solution. Typically, the answer to this second question is fairly straightforward and readily apparent, as in our Friday night example. Carol wants a quiet, peaceful evening. And I want to do something mindless, something thoroughly entertaining.

If these desires or goals had become clear, then we'd be prepared to move to our third question: *What options do we have?*

Notice again how we're doing what Paul urges—we're moving together toward agreement: What other options do *we* have? This third question helps us look for creative, win-win alternatives rather than settle for the usual either-or, win-lose alternatives. In our example, rather than get stuck in *either* staying at home *or* going to a movie, our conflict moves toward agreement when this creative alternative is discovered: What about calling friends and see if they'd like to play cards?

This fresh alternative opens up our options in an attempt to find a solution that might satisfy both of our goals. Is this option productive in helping us decide what to do with our time by fulfilling each of our wants? Playing cards is a fairly mindless, thoroughly entertaining activity for me; and it is a quiet, peaceful activity for Carol. It qualifies, then, as a mutually acceptable alternative, and it helps *get us together.*

I find it amazing that as much as 80 percent of the time, a satisfactory, win-win alternative is available if we'll just ask and use the question, *What other options do we have?*

What are we differing about? First, clarify the primary issue.

What do we each want? Next, clarify our goals.

What other options do we have? Then, seek mutually agreeable alternatives.

These three questions can guide our conflicts to face our differences and come to agreement.[28]

Truth be told, there are some situations where this three-step collaborative process of handling conflict is limited and may not work. Rare though these situations may be, only a few ways to handle conflict remain. The parties might consider taking a break from negotiations to allow for a "cooling off" period. Binding arbitration is another consideration as is appeal to a "court of last resort" (e.g., a higher church judicatory or an impartial expert). Finally, there will be situations where the parties choose to "agree to disagree." While compromise or capitulation may not be appealing alternatives, the parties may choose to live with the consequences of such partial, or even win-lose, solutions. Still, there will be situations where conflicted parties choose to walk away from each other, admit failure and defeat, and "let the chips fall where they may." Perhaps at a later date, it will be possible to restart negotiations or to create a new way of handling the conflict.[29]

As noted earlier in this chapter, paying attention to the way we build healthy relationships in conflict situations means using effective, culturally sensitive communication skills to adaptively and creatively manage the process and outcome of conflict. In *Understanding Intercultural Communication*, Ting-Toomey and Chung recommend such skills for flexible intercultural conflict management as facework management, mindful listening, cultural empathy, and mindful reframing.[30]

Facework management includes learning to save face strategically and give face appropriately. Ting-Toomey and Chung put it this way: "Self-oriented face-saving behaviors are attempts to regain or defend one's image after threats to face or face loss. Other-oriented face-giving behaviors are attempts to support others' face claims and work with them to prevent further face loss or help them to restore face constructively. Giving face means not humiliating others, especially one's conflict opponent, in public."[31]

Mindful listening means "'attending mindfully with our ears, eyes, and a focused heart' to the sounds, tone, gestures, movements, nonverbal nuances, pauses, and silence in a given conflict situation. In mindful listening facework negotiators tend to practice dialogic listening, one-pointed attentiveness, mindful silence, and responsive words and posture."[32] Such responsive listening includes the skills of paraphrasing and perception checking so as to see how things look from each other's perspective.

Next comes cultural empathy, "the learned ability of the participants to understand accurately the self-experiences of others from diverse cultures and, concurrently, the ability to convey their understanding responsively and effectively to reach the 'cultural ears' of the culturally different others in the conflict situation."[33]

Finally, mindful reframing uses language to change the way another defines or views the conflict situation. According to Ting-Toomey and Chung, "This skill uses language strategically for the purpose of changing the emotional setting of the conflict from a defensive climate to a collaborative one. Through the use of neutrally toned (to positively-toned) language, reframing can help to soften defensiveness, reduce tension, and increase understanding."[34] Suggestions for mindful reframing include restating conflict positions in terms of common interests, changing complaints into requests, moving from blaming statements to mutual problem-solving ones, realizing the benefits of a win-win alternative, and understanding the "big picture."

These four skills can lead to competent and effective intercultural conflict management that results in healthier relationships. They provide the communication flexibility and adaptation that respects different worldviews and multiple ways of dealing with intercultural conflict situations.

Identifying and Describing Feelings

When people recognize and describe their feelings, almost magically our struggles to communicate often move ahead in a positive direction. One time on the way to do some banking, I got into a heated argument with my wife about money. After stopping to do our banking, we continued our travels when seemingly out of nowhere, she said, "Right now, I just feel as though you don't love me."

Now, I could have claimed "foul" or "low blow" and ignored my wife's feeling statement. But I'll never forget the effect it had on our communication and relationship when I paused to take her seriously. Perceptive listening diminished defensiveness and increased understanding. You see, regardless of the rationality of her statement, I discovered that *unloved* is how she felt at the time. Her *feeling is a fact*. And, in reality, it became, for her, the center of our argument.

An important outcome of identifying and expressing how we feel is that it can bring us back to the primary issue we're trying to discuss. What often begins as a difference over ideas (intellectual conflict) evolves to a difference over feelings (emotional conflict). Since the primary issue about which we differ, as well as our goals or desired outcome, is dynamic and can change during the course of a conversation, we need to be careful to keep track of the evolving issues and outcomes. Otherwise, we're apt to enter hopeless, frustrating, unproductive conversation spirals—and subsequent strains on the type of conversation that creates open, satisfying, and healthy personal relationships. Invariably, whether in the congregation or in our personal lives, this behavior of identifying and expressing our feelings, when taken seriously, gets our conversation moving in a positive direction and on a path to profitable dialogue—dialogue that creates healthier relationships.

Problem Solving

Be careful to claim differences we may have with others as "*our* problem" rather than finding who is at fault. Here's an example.

One time I worked with a friend whose husband was the leader of a home-owner group trying to get a developer to abide by agreements he had made with them. Though litigation was under way, the parties were meeting in an attempt to settle their differences out of court. They could get nowhere, because every time they met they each simply blamed the other for the problem. Trust was strained between the parties. They considered themselves adversaries. At the next meeting, after learning about and adopting this collaborative approach of seeing the issue as a shared problem, they made amazing progress. My friend greeted me the next day with the exclamation, "It works; it works!"

By being careful in how he framed the conversation—by exploring *our* problem rather than continuing trying to prove who is right or wrong—my friend's husband helped get the parties unstuck from fruitless blaming sessions and on to a mutually beneficial, problem-solving outcome.

So also in the congregation, adversaries quickly get defensive and productive conversation is threatened, whereas partners can work toward a mutually agreeable solution. Notice here that it is the *attitude* or *point of view* we take toward one another that makes the difference. Is it *your* problem or is it *mine*? If it is a problem *we're* having, then it is *our* problem. This seemingly small but powerful change of attitude or point of view can make a big difference in people feeling free to engage in productive conversation and to begin working together toward a mutually agreeable solution.

Summary and Conclusion

We have now covered six ways to be careful with our communication. We've seen how careless communication results in deterioration of our relational health, and how careful communication results in building healthy relationships. More importantly, we've learned practical, sensible ways to improve the quality of our communication, including perception checking, creating meaning, fostering a supportive climate, using nonverbal communication, raising our listening IQ, and handling conflict. These six guidelines for building relationships can go a long way toward helping people become more effective in how they relate to one another.

Practical Applications

1. As a way to integrate all six guidelines, write a dialogue or narrative using a variety of careless communication behaviors. Then rewrite it using a variety of careful communication behaviors. Consider role-playing these scenarios to experience and reflect on effective and ineffective ways we relate to one another. Also, consider seeing a film such as *On Golden Pond* or *August: Osage County* as a creative way to integrate all six guidelines in action. Before viewing the movie, briefly review each guideline; during the movie notice what does and does not create healthy relationships; and afterward reflect on your observations, including connections between the six guidelines in action.

2. Create examples from real-life experience such as the conversation between Maya and Carole. Be careful to include perception checking as meaning emerges between conversational partners. Then practice the skills of bracketing your judgments and perception checking using the Paraphrasing Exercise in Appendix A.

3. Which of Gibb's six sets of defensive and supportive climates do you see most frequently affecting the building of healthier relationships? Consider in particular an experience where closed-minded, judgmental attitudes adversely affect the communication climate. How can your use of I-messages or other effective communication styles, behaviors, and skills result in better outcomes?

4. What percentage did you think words, facial expressions, and tone of voice each contribute to successful communication? Reflect on the revelation that most people underuse their huge nonverbal communication advantage, and then think of ways you can better engage facial expressions and increase variation in your tone of voice. How or in what ways does today's demand for instant communication affect the way people relate to one another? What are some important ways that cultural differences affect how we communicate and build healthy relationships?

5. Read Augsburger's paraphrase of I Corinthians 13 and then reflect on your listening strengths and challenges at home, at work, and in the church. What are the benefits of perceptive listening in your personal, social, and professional lives? How about in the church? Here are other practical applications for how to listen:

   a. Mindful that we are to be quick to listen and slow to speak, think of scenarios that illustrate how we typically practice this behavior in our congregations. Of the 70 percent of our waking hours that we spend communicating, what percentage of time did you think we devote to reading, writing, speaking, and listening? Which of the ten listening facts and fallacies are most useful in raising your listening IQ?

   b. Use the Listening Awareness and Skills Inventory in Appendix B to assess how you can make better use of your listening power. Which of your listening strengths would you like to make stronger and which listening weaknesses would you most like to strengthen?

   c. Mindful of ways diverse listening styles affect our communication, reflect on the way people process information. What are examples of ways you do or do not align your communication with the ways other people process information?

   d. How purposeful is your listening behavior? Use the Strength Bombardment exercise in Appendix C to improve the ways you listen to learn, to decide, to enjoy, and to help.

   e. How does "brainstorming" use the same meaning-making perception process that we use in listening?

6. After reading I Corinthians 1:10–17, or if you prefer, James 3:13–18, think of examples of the way you typically handle conflict in your relationships at home, at work, and in your congregation. Then practice identifying issues, goals, and options in these scenarios. Here are other practical applications to consider:

   a. Divide people into three groups or have them place themselves along a continuum according to the way they view conflict (good, bad, neutral). Then have them talk about ways they typically face and experience conflict. Notice the values of each view of conflict, noting particularly how viewing conflict as neutral is preferable.

   b. Think of a conflict situation requiring culturally sensitive communication skills to adaptively and creatively manage the process and outcome of conflict. Which skills for flexible intercultural conflict management do you find most useful?

c. What are examples where identifying and expressing feelings has a positive effect on handling conflict? What are instances where intense emotions such as anger can turn what otherwise would be painful, unproductive conflict into manageable, productive "energy"? Consider, for example, David Augsburger's insight that viewing anger as a demand can be a positive, life-affirming emotion and a creative force to confront others with their need to change unloving communication behavior. (For more information about this approach, see Augsburger, *Caring Enough to Confront*, pp. 47–53.)

d. Describe or create a conflict scenario that illustrates what happens when you do or do not take a problem-solving approach rather than an adversarial one.

For Further Study

Augsburger, David. *Caring Enough to Confront: How to Understand and Express Your Deepest Feelings Toward Others*, 3rd ed. (Ventura, CA: Regal, 2009).

———. *Caring Enough to Hear and Be Heard* (Ventura, CA: Regal, 1982).

Baab, Lynne M. *The Power of Listening: Building Skills for Mission and Ministry* (Lanham, MD: Rowman & Littlefield, 2014).

Everist, Norma Cook. *Church Conflict: From Contention to Collaboration* (Nashville: Abingdon, 2004).

Fisher, Roger, William Ury, and Bruce Patton, eds. *Getting to Yes: Negotiating Agreement without Giving In*, 2nd ed. (New York: Penguin, 1991).

Galvin, Kathleen. *Listening by Doing: Developing Effective Listening Skills* (Lincolnwood, IL: National, 1985).

Goodman, Denise W. *Congregational Fitness: Healthy Practices for Layfolk* (Herndon, VA: Alban Institute, 2000).

Lewis, G. Douglass. *Resolving Church Conflicts: A Case Study Approach for Local Congregations* (New York: HarperCollins, 1981).

Lott, David B. *Conflict Management in Congregations* (Herndon, VA: Alban Institute, 2001).

Newberg, Andrew, and Mark Robert Waldman. *Words Can Change Your Brain: 12 Conversation Strategies to Build Trust, Resolve Conflict, and Increase Intimacy* (New York: Plume, 2013).

Samovar, Larry A., Richard E. Porter, and Edwin R. McDaniel, eds. *Intercultural Communication: A Reader*, 13th ed. (Boston: Wadsworth Cengage, 2012).

Stewart, John, ed. *Bridges Not Walls: A Book About Interpersonal Communication*, 11th ed. (New York: McGraw-Hill, 2012).

Stewart, John, Karen E. Zediker, and Saskia Witteborn. *Together: Communicating Interpersonally*, 6th ed. (New York: Oxford, 2005).

Ting-Toomey, Stella, and Leeva C. Chung. *Understanding Intercultural Communication*, 2nd ed. (New York: Oxford University Press, 2012).

Ury, William. *The Power of a Positive No: How to Say No and Still Get to Yes* (New York: Bantam Dell, 2007).

Wilmot, William W., and Joyce L. Hocker. *Interpersonal Conflict*, 7th ed. (New York: McGraw-Hill, 2007).

Wolff, Florence I., and Nadine C. Marsnik. *Perceptive Listening*, 2nd ed. (New York: Harcourt Brace Jovanovich, 1993).

~

CHAPTER TWO

Leading Meetings

- *"Another committee? You must be crazy! I can't wait to retire. No more meetings!"*
- *"I'm confused. Why are we meeting and how may I participate?"*
- *"Why don't our multicultural members speak up more often at meetings?"*
- *"I think we should get rid of all our committees. We waste a lot of time and accomplish very little."*
- *"How do you deal with difficult people?"*
- *"No one has a clue about how to lead a good discussion."*

All-Too-Common Scenario

You may share the sentiment captured in Barnett Cocks's remark, "A committee is a cul-de-sac down which ideas are lured and then quietly strangled." This somewhat humorous, tongue-in-cheek analogy may have more than a grain of truth for members of many congregations' councils, ministry teams, task forces, committees, and organizations. If you want a good idea to die or a creative action plan to be stillborn, then just give it to a committee, say sarcastic naysayers. Why do people put down, scorn, or speak critically about these pervasive, established, and, at times, effective staples in most congregations?

Patrick Lencioni in his book, *Death by Meeting*, comments:

> We complain about, try to avoid, and long for the end of meetings, even when we're running the darn things! How pathetic is it that we have come to accept

that the activity most central to the running of our organizations is inherently painful and unproductive? All of this is an unnecessary shame because meetings are critical. . . . If we hate meetings, can we be making good decisions and successfully leading our organizations? I don't think so. There is simply no substitute for a good meeting—a dynamic, passionate, and focused engagement—when it comes to extracting the collective wisdom of a team. The hard truth is, bad meetings almost always lead to bad decisions, which is the best recipe for mediocrity. But there is hope. . . . We can transform what is now painful and tedious into something productive, compelling, and even energizing.[1]

My denomination, the Presbyterian Church (U.S.A.), prides itself on doing things "decently and in order" and, like other denominations and congregational bodies, conducts much of its work through meetings. It appears that the early Christian church even knew a thing or two about effective group discussion and decision-making. Consider this description by David Sawyer:

How would it have felt to attend the council meeting that day at First Church, Jerusalem, which is described in Acts 15? The debate took up the early part of the meeting with people speaking enthusiastically on both sides of the issue of circumcision for the Gentiles. After a while Peter gave his opinions and beliefs on the matter. Sometimes it is important for a leader to state his or her position clearly. Next on the docket the guests were invited to tell stories of their mission among the Gentiles. I can imagine the officers smiled and even laughed at some of the incidents, which also answered many of the questions the elders had about the matter before them. When it appeared that everything had been said, the presiding officer summarized the whole discussion and proposed a solution. A vote was taken and the resolution passed overwhelmingly. The group even remembered to assign two members to carry the decision to the Gentile churches. Everyone felt good about the meeting and about the decision. Your official board can get its work done in such a fashion, too.[2]

Perhaps, then, negative impressions of committee meetings have less to do with inherent weaknesses or failures of group work per se than they do with dysfunctional group practices and behaviors. Such factors might include ineffective group leadership, imbalance between task and teamwork, lack of member participation, and inefficient group structure.

Most people enter a group with two questions: "Why are we meeting?" and "How may I participate?" The major problems with communication in committees and discussions may be largely addressed by proper attention to these two matters: group purpose and member participation. Social scientific research on group communication often centers on these task and relationship aspects of group life.[3] Related topics include leadership style and behavior, group structure, member satisfaction, group conflict, leader-member relations, group decision-making, and group productivity. We will return to such topics in the following section—our *guidelines for leading meetings*.

Given the amount of time, effort, resources, and hope congregations invest in meetings, we expect our leaders to facilitate groups well. They must know how to avoid energyless, aimless, unproductive group work and instead make it exciting, purposeful, and productive. Given the ineffectiveness of many leaders in our congregations in leading meetings, training is urgently needed to enhance their knowledge base and to upgrade their skills. Let's see how the leaders and members of our congregations can learn healthier ways of relating to one another in their group work.

Most of our congregations are eager to help their leaders create healthier ways of relating to one another in their group work. Here are eight simple guidelines that can go a long way toward helping people lead meetings more effectively.

Guidelines for Leading Meetings

1. How We View Ourselves as Group Leaders Matters.

While leaders may emerge naturally, most groups in our congregations have a designated leader. That is, someone is identified to help the group work as a team to accomplish its task. Here is how I view myself as a group leader: *I am a member of the group designated to help the group go where it wants to go to the extent that such help is needed.*[4] You will notice several important features of this perspective.

First, rather than see myself as apart from the group, I view myself as a bona fide member of the group. I simply have a particular function to perform.

Second, my leadership role is to help the group go where *it* wants to go. Most congregational leaders have little authority to "call the shots." Such power and autonomy simply do not work in most congregational groups, because group members want a say in what a group does and how it functions. They think of the group as "ours," not the leader's, and they expect leaders to be partners, not overlords. In reality, group morale and productivity are often adversely affected by leaders who "lord it over" other group members. It's what Peter had in mind when he exhorted congregational leaders, "Do not lord it over those in your charge, but be examples to the flock" (I Peter 5:3).

Finally, I see group leadership on a sliding scale. My task may be large or small, depending on the extent to which a group needs direction and facilitation. Early in a group's life, the designated leader can be especially helpful by assisting the group to establish its purpose and making suggestions for member participation. In ongoing group life, the leader's main task is to facilitate member participation so that the group can accomplish its purposes. One person—the designated leader—may provide this leadership, or several members may share it. Ideally, other group members will soon help the group accomplish its task and work as a team.

2. People Enter a Group with Two Primary Questions: Why Are We Here? And How May I Participate?

Put clarifying the group's purpose and facilitating member participation at the top of your to-do list early in your group's life. Whenever you begin a new group, create an overview of your group's objectives, goals, purposes, and processes. In addition, develop conversational guidelines that let members know what is expected of them as participants. Moreover, regularly remind the group why it is meeting and frequently encourage member participation.[5]

Box 2.1 shows examples of an *overview* and *conversation guidelines* that one congregation created for a new spiritual formation ministry, Conversations on the Way.[6]

Box 2.1. Overview

Objective

To provide space for weekly conversations based on people's faith journeys

Goal

To provide an ongoing pathway for discipleship, including:

- Gathering and building trust
- Connecting newcomers and established members (mentoring)
- Preparing for commitment and reaffirmation

Purposes

- To have a safe place both to explore and to go deeper in our Christian faith
- To connect newcomers and established members

- To experience Christian community through small groups in the congregation
- To explore our Reformed faith tradition

Process

Meet weekly on Saturday morning
10:00 a.m.: Gathering and sharing
10:45 a.m.: Conversations on the Way

- Opening with prayer
- Reading a Bible passage
- Asking a faith question
- Taking time for silent reflection
- Inviting sharing of reflections
- Closing with prayer.

Conversation Guides

Speak your mind freely.

- Everyone's ideas are important.
- No one has your specific background of knowledge and experience.
- Share your ideas—you have a responsibility besides listening.

Try to maintain an open mind.

- Listen objectively and without judgment.
- Disagree in a friendly way.
- Remember that other people's views make sense to them.

Help others to participate.

- Let the other person talk, too.
- Show interest in what others think and invite them to speak.
- Help make sure everyone has opportunity to share.

(continued)

Keep communication clear.

- Listen to understand what others mean to say.
- Ask others to clarify unclear points.
- Perception check when communication breaks down.

Try to make the conversation a pleasant experience for all.

- A smile may do more to further discussion than your best arguments.
- Try to have fun, and make the conversation pleasant for others, too.
- A laugh or pointed joke can dispel glumness, hostility, and boredom.

3. Groups Usually Need a Balance of Task Work and Teamwork.
Some people's primary interest is in accomplishing the group's task. These task-oriented members place priority on group productivity. Other people are most interested in working together as a team. These relationship-oriented members place priority on group cohesiveness. Then there are those who place importance on both task work and teamwork—accomplishing their tasks *and* developing satisfying working relationships.

These divergent interests sometimes produce tension and create a challenging work environment. In reality, both task work and teamwork are important. So, what's needed is a balanced approach. You may need to help members become aware that both teamwork and task work are necessary for their group's success. Groups have a task to accomplish for which teamwork is a necessary complement. While most people will intuitively understand this duality, patience with one another is often required to maintain balance. In most instances, both group productivity and group cohesion are achievable expectations.

4. Groups Need Leaders Who Are Flexible and Adaptable.
Researchers have long been interested in determining why some small group leaders are effective and other leaders are ineffective. They have asked, for instance, whether effective group leaders possess certain traits, develop particular styles, or pay attention to specific situational factors. No consensus has emerged, particularly for leaders in volunteer organizations such as congregations. In recent years, however, another theory has evolved: effective

leaders are flexible and adaptable. Here, it is the behavior of leaders that matters. We can help our leaders increase their behavioral flexibility so they can adapt themselves to situational demands. Sometimes, situations will demand more task-oriented behaviors. And others require greater emphasis on relationship-oriented behaviors. What groups need are leaders who have learned both how to jettison ineffective leadership behaviors and how to practice the flexibility and adaptability of effective leadership.[7]

5. Groups Must Learn How to Deal with Members' Dysfunctional Group Behavior.

Most groups will experience periodic difficulties in the way members interact with one another. Here are some common group problems you may encounter:

- Aggressiveness
- Anxiety
- Avoidance of depth
- Backstabbing
- Cultural insensitivity
- Defensiveness
- Disgruntlement or agitation
- Distrust
- Domination
- Fearfulness
- Inappropriate settings
- Inflexibility
- Judging
- Passivity
- Stubbornness
- Superficiality
- Unfulfilled expectations

While a daunting challenge, facing dysfunctional behavior openly, directly, and creatively is generally the wisest approach. Addressing this rarely treated topic, Clyde Reid offers this advice in his classic book, *Groups Alive—Church Alive*: "In all these group problems, there is nothing like the openness and honest sharing of feelings as a general prescription for group health. This honesty has a price. It may be painful. But pain is often the necessary prelude to health."[8]

Elsewhere, I add this advice:

In my experience, Reid is right, even though the adage "easier said than done" frequently applies—especially to the problems of the dominator and superficiality. Unless groups face such major problems directly, however, they are apt to drift into mediocrity and eventually some members may quietly leave the group.

Emphasize that dominating and judgmental behaviors threaten a group's very existence. Such behaviors stifle other group members' freedom to participate and be themselves. Without a commitment to dialogue, a group simply cannot be a group.

Likewise, superficial group interaction is not fulfilling for most members and is also apt to destroy a group if members allow such behavior to continue.[9]

Perhaps the best way for a group to deal directly with dysfunctional behavior is to build regular reviews into group life. Ideally, your group will create a set of expectations for member behavior, such as the Conversation Guides, and use these agreements as a basis for evaluating group interaction. The leader can invite group members to name specific troublesome behaviors, describe how they experience such behavior, and then offer suggestions for changing the dysfunctional behavior.

I'll never forget what happened during one such review in a pastor's sharing and support group of which I was a member. Here is an exchange between two members (for the sake of privacy, we will name them Wayne and Daren):

Wayne: You know, Daren, often in our group, I notice that you speak as though what is true for you is true for all of us. For example, a little while ago you said something like, "Well, we all experience spiritual deadness this time of year." Your experience doesn't ring true for me at this time. These "all-ness" statements drive me crazy. I cringe inside and feel defensive when you seem to make your experience normative. I think it threatens my integrity—it doesn't create space for me to feel differently than you.

Daren: Wow, I'm really glad you brought this matter to my attention. I had no idea my sharing is sometimes troublesome for you. I don't think I meant to speak for you. I'm sorry, though, if I have done so.

Wayne: Well, that's good to know. Thank you for hearing me out. In the future, it will help me if you make clear that you are speaking for yourself, and not for me, too.

Daren: Okay. I'm agreeable to that. If I slip back into my old way of speaking, will you let me know so that we can deal with it right then and there?

Wayne: Yes, that's a good idea. Let's see how this new agreement about our group life works out. I think it has promise to alleviate my discomfort.

Here is an example from another group that demonstrates how regularly scheduled reviews can have surprising results. In this group, one member in particular rarely got beneath the surface during group discussion. This member's superficial sharing seemed to stifle other people's willingness to freely participate in conversation. It prevented the group from developing a sufficient level of trust that members could feel comfortable taking risks in sharing some of their deeper thoughts and feelings. Several members of the group were so disturbed by this dysfunctional behavior that they were ready to leave the group. And then an astonishing thing happened. During the group's next review, the superficiality problem was cited—but not by a disgruntled member. It seemed that the "troublesome member" was also tired of the group's superficiality. As you might expect, it didn't take long for the group to affirm a commitment to deeper sharing.

Of course, some people's dysfunctional behavior may be the result of deep-seated personality disorder or mental illness and require professional counseling. Regular reviews can offer occasion to identify such behavior, offer care and support, and recommend professional help.

Finally, certain group members' behaviors may become so egregious, disruptive, and even abusive that they must be identified and exorcised. Aggressiveness, backstabbing, disgruntlement, agitation, and inflexibility can be especially problematic for a group. Negativity and abusive behavior can squash participation, crash systems, oppress members, sap energy, kill joy, hamper work, and bind up relationships. Group members need to ask, what needs to happen so life, energy, joy, and freedom can flourish anew?

Struggling groups and their leaders often need to learn about healthy and unhealthy interpersonal, group, and organizational dynamics. This may require outside assistance from consultants and skilled denominational staff, or from training events such as Peter Steinke's Healthy Leadership seminar. Once your members "get it," once they grasp the gravity of what is happening in their group, they will be ready to deal with these problematic behaviors. Sometimes, all it takes is for one wise, courageous, kind, and caring member to confront another with their unhealthy behavior either in private or in the group. Such intervention can expose the problem, express a demand to change, and, if necessary, present an ultimatum to either cease the behavior or not return to the group. In effect, the offending person's power to influence in the group is removed, and they have a choice to change or leave. If such dysfunctional behavior is allowed to persist over a long period of time, it may take considerable time for your group to break free from its bondage, recover its energy, or renew its joy. It may also take several phases of such intervention should these serious threats to group health persist or reappear.

6. Groups Function Properly When Everyone Contributes.

The active participation of all small group members is imperative for healthy group discussion and high-quality decision-making. A group can function well if some people are talkative while others are quiet, but not if some people so dominate group discussion that opportunity for everyone to speak is sacrificed. Nor can a group be effective if some people withhold their contribution to group discussion and decision-making, forfeiting valuable insight. Diverse perspectives and opinions are necessary to create a well-functioning, inclusive, harmonious tapestry of participation. Effective group leaders are familiar with an array of strategies, such as the following eleven, for ensuring everyone participates.

Agreements about Group Life

Agreements about group life serve as a contract or covenant for group members. We have already seen that groups need clarity and agreement about group purpose and member participation. Use standards such as the overview and conversation guidelines presented earlier to evaluate the health of your group's direction and member participation. Then take appropriate steps to enhance group productivity and member interaction.

Conversation Analysis

This strategy helps people determine each member's "fair share" of group discussion time. For instance, let's say your eight-member group meets for one hour, and comments average one minute in duration. Do the math! If eight people make sixty comments, then there's time for each person to make seven or eight comments. Naturally, some comments will take less than one minute and other comments longer than a minute. Theoretically, in terms of conversation equity, those who speak more than seven or eight times during discussion take more than their "fair share" of speaking time; and those who speak only once or twice give up their opportunity for conversation parity. In practical terms, this exercise gives people a way to gain speaking self-awareness, create speaking space for all, and monitor speaking behavior. In short, it offers members a way to self-regulate the conversation flow so that everyone's contributions are valued and received. Ideally, talkative members begin to draw out contributions from quieter members, and quieter members begin speaking more frequently and carrying their share of the conversational freight.

Process Observation

Another way to gain perspective on member participation is to have someone observe what happens during the process of a group meeting. This process observer focuses not on the content of what members say, but on the group process itself. For example, the process observer may record who speaks and who doesn't, when members speak and for how long, who interrupts and who yields the floor, people's nonverbal communication, and how decisions are made. For a more comprehensive record of member participation, pre-pare a checklist to log selected effective and ineffective member behaviors, including dysfunctional member behavior. A report of observation results can help monitor the diversity of member participation in group discussion and decision-making.

Round-Robin Sharing

Round-robin sharing is a way to give everyone an equal opportunity to generate and share ideas. It is especially helpful if a few people tend to domi-nate group discussion while others normally do not contribute. Ask members to reflect silently for a few minutes and then, one at a time, to contribute one idea to the discussion. After everyone has had an opportunity to speak, begin another round of sharing, again one item per participant. Continue the rounds of sharing until everyone has shared all their ideas. Be sure to allow people the freedom to pass (not speak), but invite everyone to contribute to the discussion for each round.

Breakout Groups

Often groups are too large to permit everyone to contribute to the discus-sion and decision-making. One way to obtain wider participation is to divide into a number of small groups called breakout groups. These small groups of-fer an opportunity for more personal involvement in discussion, particularly for those who are less likely to speak in a large group. Once quieter members have talked in smaller groups, they may be more likely to speak up in the larger group. Breakout groups can also offer opportunity for more people to ask questions and to raise important concerns. If appropriate, ask each small group to select someone to serve as recorder and present a summary of the discussion to the larger group. Group leaders should set reasonable time lim-its and provide comfortable spaces for breakout groups to meet.

Open Space Meetings

Open space meetings can generate energy, passion, and an eagerness to participate. They are particularly useful when a group gets stuck or when people lose interest in the direction the group is headed. They may be used to engage small or large groups of people in productive conversation on diverse issues and questions about which they care deeply. A meeting convener invites people to discuss a particular topic or theme that serves as the focus of the gathering. After a brief opening comment, the convener "opens the space" for participants to self-organize around the issues and questions for which they have real passion and are willing to start a discussion. Anyone may post an issue or question for discussion. Then the convener invites participants to select a discussion they would like to join. Participants remain with a discussion group as long as they are learning from or contributing to the conversation. When they no longer are, they join another discussion. Discussions normally last from forty-five to ninety minutes. Each group prepares and posts a report on its discussion.

Suppose that you are part of an organization that has lost its purpose and is meeting to create a new identity. After a brainstorming session, several possible purposes surface. During an ensuing discussion, some members become frustrated and bored with the direction the discussion is taking. They feel they have been down this road before, and are fast losing interest in the conversation. So, the leader calls a timeout and the group takes a break. When the group reconvenes, the leader proposes an open space meeting process to rekindle member interest and energy. First, members identify and post topics or questions they would like to discuss about the organization's future. Next, they discover that their topics and questions cluster around several larger themes, around which breakout groups form. Group discussion is lively and passionate. Then, after everyone gathers to hear breakout group reports, fresh ideas stimulate creative alternatives for the organization's future. A consensus emerges around a new purpose that rekindles the group's vitality and excitement about its future.

Mutual Invitation

The practice of mutual invitation is a creative, simple way to engage quieter group members and restrain members who typically dominate group discussion and decision-making. Eric Law, Episcopal priest and consultant on multicultural leadership, created it to promote cultural sensitivity that leads to more inclusive group participation and decision-making in a multicultural community.

In some cultures everyone expects to participate in group discussion. Differences are expressed and freely debated with decisions reached by consensus. People from other cultures are reticent to speak up. They expect to be invited to participate in discussion and decision-making and they prefer letting someone take charge so that something gets done.

Law believes there are three typical processes of group interaction, none of which he thinks is effective in an intercultural setting. In the first type of interaction, the *volunteer process*, group members speak up whenever they have something to say. Typically, those with a strong sense of individual power are apt to speak first, followed by awkward, unbearable, and time-consuming silence. In the second process, *going around in a circle*, people take turns speaking. This process tends to create anxiety, resulting in poor listening and brief sharing. In the third process, the *commander* approach, the leader decides who speaks. This process gives too much power to one person. For instance, these leaders typically permit those who agree with them to speak, and prevent people with opposing views from speaking.

As an alternative to these three typical and problematic ways of facilitating group discussion, Law invented the process of mutual invitation to give everyone a chance to participate in group discussion and decision-making in multicultural settings. Here is how Law describes this process:

> I, as the leader, first share without projecting myself as an expert. After I have spoken, I then invite someone to share. I usually do not invite the person next to me because that might set up the precedent of going around in a circle. After the next person has spoken, that person is given the privilege of inviting another to share. The person being invited has the option to "pass" if she does not want to say anything. After a person says "pass," he is still given the privilege to invite another to share. This continues until everybody has had a chance to share.[10]

Mutual invitation decentralizes the power to participate. After the leader describes the process, shares, and invites the next member to share, the process takes over, and group members take turns giving one another permission to speak. This process may at first seem foreign or stilted to you and your group, so you may need to try it several times to determine its effectiveness in helping everyone participate in the conversation. Consider passing an object such as a talking-feather or talking-stick from person to person as a tactile way to regulate the conversation.

Robert's Rules of Order

Groups that seek an orderly, democratic, majority-based process of discussion and decision-making when consensus or compromise is unnecessary, impractical, or unlikely to succeed often adopt Robert's Rules of Order.[11] Originally created to bring order out of chaos in public meetings, Robert's Rules provide widely adopted, systematic, step-by-step procedures for groups to make decisions by majority rule. Used properly, these procedures give everyone access to group discussion and decision-making. Patience, common sense, civility, and skilled leadership are required. Used improperly, these rules of deliberation can obstruct or subvert the will of the majority since power can always be misused and abused.

Fist to Five

A quick way to gauge the level of group support for an idea or proposal during discussion and decision-making is to use the fist-to-five method. This strategy is useful when consensus is too time-consuming or unnecessary, or as a transition to reaching consensus. Everyone participates by raising their fist if they are unsupportive and will block consensus, one finger if they are not supportive but will go along with the decision, two fingers if they are moderately supportive but desire further conversation, three fingers if they are neutral or not in total agreement but comfortable going along, four fingers if they are solidly supportive and in basic agreement, and five fingers if they are fully supportive and in complete agreement. If everyone raises three or more fingers, a decision is approved. If not, objections are clarified, questions answered, and changes proposed. Then the process is repeated until no one raises a fist or one finger. The group may decide to limit the time for discussion and number of re-votes before taking a final majority-wins vote, continuing discussion and voting at another time, or deciding to try another method of discussion and decision-making.

Drama or Conflict

As we saw at the beginning of this chapter, in *Death by Meeting* Patrick Lencioni suggests that meetings are a puzzling paradox. They are both *critical*—at the center of every organization, and they are *painful*—frustratingly long and seemingly pointless. He thinks we must fundamentally rethink the way we understand and manage meetings. Here is what he recommends:

> We must abandon our search for technological solutions that will somehow free us from having to sit down face to face. And we have to stop focusing on

agendas and minutes and rules, and accept the fact that bad meetings start with the attitudes and approaches of the people who lead and take part in them.[12]

Lencioni identifies these two problems with most meetings: they are boring and they are ineffective. He believes meetings are boring because they lack *drama* or conflict, and are ineffective because they lack *contextual structure*. And to better manage meetings, he offers a simple two-part model to transform painful and pointless meetings into compelling, productive, and energizing ones—meetings with increased member participation, higher morale, faster and better decisions, and greater results.

Here is the first part of Lencioni's model: "To make meetings less boring, leaders must look for legitimate reasons to provoke and uncover relevant, constructive ideological conflict. By doing so, they'll keep people engaged, which leads to more passionate discussions, and ultimately, to better decisions."[13] And here is the second part of his theory: "To make our meetings more effective, we need to have multiple types of meetings, and clearly distinguish between the various purposes, formats, and timing of those meetings."[14]

We will consider his first approach here because of its relevance for keeping everyone engaged in group discussion, and his second approach in guideline 8, since it relates to sensible group structure.

In chapter 1, we see that conflict is a normal and natural part of human interaction. We also learn how to effectively handle the "energy" produced when strong differences of opinion meet. The point is made that sufficient conflict exists in most groups to keep people engaged in lively discussion without precipitating it. Lencioni, on the other hand, suggests that in order to keep boredom in check, we should find legitimate ways to spark or raise the lid on conflict.

Here is his perspective about the importance of group conflict:

> Meetings are not inherently boring. By definition, they are dynamic interactions involving groups of people discussing topics that are relevant to their livelihoods. So why are they so dull? Because we eliminate the one element that is required to make any human activity interesting: conflict.[15]

And here is the importance he places on facing group conflict:

> When a group of intelligent people come [*sic*] together to talk about issues that matter, it is both natural and productive for disagreement to occur. Resolving those issues is what makes a meeting productive, engaging, even fun.

Avoiding the issues that merit debate and disagreement not only makes the meeting boring, it guarantees that the issues won't be resolved. And this is a recipe for frustration. Ironically, that frustration often manifests itself later in the form of unproductive personal conflict, or politics.[16]

Lencioni suggests that the way to provoke or uncover conflict is for a leader to remind team members to expect conflict and to engage in it as it occurs. Surely there is wisdom in including an expectation to experience and face conflict in a group's agreements about group life. However, even though we remind people to expect conflict and give them permission to face conflict when it does occur, we still are left with the need to facilitate the productive handling of group conflict—such as the three-step *modus operandi* you may find in chapter 1.

Cultivating Curiosity

Cultivating curiosity is yet another way to facilitate full participation in your group. Especially evident in the Gospel of Mark, Jesus often teaches by focusing on people who stay around after the crowd is gone to ask questions. He seeks people who are eager to ask questions in a safe environment, people who are lifelong learners.

Here is an example from a Sunday morning adult education class I facilitate in my congregation. Over the last ten years this class has grown to include nearly 40 percent of the adults in our congregation. Two characteristics of our success are our *style* or *approach to learning*, and the *simplicity of our group process*. We will examine our style of learning here, and our simple group process in guideline 8.

What most attracts these adult learners is their freedom to ask questions. As Indira Gandhi points out, "The power to question is the basis of all human progress." These adults are curious learners. Our style of learning includes an openness to listen to views different from one's own, and an eagerness to learn something new. Simple-though-profound, this learning style is vastly different from the simple-answers approach that is attractive to many of today's churchgoers.

Sadly, many people want easy answers to complex questions. They want to be told what to think, believe, and do. Not Jesus' disciples, and not the learners in our adult education class. They thrive on asking and living the questions of faith. Perhaps, then, this class is doing just what Jesus intends for us to do as people of faith. We are becoming just the type of followers Jesus seeks. Indeed, our discipleship, our spiritual formation, is being nurtured in attractive, healthy ways through cultivating curiosity.

7. Groups Can Profit from Collaborative Leadership for Group Discussion and Decision-Making.

Most groups have topics to explore, discussions to engage, problems to solve, and decisions to make. In order for these groups to accomplish such tasks, members learn how to work together as a team. Normally, these group activities require collaboration between leaders and members. For instance, joint ownership and implementation of group decisions often require collaboration. Traditional patterns of organizing and leading are often unable to deliver these results. Unfortunately, old habits can be hard to break. C. Jeff Woods offers this perceptive overview and cogent critique in *We've Never Done It Like This Before: 10 Creative Approaches to the Same Old Church Tasks*:

> Church leaders often follow "tradition." For some that means continuing the same old bureaucratic organizational patterns that have endured since the beginning of this [twentieth] century. Yet the bureaucratic model, developed by Max Weber as he analyzed the hierarchy of the ancient Catholic Church and the military system, is seldom helpful for churches today. Church leaders need a new way to lead.[17]

Woods continues:

> The dominant paradigm of today is still the bureaucratic model. The bureaucratic model claims to operate in an efficient, predictable, and rational way. Even when we discover that organizations are no longer operating in this manner (if they ever did), it is scary to announce that we are about to adopt a new viewpoint, one that views organizations as inefficient, unpredictable, and irrational! As the reader can easily see, along the way we will need to develop new language for our new paradigm of organizing.[18]

Woods concludes:

> In our changing world, church leaders must look for new ways to lead. We must also begin breaking down the barriers between professional church leaders and laity and learn to lead together.[19]

In our postmodern, post-Christian, post-denominational era, people are often more receptive to and interested in practicing collaborative leadership than people in previous generations. For congregations in the Reformed tradition that value "the priesthood of all believers," collaborative partnering between clergy and laity is a long-valued best practice. Nonetheless, the top-down, corporate model of directive leadership is common in many quarters. While some people may resist the movement from top-down to collaborative leadership, this shift will be particularly beneficial for leading meetings in congregations.

8. A Simple Agenda and Sensible Structure Can Create Lively Conversation and Efficient Meetings.

I am often amazed by the way lively discussion and efficient meetings can emerge when groups are given a simple agenda and a sensible structure. Here is an illustration of how a simple agenda creates lively conversation.

Simple Agenda

Earlier, in guideline 6, I referred to an adult education class I facilitate at my congregation. There, I mentioned the first of two characteristics of our success—our *style* or *approach to learning*. Here we will consider the second characteristic—the *simplicity of our group process*.

Often we view a stimulating fifteen- to twenty-minute video presentation, then enjoy thirty-five to forty-five minutes of lively group discussion.[20] Two factors are largely responsible for creating this lively conversation: *compelling content* and *simple group direction*. In fact, stimulating content seems to produce substantive group discussion. I simply ask class members to make a mental note of what especially strikes them as they view the video presentation. Whereas most video resources provide questions for group discussion, I find that this simple question almost always results in stimulating, productive discussion: "What strikes you in the video?" Almost everyone is willing and eager to share observations and reactions. My task is simple: I merely invite reflections and then moderate the sharing of reactions both to the video and to one another's contributions. In short, I help group members learn from one another. This experience is a classic demonstration of the adage, *the process is the product*.

Sensible Structure

In guideline 6 we considered Lencioni's theory that *drama or conflict* can make for lively rather than boring meetings. Now we see how a sensible structure creates efficient meetings.

Here is the problem with how we typically structure our meetings from Lencioni's perspective:

> No matter what kind of organizations I work with—regardless of size, industry, or geography—the same general experience drives people crazy when it comes to meetings. . . . The single biggest structural problem facing leaders of meet-

ings is the tendency to throw every type of issue that needs to be discussed into the same meeting, like a bad stew with too many random ingredients.[21]

More specifically, he says:

Unfortunately, this only ensures that the meetings will be ineffective and unsatisfying for everyone. Why? Because some people want the meeting to be informative and quick, an efficient exchange of data and tactical information. Others think it should be interactive and strategic, providing key analysis and data to make critical decisions. Others would like to step back, take a breath, and talk meaningfully about company culture and people. Others just want to make clear decisions and move on. Who's right? Everyone. And that's the point.[22]

Lencioni's solution to the structural problem facing most group leaders is to have different meetings for different purposes. To ensure that meetings will be effective and satisfying for everyone, he proposes adopting four basic types of meetings: the daily check-in, the weekly tactical, the monthly strategic, and the quarterly off-site review. While not a one-size-fits-all solution, these four types of meetings are worth a closer look.

Daily check-ins are very brief, five-minute meetings to share daily schedules and activities. Don't sit down and don't cancel even if some people can't attend. And above all, keep it administrative.

Weekly tactical meetings take forty-five to ninety minutes to review weekly activities and progress, and to resolve tactical obstacles and issues. Don't set the agenda until after the initial reporting, and postpone strategic discussion.

Monthly strategic or ad hoc strategic meetings require two to four hours to discuss, analyze, brainstorm, and decide upon critical issues affecting long-term success. Limit these meetings to one or two topics, prepare and do requisite research, and engage in good conflict.

Quarterly off-site reviews are one- or two-day-long meetings to review strategy, trends, competitors, personnel, and team development. Get out of the office, center on task more than social activities, and don't overburden the schedule with too much structure.

Lencioni is well aware that some people will think, "This is crazy. Where am I going to find the time to do all this? I'm already going to too many meetings."[23] Here is his answer to what he sees as the myth of too many meetings:

While it is true that much of the time we currently spend in meetings is largely wasted, the solution is not to stop having meetings, but rather to make them better. Because when properly utilized, meetings are actually time *savers*. That's right. Good meetings provide opportunities to improve execution by accelerating decision making and eliminating the need to revisit issues again and again. But they also produce a subtle but enormous benefit by reducing unnecessarily repetitive motion and communication in the organization.[24]

It is important to recognize that Lencioni's innovative two-part model emphasizing *drama* and *contextual structure* is geared to profit-making, business organizations. As such, it may be too radical or impractical for some of your group contexts, including some nonprofit, volunteer organizations like congregations. Nonetheless, you may be able to adapt some of Lencioni's outside-the-box thinking and creative approaches to make some of your congregation's meetings more lively and decision-making more effective. Perhaps our biggest takeaway is to match our meeting type and duration to our meeting purpose and format.

In chapter 1, we learned that the costs of poor listening are immense and the benefits of effective listening enable us to grow, learn, and prosper. So, too, are there far-reaching costs of bad meetings and benefits of lively and effective ones. Lencioni's final thoughts are a poignant and fitting way to conclude this chapter:

> Bad meetings exact a toll on the human beings who must endure them, and this goes far beyond mere momentary dissatisfaction. Bad meetings, and what they indicate and provoke in an organization, generate real human suffering in the form of anger, lethargy, and cynicism. And while this certainly has a profound impact on the organizational life, it also impacts people's self-esteem, their families, and their outlook on life.
>
> And so, for those of us who lead organizations and the employees who work within them, improving meetings is not just an opportunity to enhance the performance of our companies. It is also a way to positively impact the lives of our people. And that includes us.[25]

Summary and Conclusion

While negative impressions of committee meetings are prevalent, the real culprits are dysfunctional group practices and behaviors rather than inherent weaknesses or failures of group work per se. Eight guidelines were presented to help people lead meetings more effectively.

We learned the importance of viewing leaders as members of a group designated to help a group go where it wants to go to the extent that such help is needed. Effective group leaders are flexible and adaptable.

It is essential that people know why they are meeting and how they may participate. When you begin a new group, create an overview of your group's objectives, goals, purposes, and processes and develop conversational guidelines that let members know what is expected of them. Regularly remind your group why it is meeting and frequently encourage member participation.

Groups must learn to face dysfunctional behavior openly, directly, and creatively. Eleven strategies were presented to ensure healthy participation in group discussion and decision-making.

In order for groups to accomplish their tasks, members learn how to work as a team. Normally, group activities require collaboration between leaders and members.

A simple agenda can create lively conversation, and sensible structure results in efficient meetings.

The costs of poorly led meetings are far-reaching even as the benefits of effectively led ones are readily apparent and accessible. In short, as people in our congregations learn to lead meetings more effectively, they will experience healthier ways of relating to one another in their group work.

Practical Applications

1. How do you view yourself as a group leader? What are the advantages and disadvantages of collaborative leadership over and against directive leadership?
2. Can you think of instances where a group has floundered because members don't know either how to participate or why they are meeting? If so, how might you deal with the challenge? How might you handle it differently in the future?
3. How might you adjust the balance between task work and teamwork in a group you lead?
4. How can you increase the flexibility of your approach to leadership? See note 7 for resources.
5. How might leaders in your congregation deal with a particularly troublesome dysfunctional member's behavior? Use the Conversation Guides to evaluate and improve group interaction. For an additional resource, see note 5.
6. In which of the groups you work with are the ten strategies for achieving full-group participation applicable? How about in culturally diverse situations?
7. In which congregational groups might a simple agenda and sensible structure create lively conversation and efficient meetings?

For Further Study

Bellman, Geoffrey M., and Kathleen D. Ryan. *Extraordinary Groups: How Ordinary Teams Achieve Amazing Results* (San Francisco: Jossey-Bass, 2009).

Kirkpatrick, Thomas G. *Small Groups in the Church: A Handbook for Creating Community* (Herndon, VA: Alban Institute, 1995).

Law, Eric. *The Wolf Shall Dwell with the Lamb: A Spirituality for Leadership in a Multicultural Community* (St. Louis: Chalice, 1993).

Lencioni, Patrick. *Death by Meeting: A Leadership Fable* (San Francisco: Jossey-Bass, 2004).

Sawyer, David. *Work of the Church: Getting Jobs Done in Boards and Committees* (Valley Forge, PA: Judson, 1986).

Scheidel, Thomas M., and Laura Crowell. *Discussing and Deciding: A Desk Book for Group Leaders and Members* (New York: Macmillan, 1979).

Woods, C. Jeff. *We've Never Done It Like This Before: 10 Creative Approaches to the Same Old Church Tasks* (Herndon, VA: Alban Institute, 1994).

CHAPTER THREE

~

Experiencing Trust

- *"I do believe your intentions to help me are good, pastor, but I don't feel very confident that you can get me out of my depression this time."*
- *"It feels very satisfying to be able to be this risky and trusting in our relationships. There's a climate of openness and acceptance; such bonds of warmth and support."*
- *"I'm not sure I know enough about the situation to predict what they will do. I have a suspicion they could deceive us; then too, we might end up relying on their support."*
- *"Our trust built a little bit at a time in my group." "Oh, really? Trust was never an issue for us, even right from the beginning."*

All-Too-Uncommon Scenario

Imagine with me that it is Monday night, time for a new sharing and support group to meet for the first time. With favorite beverage in hand, people finish their greetings and chitchat. As they settle into comfortable living-room chairs, the group's purpose and conversational guidelines are clarified and affirmed.

Everyone is then invited to share one of the more important things that have happened in their lives in recent weeks. After people have time to gather their thoughts, the leader goes first.

"Recently, I've begun to get a handle on something I've been struggling with for quite some time. During the last several years, I've been waiting to discover where my passion for human justice can be expressed. Over the last twenty years, I've served on the board of several organizations that provide services to victims of domestic violence. One such program was in a small Midwest town where citizens were outraged at what they perceived as a huge miscarriage of justice in a domestic abuse case. Soon, outrage turned to action. Since there were no social service organizations providing assistance to victims of domestic violence, citizens decided to form an organization to offer services for family peace and justice. For twelve years I devoted considerable time and energy to this organization that now offers the type of services that may have prevented the violence that so deeply touched our community. Since we moved here eight years ago, I've completed a six-year term on another domestic violence services board. So, for the last several years, I've been looking for a new way to express my passion for human justice. Just this week, it occurred to me that I may have discovered a new passion quite some time ago, but haven't given myself permission to pursue it wholeheartedly. You see, when I wake up in the morning, I can't wait to get to my computer and write. Finally, I have time to devote to a passion that's been on the back burner far too long. It feels okay to back off major human justice efforts for now. I'm sure I'll reengage down the road, but I need to move from a season of activism to a season of writing at this time in my life."

"Wow, Maisie, that's an amazing story," comments Raul.

"Thanks for telling us about this exciting passage in your life," says Joyce.

Eka speaks next. "You all know my mother passed away last year. As I think most of you know, she died from a rare degenerative brain disease. What you may not know is that this disease currently is incurable, and it is hereditary. It means that my brother and I each have a 50/50 chance of carrying the same gene. Recently, we both decided to undergo genetic testing. Test results show that both of us carry this gene. It means that both of us will get this disease—sooner or later. After much thought and prayer, we've both decided to participate in a research project that seeks a cure for this disease. A cure might not come in our lifetime, but our participation might help people down the road. As you might expect, we weren't prepared for this whole ordeal. I don't know how much time I have left to be with my husband and kids, and they with me. The uncertainty is stressful, and we're all trying to learn how to live one day at a time."

Stunned at the depth of Eka's sharing, and grateful she confided so readily and intimately in people she didn't know too well, Raul decides to tell the group about a dream. "Last night, I had quite an extraordinary dream. In it, I saw an intense, bright white light. It surrounded me with warmth like a blanket surrounds a baby. I awoke this morning with a calm that is nothing short of a miracle. As I reflect on this experience, I think this may have been a God-inspired dream. You see, my physics doctoral dissertation centered on light particles. I'm a physicist who specializes in light refraction. Is this mere coincidence, or God's amazing whimsy—a dream about something to which I'm deeply connected? And then there is this reality. For far too long, I've felt disconnected to God. It's as if I've been on a very long, dark journey in my soul. So, when I awoke from this very bright light experience feeling surrounded by a calm warming in my parched soul, I guess I think I had more than just an ordinary dream. I'm choosing to be grateful to God for an extraordinary connection to my long love affair with light, and to the beginning of healing in my soul."

Joyce decides to share a similar story of gratitude. "You know, I'm grateful just to be alive. About a year ago, I nearly died from a massive infection in my lower leg. I had underestimated the debilitating power of diabetes such that one day, I entered a stupor from which I likely would not have awakened if it were not for a 911 call from a member of our congregation. No one had heard from me for days, so when someone came to check on me and got no response, they decided emergency measures were needed. That 911 call no doubt saved my life. EMTs quickly realized the infection was so advanced that I had only hours to live, and even with emergency treatment, I might not survive. I did survive, but not without the loss of one of my lower legs. Through rehab and physical therapy, I've learned to get around quite well with my prosthetic leg. I now have tremendous respect and appreciation for skilled, patient rehab therapists. I tell them often how grateful I am for their part in my return to normalcy."

Leonardo is the last to speak. "I've been a stay-at-home dad for nearly four years. I do enjoy most days, though as our last child nears kindergarten, I don't know what's next for me. I've been out of the paid workforce so long that I'm not sure how to reenter the education field. I'm not even sure if I'd like to return to full-time classroom teaching. I'm not feeling pressure to decide right now, but I think I'll need to make some career decisions before too long."

As the sharing time comes to a close, Maisie comments, "The depth of our sharing is remarkable. I'll bet a book acquisitions editor would love to have been a fly on the wall listening to the stories we've each told. Our quality of sharing is a 'textbook model' for how to begin a new sharing and support group."

To which Raul observes, "Well, Maize, the reason our sharing was so intimate is because you set the tone for our sharing with your openness. You risked sharing at a gut level with people you really didn't know very well. It helped establish a level of trust that invited the rest of us to also risk sharing some below-the-surface things that have happened in our lives in recent weeks."

Maisie is right in her observation that this group's quality of sharing represents a rather all-too-uncommon scenario. But why is this depth of sharing so unusual? Can it become normative? This chapter helps us see what conditions are necessary to replicate this experience in real life.

Shall we trust or shall we not trust? This is our question. Since most people are eager to create healthier ways of relating with one another, here are seven sensible, practical guidelines that can go a long way in helping people become more effective in how they experience trust in our congregations and everyday relationships.

Guidelines for Experiencing Trust

1. Check Your Understanding of Trust Against Reality.
How do you understand what it means to trust someone?

In its simplest form, trust means being able to rely on someone. This basic understanding of trust reflects what Scottish novelist, poet, and minister George MacDonald said when he noted, "Few delights can equal the presence of one whom we trust utterly." In the Bible, trust, faith, and belief are closely related. In reality, the experience of trust is multifaceted and includes considerable ambiguity. For example, trust researcher Bart Nooteboom identifies these nine paradoxes of trust[1]:

- It goes beyond self-interest but has limits.
- It entails a state of mind and a type of action.
- It may concern competence or intentions.
- It is based on information and the lack of it.
- It is rational and emotional.
- It is an expectation but not a probability.
- It is needed but can have adverse effects.
- It may be broken and deepened by conflict.
- It is both a basis and an outcome of relations.

So, while there is a common, straightforward meaning of trust, much complexity must be taken into account. Notice that Nooteboom's paradoxes are presented as both-and polarities rather than either-or opposites. For instance, while some may emphasize the rational side of trust and others focus on its emotional dynamics, both rationality and emotion are involved. At times they must be held in tension or kept in balance. As we will see in the guidelines to follow, it is important to acknowledge and manage these polarities.

Based on these paradoxes as well as concepts introduced in subsequent guidelines, test your knowledge about the experience of trust using the following list of myths and realities:

Myths (Partial Truths)	Realities (Complementary Truths)
Self-interest is compatible with trust	Self-interest can take advantage of trust
Trust is a state of mind	Trustworthy action also is essential
People should trust your good intentions	Your competence also is required
Trust is based on information	Trust is also based on lack of information
Trust is mainly rational	There is an emotional side to trust
Trust leads to confident expectations	Trust includes doubt and probabilities
You can never have enough trust	Trust can be excessive
Intense conflict causes broken trust	Trust can deepen through conflict
Trust is the basis of relationships	Relationships also shape trust
Trust should overcome suspicion	Healthy suspicion is beneficial
It is smart to trust	It can be naïve to trust
Trust takes time	Trust can emerge quickly
Trust leads to taking risks	You can't have one without the other

We turn now to guideline 2, where we will see the linkage between risk and trust.

2. Link Risk and Trust.

Trust and risk are closely related. In fact, they are bound or linked together. You cannot have one without the other. You cannot trust someone unless risk is involved. And you cannot risk being vulnerable unless you can trust someone. In short, *without trust there is no risk, and without risk there is no trust.*

Trust researchers typically define a trusting relationship as one of interdependence where at least one party is vulnerable to the opportunistic behavior of least one other party to the relationship. At the same time, the vulnerable party also voluntarily accepts the risks of its vulnerability.[2] In this sense, trust includes *mutual vulnerability, sufficient information, and ethical conduct.* Let us consider each of these three dynamics of the experience of trust.

Mutual Vulnerability

The experience of trust normally is a reciprocal or two-step process involving trust and risk. First, all parties open themselves to risk of personal loss. Second, when all parties forego personal gain and cause no harm to the others, trust is experienced. Personal loss might include damage to reputation, violation of confidence, opportunistic self-interest, betrayal, or rejection. For instance, Raul became vulnerable to being perceived as lacking sensibility when he opened up about having a dream. Another group member could discount Raul's experience as craziness or mere figment of imagination. After all, do normal people still have dreams in the twenty-first century? Raul is also vulnerable to being perceived or judged as not being spiritual enough. When the group seems to accept Raul's risky story as legitimate and his spiritual journey as normal, he can relax as Joyce decides to share a similar story of gratitude. Notice, too, what precipitates Raul's confidence to tell his dream story in the first place—his surprise at the depth of Eka's sharing and his appreciation of her readiness to confide intimate information to people she didn't know very well. In other words, his response communicates that Eka's risky sharing both warrants his trust, and leads him to open himself to similar risky sharing. So, risky sharing warrants trust, and trusting behavior leads to risky sharing. *Mutual vulnerability*, then, helps lead to the experience of both risk and trust.

Sufficient Information

Predictability also is integral in our experience of trust. There is an expectation that it is safe to trust one another's goodwill based on sufficient information about each other's trustworthiness. Similarity of beliefs, common group norms, and prior history sometimes provide sufficient information for people to have confidence to readily share risky information. In our congregations, where we supposedly share a common core of values and commitments, trust should come more easily—and in healthy congregations it does.

Similar religious beliefs about healthy spirituality leads sharing group members to accept Raul's dream as legitimate and his spiritual journey as normal. Such predictability also is warranted based on the conversational guidelines the group adopts prior to their initial sharing. Confidentiality, for instance, is affirmed as an agreement about group life. Although the members of the group have no prior history as a group, they do belong to the same congregation. This common life partially explains how these group members so readily trust one another, whereas people in another group without shared history may require that trust emerge slowly and incrementally. Different circumstances, then, lead to different or variable timeframes in our experience of trust.

Sometimes we hear people say they have implicit trust in someone as if trust were a one-sided or one-step formation process. It may be more accurate to say that trust can develop quickly. As in our sharing group experience, trust develops when there is sufficient information to predict that everyone will act in one another's best interests rather than take advantage of each other's vulnerability. In short, while trust may be considered implicit, nonetheless, it is based on sufficient information to warrant reliance on another's goodwill. And if relational trust is the goal, then a reciprocal, two-sided process involving trust and risk between all parties is still required.

Notice, too, that just as trust and risk are intertwined, so are trust and relationships linked: *without trust there are no relationships, and without relationships there is no trust.* Trust is necessary to create relationships, and relationships are necessary for trust to be experienced. Trust is, therefore, both a means and an end. Put another way, trust is both a cause of relationships and an effect of relationships. In sum, trust produces relationships and relationships produce trust.

Ethical Conduct

The presence of sufficient information to warrant confidence in one another's goodwill implies ethical behavior in trust formation. How so? Because a trustworthy person ought not exploit the vulnerabilities of the other parties in a relationship. Reliance on another's goodwill requires that we must decide what counts as unjust or unfair exploitation of the vulnerability of trusting partners. In other words, we must deal with such ethical issues as what constitutes goodwill, and how we ought to act. One answer might be not to renege on or violate the fairness norms affecting one another's vulnerability in the situation. Examples of clear, transparent fairness norms are discussion and conversation guidelines such as those found in chapter 2 to which support group members obligated themselves.[3] For instance, promises to speak one's mind freely, maintain an open mind, and help others participate establish conversation rights and responsibilities for reciprocal, considerate, and safe sharing. Violations of such norms or customary ways of communicating ought not happen, thereby preventing members from being treated improperly, e.g., judged, silenced, or ignored.

3. Good Intentions May Be Necessary but Insufficient to Experience Trust—Competent Behavior May Also Be Required.

Sometimes the best of intentions are not sufficient to experience trusting relationships. Sometimes one party is unable to fulfill the obligations necessary to experience trust. For example, on an organizational level, let's say that you volunteer to take on the duties of your congregation's treasurer while she is on vacation. The congregation's bills must be paid whether or not the treasurer is available to write the checks. You are willing to fill in for her—after all, you know how to write checks. However, your best of intentions are insufficient to experience trust when you learn that there's more to the job than simply paying the water and electricity bills. Staff payroll also is included, for which computation of worker compensation, health deductions, and retirement contributions is required. It is apparent that you will be in over your head as your congregation's temporary treasurer and that you can't be trusted to fill in after all. Your intentions are well meaning while your professional competencies are lacking.

Or, on a social level, suppose that you ask a neighbor to take your kids to soccer practice after school on the days you visit your mother after work. Your neighbor is perfectly willing to help out and intends to do so. Then you discover that your neighbor forgot to mention that his work sometimes takes him out of town unexpectedly, without warning, and for days at a time. In this instance, you are grateful for his willingness to help, but you decide you can't trust his work schedule to allow him to transport your kids when necessary.

Or, on a personal level, suppose that your best friend is dealing with clinical depression yet again, and she confides in you to help her deal with her mental illness. She knows she can trust you to not tell anyone else about her mental state, and you are certainly willing to help provide the support she needs. However, it soon becomes clear that you do not know enough about depression and mental illness to understand why she does not just get back on her medication and snap out of it. You quickly learn that your best of intentions to be supportive are not sufficient to provide the help she needs. You do not have the ability to help her sort through choices that lead to mental health. Again, both intentions and competence are required. You simply cannot behave in a way that fulfills your friend's initial trust in coming to you for help to deal with the experience of mental illness. In short, your intentions are good, but your skill level is lacking.

4. Find the Optimum Level of Experiencing Trust.

So far, we have emphasized the benefits of experiencing trust. However, trust doesn't always have positive outcomes. Sometimes, excessive trust can be harmful. Likewise, deficient trust can result in lost opportunities. In reality, there is both a naïve side and a reluctant side to experiencing trust. Trust, like conflict and power, is neither inherently good nor bad. Trust itself is neutral and depends on how it is experienced. This is why chapter 3 is about *experiencing trust* rather than *building trust*. Building trust implies that trust is good and should be our aim. As we will soon see, though, sometimes it is wise to be suspicious and withhold or refuse to trust rather than be reliant and build or develop it. Consequently, our aim should be to discern when to trust and when not to trust. English hymn writer, theologian, and logician Isaac Watts got it right when he said, "Learning to trust is one of life's most difficult tasks." Our attention should focus on finding the optimum level of experiencing trust.

Continuum Perspective

There are several ways to look at the benefits and liabilities of experiencing trust, or the positive and negative sides to our experience of trust. One way is to view our experience of trust on a continuum where there's more and less trust on a linear sliding scale depending on certain circumstances. From this perspective, it is wise to "trust always or completely" at one side of the continuum to maximize the positive outcomes of trust, and to trust "never or not at all" at the other side of the continuum to minimize the negative consequences of trust.

Bell Curve Perspective

A second way to view our experience of trust is on a bell curve where there's an optimum level in the middle between two negative extremes. From this perspective, there is too much trust at one end of the curve and too little trust at the other end. Consequently, it is wise to move away from the negative consequences or liabilities at each extreme to an optimal middle point that maximizes the positive consequences or benefits of trust.

Notice that both of these ways of viewing our experience of trust are useful to maximize or optimize the positive, beneficial outcomes of trust on the one hand, and to minimize or ameliorate the negative, harmful outcomes of trust on the other hand. Both views seek a balance between extremes, neither of which is wise, warranted, desirable, or beneficial. However, there are circumstances where it is appropriate, even wise, warranted, desirable, and beneficial to not trust at all. There are circumstances where trust is excessive—circumstances where it is naïve or dangerous to trust at all. In short, there are situations where it is wise to be suspicious and totally distrusting. Conversely, there are circumstances where trust is deficient—circumstances where it is advantageous or completely safe to rely on someone. In sum, there are situations where it is wise to be reliant and fully trusting.

Here is an example that demonstrates the tension or dilemma between suspicion and reliance. My denomination, the Presbyterian Church (U.S.A.), is in turmoil over our years-in-the-making decisions to permit Presbyteries to ordain candidates for ministry regardless of sexual orientation, to redefine marriage from "between a man and a woman" to "between two people," and to permit ministers to marry same-sex couples. This struggle creates deep dissension, saps our energies, and threatens our common life. Schism is under way with decisions by more than one-third of the churches in my Presbytery to leave our denomination, reducing our membership by nearly one-half. During this turmoil, trust has been strained and broken seemingly beyond repair between churches, pastors, and lay leaders. There are times when I've wanted to challenge colleagues privately and publicly about their reasons for leaving our denomination. However, I have not felt safe to do so. My uncertainty and fear over how our conversation might transpire prevent me from initiating the mutually beneficial dialogue we are committed to have as partners in ministry.

You can see my dilemma, one not uncommon in such challenging circumstances. On the one hand, by failing to rely on our common bond in ministry, we're unable to have the type of dialogue we should expect of one another. By trusting too little, we've sacrificed the benefits of frank, respectful debate. On the other hand, by succumbing to our suspicion of one another's goodwill and intentions, our civility and surface-level respect remain intact. By trusting too much, we run the risk of angry harangues and defensive behaviors.

Polarity Perspective

Perhaps, then, we need to invent a third way to view the experience of trust, a perspective that captures the nuances of trusting attitudes and behaviors. Let us consider the perspective of polarities between two equally wise, desirable, warranted, and beneficial choices. We will name these polarities *suspicion* and *reliance*. Rather than find an optimum level of trust using either-or thinking as in the first two views, polarities find balance using both-and thinking. Polarity thinking offers a way to frame and manage choices that are equally wise and beneficial. It offers choices to navigate between maximizing or embracing positive or valuable outcomes, and minimizing or eschewing negative or fearful outcomes. To see how polarity thinking works, we will create a process to map out our *suspicion* and *reliance* polarity.

Polarity Map First, we will identify an *overall purpose* for managing our polarity. Then we will create a polarity map with four features for both *suspicion* and *reliance*: *values, fears, alerts,* and *actions*. *Values* are the positive results from focusing on one pole or the other. *Fears* are the negative results from overfocus on one pole to the neglect of the other. *Alerts* are warning signs of approaching the downsides of either pole. And *actions* are ways to gain or maintain positive results of either pole. Third, we will learn how to navigate a path or chart the movement between values, fears, alerts, and actions, in order to achieve the overall purpose.

The overall purpose states the desired outcome or result we would like to achieve. It states why we seek to balance or manage our polarity. In order to successfully navigate our polarity, suspicion and reliance, we begin with this overall purpose statement: to help people create healthier ways of relating to one another by becoming more effective in how they experience trust; in short, *healthy relationships*.

Box 3.1 shows our map for creating healthy relationships by experiencing the optimal level of distrust and trust between suspicion and reliance, featuring values, fears, alerts, and actions for each pole.

Box 3.1. Healthy Relationships

(Overall Purpose)

Suspicion (Distrust)
Values: positive results from focusing on the left pole

- Protection from ill will
- Avoid false sense of security
- Avoid taking unwarranted risks
- Create space for healthy confrontation
- Guard against incompetent behavior

Fears: negative results from over-focus on left pole to neglect of right

- Appear selfish or opportunistic
- Miss opportunities
- Be obstinate or inflexible
- Be deceptive or devious
- Failed expectations

Alerts: warning signs of approaching downsides of the left pole

Reliance (Trust)
Values: positive results from focusing on the right pole

- Reap benefits of goodwill
- Signal good intentions
- Offer peace of mind
- Find freedom to risk
- Expect competent behavior

Fears: negative results from over-focus on right pole to neglect of left

- Take unwarranted risks
- Have overconfident expectations
- Feel foolish or naïve
- Be ignored or alienated
- Feel let down

Alerts: warning signs of approaching downsides of the right pole

---

(continued)

- Others are resentful or threatening
- Miss too many opportunities
- Too much resistance or defensiveness
- Others feel betrayed or put down
- Others express anger or frustration

- Resent opportunistic behavior
- Question others' integrity
- People laugh at your gullibility
- Cannot take people at their word
- Manipulative or controlling behavior

Actions: ways to gain or maintain positive results of left pole

Actions: ways to gain or maintain positive results of right pole

- Use caution about good intentions
- Confirm signs of ill will
- Confirm suspicions are well founded
- Engage in caring confrontation
- Gain sufficient information

- Convey appreciation for goodwill
- Confirm others' willingness to risk
- Be satisfied with your relationship
- Be spontaneous and non-defensive
- Confirm judgments as well founded

Movement Between Values, Fears, Alerts, and Actions to Achieve Purpose Psychologists Daniel Kahneman and Amos Tversky study the way people manage risk and uncertainty.[4] They discovered an unconscious and uncontrollable tendency toward *loss aversion*. Loss aversion is the notion that fear of disadvantage far outweighs the prospect of advantage. Negative possibility often trumps the positive in our minds. That is just what happened in my Presbytery meeting—our fear of incivility outweighed the prospect of mutually beneficial dialogue. We even favor the status quo because we fear the disadvantages of change rather than the advantages.

Notice how this notion affects the dynamics of our choices to be suspicious and reliant. It informs us that our fears of negative results from over-focus on one pole to the neglect of the other are more important than the positive results we value from focusing on either pole alone. This dynamic may explain why we become conflicted in deciding whether or not to be suspicious or reliant. It explains why we pause to evaluate the wisdom of our decision in light of what we'll miss out on if we cling too tightly to either pole. It can have a leveling affect. As with my Presbytery colleagues, when our fear of loss trumps the value of gain, it helps us guard against overfocusing on either pole by factoring in the advantages we'll sacrifice by ignoring the other. It is a way to balance possible gain and possible loss. What advantages of the other pole will I sacrifice? In short, it is a way of balancing advantages and disadvantages wherein our tendency is to fear disadvantage more than claim advantage.

One way to manage this quandary is to look for the most appropriate solution rather than try to find a perfect solution. In other words, we can assess the advantages and disadvantages of both poles before deciding how best to experience trust—with suspicion or with reliance. It also leaves open the possibility of being suspicious of certain factors while relying on other aspects of the situation. For example, on less controversial topics at our Presbytery meetings, we could rely on one another's capacity for productive dialogue without fear of angry harangues or suspicion of defensive behaviors.

Paying attention to warning signs about impending loss or negative results and taking steps to acquire gain or positive results are other ways to help us manage our quandary. These are ways to be proactive in warding off unwanted outcomes and in achieving desired outcomes. Again, we need not make this an either-or decision—to trust or not to trust. Rather, we are free to be suspicious when it is to our advantage to do so, and to be reliant when it is in our best interests to do so. This path helps us deal with our fear that we'll miss out on something beneficial. It gives us perspective for deciding when to be suspicious and when to be reliant. It also helps us guard against our unconscious and uncontrollable tendency to fear what we might miss more than value what we might gain from suspicion or reliance alone. Taking this course with my Presbytery colleagues may provide a path toward cautious dialogue.

One way out of our quandary about whether or not to trust or distrust might be to try to have a civil discussion about the least controversial topic. We could risk talking about the ordination issue, and if all goes well, approach the definition of marriage issue. As we take this first step toward civil dialogue, we can keep *alert* to signs of defensive and supportive behaviors, and then take safe *actions* as appropriate, thereby balancing the dangers of loss against the benefits of gain. If warranted, we could take the next step forward or decide to back off for now. This incremental approach offers a pathway to experience trust that moves us toward the advantages of fruitful dialogue and away from the disadvantages of uncivil conversation.

5. Trust Is Fragile—Easily Broken and Requires Forgiveness to Restore.
Research from social scientists reveals an ever-widening and disconcerting societal breakdown in trust: "Ironically, and unfortunately, while the need to rely on trust and the benefits that flow from trust are clear, there is extensive evidence that trust is declining in many (but not all) societies and within many organizations. Bruhn (2001, p. 3) describes the many polls and studies showing that trust and its allies—honesty, integrity and commitment—have been declining in the USA as well as in other countries over the last 50 years."[5]

Recall, for instance, the recent all-time-low voter approval ratings of our political institutions and elected officials, the mean-spirited and fear-based political campaigning, the misleading and deceptive advertising, and the incivility of our public discourse. Similar evidence of declining trust, honesty, integrity, and commitment includes the following:

- Closed-minded and absolutist thinking
- Opportunistic and selfish behavior
- Self-deception and poor judgment
- Despicable and immoral acts
- Illegal and unethical business practices
- Corrupt and greedy leaders
- Misuse and abuse of power
- Hateful and intolerant attitudes
- Denigration and betrayal of others

Like many societal institutions, the Church has been beset by major seasons of discontent in recent decades. It took the suffragette movement to spur the Church to ordain women, the civil rights movement to spur the Church to integration, and, more recently, the LGBTQ movement to spur the Church to redefine marriage and to ordain members without regard to sexual orientation. The discrimination against women, people of color, and the LGBTQ community has left a legacy of pain and suffering from which healing and change may take years, even generations. Central to building healthy relationships in the Church is the repair and restoration of trust where it has been fractured and broken.

Unfortunately, as business management and organizational behavior social scientists Andrew H. Van de Ven and Peter Smith Ring conclude, "Trust is often easier to breach than it is to build. No relationship is perfect, and most relationships are not expendable. As a result, seldom can parties terminate a relationship in the event a breach in trust occurs (as the literature implies)."[6] How, then, are relationships to heal and thrive when violations of trust occur?

These scholars pose three choices: do nothing, tighten structures to deal with abuses of trust, or repair and restore trust in ongoing interpersonal relationships. With respect to the first two options, here is their conclusion:

> In the final analysis, however, these kinds of interventions will never substitute for high commitment interpersonal relations. As stated before, human beings and their institutions are fallible. No relationship is perfect, and most relationships are not expendable. With their "backs against the wall," reasonable people often can and will work out their differences and failings. Even after serious violations, it is possible to reconstruct trust in relationships. Reconstruction can occur when the parties involved believe the relationship is worth salvaging, so they engage in a negotiation process that involves an extended period of time during which they assess the violation and the intent of the violator, and they offer an apology and render forgiveness.[7]

It might surprise the leaders and members of our congregations to learn that these social scientists know that healing begins with forgiveness. Sociologist John G. Bruhn says this about forgiveness: "The act of forgiveness, even though it may not be accepted by the other party, always makes a difference to the forgiving individual and creates a permanent difference in the relationship, which, over time, can lead to a full conflict resolution and restoration of the relationship."[8] Van de Ven and Ring suggest that the daughter of trust is forgiveness and identify these four characteristics of authentic forgiveness:

- It is unconditional; it is offered to the other person regardless of the response.
- It is self-regarding as well as altruistic; forgiveness is offered for the well-being of the relationship and requires that the persons break free of the old habits and feelings.
- It does not take place instantaneously.
- It is not symmetrical; one party usually instigates the process and becomes the prime mover in restoring the relationship.[9]

Theologian Lewis Smedes captures these truths well with this admonition: "While it takes one person to forgive, it takes two people to be reunited."

Van de Ven and Ring conclude, "If forgiveness is to be an effective intervention, full conflict resolution is necessary. Forgiveness is a transforming process that empowers the forgiver and forgivee."[10]

In sum, while trust may be fragile and easily broken, healing fractured relationships requires restoration of trust. Once trust is broken, it often requires conscious, deliberate, painstaking effort to reestablish trust. Moreover, restoration of trust requires forgiveness, including effectively dealing with the underlying conflict in which the breach of trust occurs.

So, how does the practice of forgiveness repair and restore broken trust in real life? Consider this illustration.

When Archbishop Elias Chacour of Galilee was first sent to his church in Ibillin, Israel, a deep rift existed between a policeman and his three brothers that divided the congregation. As told by Jim Forest based on an interview with Father Chacour, something surprising happened in worship during his first year as pastor of Ibillin. During the service, he padlocked the door and told his parishioners: "Sitting in the building does not make you a Christian. You are a divided people. You argue and hate each other. You gossip and spread lies. Your religion is a lie. If you can't love your brother whom you can see, how can you say that you love God who is invisible. You have allowed the Body of Christ to be disgraced. I have tried for months to unite you. I have failed."[11] Reminding them Jesus can bring them together in unity through the power of forgiveness, he concluded, "So now I will be quiet and allow him to give you that power. If you will not forgive, then we stay locked here. If you want, you can kill each other, and I'll provide your funeral gratis."

Stunned, the congregation sat in silence until the policeman stood before the congregation and said, "I am sorry. I am the worst of all. I have hated my own brothers. I have hated them so much that I wanted to kill them. More than any of you, I need forgiveness." Upon his confession and request for forgiveness, the policeman and Elias embraced each other with the kiss of peace. Next, the four brothers met in the aisles and, in tears, forgave each other. Instantly, worshippers erupted in the chaos of embracing and repentance. At the conclusion of the service, Elias unchained the door, and, as he recalls, "For the rest of the day and into the evening, I joined groups of believers as they went from house to house. At every door, someone had to ask forgiveness for a certain wrong. Never was forgiveness withheld."

Earlier, we learned from social scientists that the process of forgiveness requires that it be unconditional, is offered for the well-being of the relationship, does not take place instantaneously, requires people to break free of old habits and feelings, and is not symmetrical. The surprising experience in Ibillin resulting in healing a rift and restoring trust between four brothers includes most of these characteristics: one brother initiated the process and became the prime mover in restoring the relationship between brothers; his confession breaks free of old habits and feelings; forgiveness appears to be offered unconditionally, regardless of the response; and forgiveness is offered for the well-being of relationships in the community. While the moment of restoration appears unusually instantaneous, it was nonetheless months in the making. In any event, underlying conflict between brothers is fully addressed. Indeed, forgiveness is a transforming process that empowers all parties to repair broken trust through the healing of relationships. It should be noted that while we have been discussing the process of forgiveness here in chapter 3, much more is said about practicing forgiveness in chapter 4.

Finally, a further comment about the speed of trust is warranted. There are a number of factors that affect the amount of time it takes to restore trust. For instance, a catharsis amid crisis such as occurred in Ibillin might result in sudden, deep-level repair of broken relationships. Other situational factors result in considerable variation in the duration of restoration, including:

- Levels of intention
- Competency
- Awareness
- Loss
- Commission
- Omission
- Triviality
- Naïveté
- Morality
- Judgment
- Control

Sometimes these factors result in restoration being fast or slow, incremental or episodic, deliberate or unintentional, one-time or repetitive, partial or complete, conscious or unconscious, behavioral or attitudinal, and superficial or deep-rooted. Moreover, different types of relationships (e.g., strangers, acquaintances, friends, good friends, and intimates) may experience different levels of intensity or importance regarding what is at stake. Then, too, the seriousness of the breach, cause of the breakdown, genuineness of the apology, and severity of the consequences may affect the time required to heal and repair broken trust.

6. Find Common Ground.

Often trust is strained and broken during times of disagreement in discussion and decision-making. Frequently, mishandled conflict is the culprit. Few things are as toxic to trust as conflict. We get locked into "either-or," "I'm-right-you're-wrong" accusations rather than finding "both-and" common ground. We get stuck and lack direction in our search to find a path through conflict that leaves trust intact. Here are eight ways to experience trust by finding common ground.

- Discover the 80%–100% rule
- Find unity amid diversity
- Follow the 75% rule
- Complement rather than oppose
- Use mutual invitation
- Agree on criteria
- Use open space meetings
- Share life-stories or faith journeys

Discover the 80%–100% Rule

Sometimes, we must settle for compromise during times of disagreement and decision-making. However, I have discovered that as much as 80 percent of the time, a 100 percent mutually agreeable, creative, win-win alternative is available if we'll just ask and use the question, *What other options do we have?* Before getting to this question, however, as we saw in chapter 1, it helps to keep our differences clear by asking a prior question, *What is the primary issue about which we're differing?* Next, it helps to clarify what we each want by asking the question, *What are the goals we each seek?* These two questions provide the necessary groundwork for finding a mutually acceptable solution. They are part of a process or pathway to constructively navigate our conflicts. The Friday night conversation between my wife, Carol, and me from chapter 1 is a good example. To review, here is our conversation:

Carol: I'd like to stay home tonight.

Tom: No, I want to go to a movie.

Carol: Come on, we did that last week. Let's just stay home.

Notice how our accusations strain our trust in each other's fairness: "We always do what you want" (Tom), and "Come on, we did that last week" (Carol). If we had clarified the primary issue (how we'll use our time on Friday night), then our conversation would have a focus; we could have made progress. Clarifying the issue also helps us find common ground: how shall *we* spend *our* time, rather than fighting over our positions or express suspicion about each other's fairness. It gets us working together rather than working in opposition to one another.

In our example, rather than getting stuck in *either* staying at home *or* going to a movie, and in trust-straining accusations about each other's fairness, our conflict moves toward agreement when this creative alternative is discovered: calling friends to see if they'd like to come over and play cards.

As we saw in chapter 1, this fresh alternative opens options that might satisfy both of our goals. Carol wants to have a quiet, peaceful evening. And I want to do something mindless, something thoroughly entertaining. Playing cards with friends is an engaging activity for me and it is a laid-back activity for Carol. It qualifies, then, as a 100 percent satisfactory, mutually agreeable alternative. It brings us together by finding common ground. And our level of trust is not compromised or strained in the process. It is kept intact. You should be able to find such alternatives in a large majority of similar cases.

Find Unity Amid Diversity

Ubuntu is a philosophy of African tribes that can be summed up, "I am, because we are." It is an attitude we may take to find common ground by keeping the nature of our relationships in focus. Community shapes our identity. *We become who we are in relationship with one another.* Our unity in Christ calls forth and shapes the unique and diverse gifts that create our identity. Each is needed for the common good. In reality, our unity creates our diversity, and our diversity creates our unity. Indeed, our common ground is found in our unity amid diversity. Philosopher John W. Gardner puts it well: "Wholeness incorporating diversity." Or, as it says on our US currency, *E pluribus unum*—from many, one. Similarly, Rabbi Abraham Joshua Heschel asserts, "The problem to be faced is how to combine loyalty to one's tradition with reverence for different traditions."

In cross-cultural situations, a synthesis of seemingly contradictory value differences is another way to find common ground. Typically, individualistic cultures value self-reliance while collectivistic cultures value cooperation. However, self-reliance can lead to egoism and cooperation can lead to conformity. So, to highlight the positive values of each culture and ameliorate the negative tendencies, international politics and economics scholar Richard Evanoff points out:

> Self-reliance can be combined with cooperation without contradiction, while egoism and conformity can be discarded. This new synthetic position constitutes a "third culture" which combines aspects from each of the original cultures but also transforms them in creative ways. Third cultures have the

potential to provide a common ground for coordinated action across cultures and can be applied to a wide variety of cultural disputes related to value differences.[12]

Stella Ting-Toomey and Leeva Chung also recommend a third-culture approach for bridging cultures:

> It also takes a well-balanced heart to move beyond the practices of both cultures and utilize a third-culture approach to sensitively bridge cultural differences. An individual with an open mindset and elastic communication skills is able to flex her or his communication muscles with good timing and can stretch intentionally to interact competently through a diverse range of intercultural terrains.[13]

Another way to find unity amid diversity is to follow the dictum: *In essentials, unity; in nonessentials, liberty; in all things, charity.* This practice offers a way to find common ground through tolerance and understanding. It is a way that honors our peace, our unity, and our purity. It frees us to identify those few essentials that bind us together in community, and then to agree to disagree on the majority of nonessential beliefs and practices that too often strain or fracture our trust of one another. It also reminds us that the way we conduct our conversation matters: we are to treat each other with respect and dignity. We keep our communication open and accepting such that each person's views and feelings are taken seriously. By acknowledging that some things are important enough to demand agreement, purity is served. And by acknowledging that most things are not important enough to demand agreement, peace and unity are maintained. Inclusiveness is experienced without the sacrifice of anyone's integrity. As Hillary Clinton counsels, "What we have to do . . . is to find a way to celebrate our diversity and debate our differences without fracturing our communities." Here is an illustration.

During debates over differences in polity and theology, I find a remarkable thing happens when we stop and listen to one another's faith stories. Hearing one another's story builds sufficient trust to work together when differences threaten our common life. If we can trust one another's essential faith commitments, then we form a bond of trust that sustains us during times of debate and disagreement over nonessential beliefs and practices. Our unity in essentials gives us sufficient common ground to respect our diversity in nonessentials.

Follow the 75% Rule

In practicing the gospel we preach, we know that at times it is necessary to sacrifice a degree of personal preference to make space for the other. Corey Widmer reports a way his multiethnic congregation in an inner-city neighborhood creates space for all[14]:

> In our congregation we have something we call the 75% rule. It goes like this: When we gather during the worship service on Sundays, everyone should be happy with no more than 75% of what is happening during the worship service. Why such a strange rule? Because we realize that in our culturally diverse congregation, if you are happy and comfortable with more than 75% of what is going on, it most likely means that your personal cultural preferences are being dominantly expressed. So we've decided that no one cultural form will be dominant and everyone will be equally unhappy with the worship!

Widmer continues:

> We believe this "rule" is true to the pattern of the gospel. Even though there is one, true, unchanging gospel, there is no one single way to express the Christian faith that is universal for everyone in all cultures. In fact, one of the most beautiful things about Christianity is that the Holy Spirit is at work in every culture under heaven to create God-pleasing worship that is expressed in all the many particular cultural forms of all the nations of the earth.[15]

Widmer also knows this approach rubs some people the wrong way and goes against the way many people tend to think about worship in their congregation. To which he cleverly responds:

> So go on: embrace the uncomfortable. Be willing to endure a song you don't like or a worship form that seems awkward or out of place. In doing so, you may be opening the door to a person to know Christ and to be welcomed in your community that, were it not for your own worship displeasure, would never have felt at home.[16]

Complement Rather Than Oppose

Distrust between conservatives and liberals is commonplace. It is what divides my Presbytery. Fortunately, there is a place in the middle between the extremes of liberal or progressive on the left, and conservative or evangelical on the right. In reality, a growing number of Christians find themselves being both liberal or progressive *and* conservative or evangelical. Perhaps there is a way to complement rather than oppose each other. These moderate Christians are finding common ground by combining the compassionate openness and social activism of progressive, liberal Christianity with the magnetism and spiritual passion of evangelical, conservative Christianity.[17] Such common ground helps create a climate of trust between people who are partners rather than opponents.

Use Mutual Invitation

Organizational development consultant Eric Law has studied the tendency of whites of Northern European origin to dominate discussion in multicultural situations, driving those of other races and ethnic groups to silent rage or outright rebellion. Trust among cultures is very difficult to create and sustain when such power imbalances exist. As we saw in chapter 2, Law invented mutual invitation as a process to achieve more inclusive group participation in a multicultural setting. This process is a way of finding common ground in group discussion and decision-making by decentralizing the power dynamic and creating an environment for experiencing trust among people.[18] More will be said about how power differences affect intercultural communication in chapter 5.

Agree on Criteria

A Sanskrit proverb says, "To judge a thing, one must first know the standard." Often in our feuding we haven't identified the standards we're seeking.[19] One way to get beyond our fractious worship wars over acceptable music in the church is to reach agreement on the criteria by which to judge "good music." This is another means of getting beyond either-or thinking to both-and mutually agreeable alternatives that build rather than destroy trust. For instance, rather than decide between either contemporary or traditional music, use of agreeable criteria about what constitutes "good music" frees people to select music regardless of whether it is traditional, contemporary, or blended. If a hymn is musically well written, the content is theologically sound, and it is singer-friendly, then it qualifies as "good music" for use in worship. This approach shifts the conversation about acceptable music for use in worship from people's personal preference to mutually agreeable criteria. It offers a way to prevent distrust from fracturing relationships during times of disagreement. Judgment is still required, but it is amazing what happens when decision-making is based on criteria on which everyone agrees. Trust-straining worship wars over music become less frequent because a path to find common ground is taken.

Here is another example. A church located on a six-acre parcel of land was in turmoil over selling an unused portion of its property to a nonprofit organization to build low-income housing. Conflict over the decision-making process resulted in a loss of trust in church leadership by a sizable number of parishioners. The primary issue that divided the congregation was over which portion of the church's land to sell. The goal was clear: to reach a decision on a portion of land to sell that had the congregation's support and that was acceptable to the developer. A surprising thing happened when the congregation was invited to create parameters for the sale. A path to reach a near-unanimous decision was created. Agreement was reached on these three criteria: the church's visibility would remain intact, the church's parking would not be compromised, and utility easements for the developer would be satisfactory. Three portions of land for sale were presented to the congregation. Near-unanimous support for one portion was reached. Agreement on criteria resulted in addressing the issue, meeting the goals, and creating a mutually agreeable option. This process also resulted in the beginning of a restoration of trust by the congregation in the congregation's leadership.[20]

Use Open Space Meetings

This meeting format offered me opportunity to address the lack of trust in my Presbytery. After a convener "opened the space" for participants to self-organize around pertinent issues, I identified and led a small group discussion on this topic: How can we rebuild trust in our Presbytery? I began our conversation among a dozen diverse-thinking colleagues by pointing out that risk and trust go together, and by revealing my previous failure to risk open dialogue. My risk-taking openness created a climate in which people felt free to disclose long-kept silent thoughts and feelings. It became a safe place to speak openly and freely about "the elephant in the room." Risky conversation occurred in an atmosphere of careful listening and respectful dialogue. A rebuilding of trust was under way.

Share Life Stories or Faith Journeys

A final way to experience trust by finding common ground is to take the time to learn each other's life story or faith journey.[21] As we saw earlier in the example about debate over differences in polity and theology, such sharing builds trust by bringing us together around something that is essential in our lives. Our life stories and faith journeys are sacred, and sharing them puts us on holy ground. It is an experience of ubuntu: I am, because we are. We remember that each is necessary for the common good. We discover a unity amid our diversity. It helps us keep things in perspective and find a way to practice what that wise maxim we have visited before urges: in essentials, unity; in nonessentials, liberty; and in all things, charity. All are ways that build and maintain trust through finding common ground.

7. Experiencing Trust Creates an Openness, Acceptance, Warmth, and Support in Our Communication That Leads to Relational Health.
What makes our relationships meaningful, fulfilling, or satisfying? My research shows that these four factors are at the heart of relational health[22]:

- Openness
- Acceptance
- Warmth
- Support

These four qualities of healthy relationships are all rooted in trust. An *openness* or freedom to be oneself, to share what one wants to say in the way one wants to say it, requires a vulnerability that only trust can provide. Openness requires risk, and risk requires trust. Likewise, *acceptance* implies that the risks associated with openness are worth taking. In other words, when one is open to share what one wants to share in the way one wants to share it, there is a risk of rejection or judgment. Acceptance is a product of trust: it's okay to be oneself.

A climate of openness and acceptance in our communication leads to our other two factors: the bonds of warmth and support. *Warmth*, a feeling associated with intimacy, is a relational bond that trust creates through openness and acceptance. Likewise, *support*, an experience of counting on help from others, is also a relational bond that trust creates through openness and acceptance. If openness and acceptance are rooted in trust, then the bonds of warmth and support are the stepchildren of trust.

So, trust creates a climate of openness and acceptance in our communication, and through them the bonds of warmth and support are produced. And when openness, acceptance, warmth, and support are present in our communication, healthy relationships are created—relationships that are meaningful, satisfying, and fulfilling.

Summary and Conclusion
The experience of trust is multifaceted, complex, and includes seeming contradiction between myth and reality. There is a reciprocal relationship between risk and trust characterized by mutual vulnerability, sufficient information, and ethical conduct. Good intentions and competency are required.

An optimal level of trust is reached by finding a balance between positive outcomes and negative consequences. Healthy relationships are created by successfully navigating the risks and uncertainties associated with suspicion and reliance.

Trust is often strained or broken during times of disagreement in our conversations, discussions, and decision-making. There is considerable variation in the time it takes to heal, repair, and restore broken relationships and a variety of ways to find common ground.

Trust produces an openness, acceptance, warmth, and support in our communication that creates healthier relationships.

Practical Applications

1. Which of the nine paradoxes of trust most surprise you? Test your knowledge about the experience of trust using the list of myths and realities.
2. Can you think of examples where trust and risk are linked to create a healthy relationship? If so, how or in what ways are the dynamics of mutual vulnerability, sufficient information, and ethical conduct present?
3. What is lacking in situations where your good intentions are insufficient to experience a trusting relationship?
4. Use the polarity map for creating healthy relationships to balance the advantages and disadvantages of suspicion and reliance for a quandary about how best to experience trust. Pay attention to the movement between values, fears, alerts, and actions.
5. Think of a time when the practice of forgiveness was necessary to repair and restore broken trust. Which of the four characteristics of authentic forgiveness were or were not present? What can be done differently to experience a better outcome?
6. In which of the groups you work with are the eight ways to experience trust by finding common ground useful or applicable?
7. Describe an experience where trust created a communication climate of openness, acceptance, warmth, and support resulting in a satisfying, meaningful, or fulfilling relationship.

For Further Study

Backmann, Reinhard, and Akbar Zaheer. *Handbook of Trust Research* (Northampton, MA: Edward Elgar, 2006).

Bruhn, John G. *Trust and the Health of Organizations* (New York: Kluwer, 2001).

Covey, Stephen M. R. *The Speed of Trust: The One Thing That Changes Everything* (New York: Free Press, 2006).

Kahneman, Daniel. *Thinking, Fast and Slow* (New York: Farrar, Straus and Giroux, 2011).

Kirkpatrick, Thomas G. *Small Groups in the Church: A Handbook for Creating Community* (Herndon, VA: Alban Institute, 1995).

Widmer, Corey. "The 75% Rule" (*Presbyterian Outlook Magazine*, InSights Opinion/Outpost Blog, June 19, 2013).

Wildman, Wesley J., and Stephen Chapin Garner. *Found in the Middle! Theology and Ethics for Christians Who Are Both Liberal and Evangelical* (Herndon, VA: Alban Institute, 2009).

CHAPTER FOUR

∼

Practicing Forgiveness

- *"Forgive and forget? Not necessarily so!"*
- *"Premature forgiveness is false forgiveness."*
- *"There's no 'one size fits all' formula for forgiveness."*
- *"One of you needs to take the first step toward forgiveness."*
- *"I've let it go so the power to hurt me over and over is cut off."*
- *"You must say, 'I'm sorry,' and really mean it before I can forgive you."*

All-Too-Uncommon Scenario

In John 7:53–8:11, a woman caught in the act of adultery is brought before Jesus-the-Rabbi to test him and to perpetrate a conspiracy to bring false charges against him.[1] He is presented with a conflicted lose-lose, either-or proposition: Should the woman be stoned as the Hebrew Scriptures stipulate, or will he be "soft on crime" and let her off the hook? Should she be forgiven or condemned? Notice how Jesus cleverly sidesteps this dilemma by posing a new issue, one that completely changes the negotiating situation. Jesus transforms the conflict by raising the issue about who among them is without sin. He says to let the person without sin cast the first stone.

Jesus effectively redefines the issue and redeems the situation. First, he slows down the proceedings. When he bends down to write in the sand, Jesus buys time to discover a new, creative option.

Next, he separates the parties by placing himself between the woman and the hostile crowd. He uses restraint to protect the woman. Notice that this act not only saves the woman's life; it also saves the crowd from itself. Under Roman law only Caesar is permitted to carry out capital punishment. The crowd would be guilty of insurrection, behavior swiftly and harshly punished by their Roman rulers. So, Jesus offers the crowd a life-saving alternative. They are free to repent of their actions—they may turn around and walk away. He doesn't tell them what to do or offer them a forced choice. Rather, he offers them a fresh, creative, imaginative alternative. The hostile accusers choose to take this path, leave the scene, and return to their homes.

Finally, Jesus restores the woman's dignity by asking her where are her accusers. Seeing none, Jesus sets her free. Yes, she can be forgiven rather than condemned—apparently even without formally asking, even without actually confessing, even without explicitly receiving pardon. Free from condemnation even by Jesus, she is free to turn around and start a new life. She can face the truth about herself, forgive herself, rid herself of bitterness, blame no one else for her predicament, and choose to follow the right path: to go and sin no more.

Jesus' behavior demonstrates how to create healthy relationships by practicing forgiveness. Moreover, it models a way of relating that is central to our lives as people of faith. As we shall see, it also reveals much about the process, challenge, theology, and opportunities of practicing forgiveness. Most people are eager to create healthier ways of relating to one another. But how to do so? Here are twelve guidelines that can go a long way in helping people become more effective in how they practice forgiveness.

Guidelines for Practicing Forgiveness

1. Forgiveness Is Multifaceted.

Common Understandings

Forgiveness is neither a simple concept to grasp nor an easy journey to travel. It can be complicated to understand and challenging to practice. It is not a static, single-tiered, one-dimensional phenomenon. Rather there is a dynamic, many-layered, multidimensional pathway through the processes of forgiveness. For example, forgiveness may include restraint or forbearance of resentment, indignation, or anger stemming from a perceived offense, disagreement, or mistake. It may involve ceasing to demand punishment or restitution, or it may include an expression of sorrow and completion of reparations. It may be offered and it may be sought. It may be available whether or not we know we need to be forgiven. And perhaps most surprisingly of all, it may or may not be accompanied by explicit request, confession, pardon, or reconciliation as we saw in the case of Jesus, the woman, and her accusers.

Forgiveness has traditionally been understood as ceasing to feel anger or resentment toward an offender, or forgoing a desire for revenge or restitution for a wrongdoing. The Oxford English Dictionary defines forgiveness as granting free pardon and giving up all claims on account of an offense or debt. Forgiveness may also be viewed as an intentional and voluntary process by which a victim experiences a change in feelings and attitude about an offense or offender, letting go of negative emotions such as revenge, and wishing the offender well.

Religious Understandings

In both the Hebrew and New Testament scriptures, an offense, wrongdoing, or sinful behavior usually creates a barrier or break in relationships both human and divine. Forgiveness is seen as a gift in which grace offers the means to remove, cover up, or send away the guilt of wrongful behavior. This grace does not emanate from human power alone—it requires divine empowerment. While grace offers the means of forgiveness, repentance is always required. Repentance involves a real and genuine change of mind, heart, will, and behavior to activate forgiveness and to restore broken relationships. The practice of forgiveness might or might not include reparations, reconciliation, justice, and peace.

From empirical research on forgiveness, we know that most religious groups promote forgiving attitudes and that people who are more religious, especially Christians, report having a forgiving disposition. Clearly, though, most people of faith find it harder to forgive some behaviors than others. For instance, some religious people have strong feelings about desecrated sacred objects and they are reluctant to forgive such transgressions. Studies about people's anger and disappointment with God reveal that people usually resolve their anger satisfactorily—though some do so by rejecting their faith.

While forgiveness has been studied largely apart from its religious roots, there are hard questions about the intersection of religion and forgiveness that remain unanswered. For example, we don't know whether forgiveness affects spiritual transformations or whether spiritual transformation affects forgiveness. Negative effects of forgiveness have not been studied, nor have the mental, physical, relational, and spiritual effects of making a decision to forgive been tested. In reality, many Christians believe that their forgiveness by God depends on their forgiveness of others. Might this tension or religious pressure lead people to say they forgive while holding emotional unforgiveness, to the detriment of their overall health and well-being? Might this impulse also deflect legitimate resentment, resulting in premature forgiveness without holding wrongdoers accountable, or in wrongdoers taking advantage of victims repeatedly if they assume they'll be forgiven anyway? Might guilt-ridden religious people be reluctant to forgive themselves, and self-absorbed and narcissistic religious people let themselves off the hook through glib forgiveness that short-circuits repentance, confession, apology, restitution, and making amends? We also know little about how people forgive when religious differences are strongly entrenched in historical conflict between religions.

Social Science Understandings

Academic fields such as speech communication, psychology, organizational development, psychiatry, philosophy, and religion all seek to understand what people go through when trying to forgive in order to benefit their overall health and well-being. Forgiveness researcher Everett Worthington points out that the study of forgiveness by clinicians and social scientists began in the mid-1980s after the publication of theologian Lewis Smedes's book, *Forgive and Forget: Healing the Hurts We Don't Deserve.*[2] He goes on to comment, "Ironically, Smedes was neither clinician nor scientist. He was a theologian. Yet he started a movement within therapy and science that revolved around the idea that forgiveness can benefit a person's mental health and well-being."[3] Worthington also notes the irony that the study of forgiveness in religion lags the study of forgiveness in nonreligious contexts.[4]

Several schools of social science researchers and practitioners have made significant strides in advancing our understanding of what forgiveness is, and how it works. The multifaceted nature of forgiveness is a common feature in the work of these social scientists and in the forgiveness literature. First, there is Worthington, a clinical psychologist and professor of psychology, and his colleagues at Virginia Commonwealth University. They see forgiveness as a choice we can make with or without forgetting or pardoning an offense. They believe we can learn to forgive by changing our response from negative emotions such as resentment, hostility, anger, hatred, and vengeance to positive feelings of care, compassion, and conciliation. Their focus is on three components of forgiveness: empathy, humility, and commitment. They help people reach emotional forgiveness using a five-step intervention process using the acronym REACH: "recall" the hurt, "empathize" with each other, "altruism" with the gift of forgiveness, "commit" verbally to forgiveness, and "hold on" when remembering past hurts.[5]

Then there is Michael McCullough, director of the Evolution and Human Behavior Laboratory and professor of psychology, and his colleagues at the

University of Miami. They believe a foundational and uncontroversial factor of forgiveness is putting the past in the past by changing one's motivations or emotions toward a transgressor over time.[6] They identify four predictors for the likelihood of forgiveness in close relationships, including personality, relational quality, nature of offense, and social behavior.[7] More will be said about this approach later.

Next, there is Robert Enright, professor of educational psychology and co-founder of the International Forgiveness Institute, and his colleagues at the University of Wisconsin-Madison. They also view forgiveness as a choice to release anger and live a healthier life. Their research interests center on the moral development of forgiveness, including a process model that includes four phases: uncovering, decision, work, and outcome.[8] Look for more information about this process in guideline 2.

Finally, there is Fredrick Luskin, director of the Stanford University Forgiveness Projects, and his colleagues at the Institute for Transpersonal Psychology and the Greater Good Science Center at University of California, Berkeley. They have developed and tested nine steps for practicing forgiveness that help people give up their grudges, which results in improvement of physical and emotional well-being. These include[9]:

- Tell trusted people how you feel
- Commit to feeling better
- Recognize present distress
- Practice stress management
- Hope for change without demanding it
- Find alternate ways to move on
- Remember that a life well lived is the best revenge
- Remember that forgiveness is a choice
- Seek peace and understanding even without reconciling or condoning hurtful actions by blaming people less and taking offenses less personally

Consensus Definitions

Since the birth of interest in forgiveness by psychologists, counselors, psychiatrists, researchers, religious leaders, and the general public, forgiveness has been defined in multifaceted ways and approached in a variety of pathways. Nonetheless, there is a common core of beliefs about what forgiveness is, and what it is not, that remains constant (regardless of whether researchers agree in every detail or circumstance).

There seems to be agreement that forgiveness is different from *forgetting*—removing awareness of an offense from consciousness, *excusing*—not holding an offender accountable for wrongful behavior, *exonerating*—clearing of blame, *justifying*—covering up wrongdoing, *condoning*—failing to see a behavior as wrong and in need of forgiveness, *pardoning*—granting forgiveness by a societal representative such as a judge, and *reconciling*—repairing and restoring relational health.

By contrast, there is a common approach to forgiveness reflected in a classic definition by Robert Enright and Robert D. Fitzgibbons. After studying the topic since 1985, these educational psychologists approach forgiveness as an integration of thinking, feeling, and behavior and define forgiving this way: "People, upon rationally determining that they have been unfairly treated, forgive when they willfully abandon resentment and related responses (to which they have a right) and endeavor to respond to the wrongdoer based on the moral principle of beneficence, which may include compassion, unconditional worth, generosity, and moral love (to which the wrongdoer, by nature of the hurtful act or acts, has no right)."[10]

A more concise consensus definition views forgiveness as "a prosocial or positive change in people's thinking, feeling, motivation, and behavior after a transgression."[11] In reality, there may be not one but several definitions of forgiveness depending on different types of forgiveness and different types of relationships. See table 4.1 for a summary of three types of forgiveness (decisional forgiveness, individual experience of forgiveness, and interpersonal processes of forgiveness), and two types of relationships (strangers or non-continuing relationships, and close or continuing relationships).[12]

Decisional Forgiveness   In decisional forgiveness, victims make a willful choice or an intention statement to control their behavior toward a wrongdoer by eliminating their negative behavior in non-continuing relationships and also by restoring positive behavior in ongoing relationships. Injured parties might or might not later experience forgiveness, and they might or might not express their decision to their offender.

There is much we do not know about decisional forgiveness. For instance, in wrongdoing by a stranger, we don't know how victims' decision to forgive affects their internal experience of forgiveness—emotionally, behaviorally, or cognitively. Likewise, we don't know how granting decisional forgiveness affects expressing forgiveness in non-continuing relationships. And in restorative justice, we don't know what effects either granting or not granting forgiveness has on the victim, offender, and involved observers. Moreover, we know little about decisional forgiveness of a stranger from the offender's point of view. To date, we know nothing about how wrongdoers experience guilt, blame, or self-forgiveness—whether or not they know their victim has granted forgiveness or still holds a grudge.

Table 4.1. Definitions of Forgiveness (Types of Forgiveness and Relationships)

TYPES OF FORGIVENESS	TYPES OF RELATIONSHIPS	
	Strangers or Non-Continuing Relationships	**Close or Continuing Relationships**
Decisional Forgiveness	Private decision not to get even, seek revenge, bring harm, or disadvantage.	Private decisions to (1) not get even, seek revenge, avoid, bring harm or disadvantage and (2) heal relational harm and strengthen the relationship.
Individual Experience	Give up a grudge and eliminate negative motivations, behaviors, thoughts, and feelings.	(1) Give up a grudge and (2) reach net positive motivations, behaviors, thoughts, and feelings.
Interpersonal Process	Achieve internally or through a third party.	Interactions surrounding wrongdoing: (1) the wrongdoing, (2) restraint or forbearance, (3) blame or justification (4) repentance (i.e., apology, confession, request for forgiveness), (5) decisions to or not to forgive, (6) acceptance or rejection of forgiveness, (7) self-forgiveness, and (8) divine forgiveness.

Source: Adapted from Everett L. Worthington Jr., "More Questions About Forgiveness: Research Agenda for 2005–2015," in *Handbook of Forgiveness*, ed. Everett L. Worthington Jr. (New York: Routledge, 2005), 566.

Individual Experience   In an individual experience of forgiveness, victims experience forgiveness internally. In relationships with strangers, acquaintances, or if a continuing relationship is not expected or desired, forgiveness includes giving up a grudge, resentment, or bitterness, and not holding an offender's injustice against them. When a continuing relationship among romantic partners, family members, close friends, or certain work group members is required or desired following betrayal or major disappointment, forgiveness includes both giving up negative thoughts, feelings, motivations, and behaviors toward an offender and also replacing them with positive ones. Sometimes this replacement is a means to experience forgiveness, and in other cases, it is the result of forgiving.

Interpersonal Process   Unlike the individual experience of forgiving, an interpersonal process of forgiveness occurs between injured parties and wrongdoers. In such relationships many processes are at work and many ways exist to deal with wrongdoing or perceived wrongdoing. While victims may practice restraint or forbearance, or may silently grant decisional forgiveness, they might also decide to deal with wrongdoing in such ways as:

- Getting even
- Being vengeful
- Seeking justice
- Justifying the offense
- Excusing
- Exonerating
- Attempting to reconcile after the wrongdoing.

Immediate reactions to wrongdoing by both parties might include exits from interaction or discussion about the wrongdoing. Later, injured parties might ask wrongdoers to explain why they offended. Wrongdoers might make excuses, deny wrongdoing, or try to justify wrongful behavior. They may also:

- Experience guilt or shame
- Decide to repent or change their ways
- Confess
- Apologize
- Ask for forgiveness
- Make restitution

Victims who decide to forgive and begin to experience forgiveness may or may not communicate their forgiveness to their offender. If so, wrong-doers might then accept forgiveness from their victim and either forgive themselves or remain trapped in their guilt and shame. Forgiveness is usually offered without expectation of restorative justice and without any response from the offender, although some form of acknowledgment, apology, sorrow, or request for forgiveness may be necessary for the wronged person to believe forgiveness is genuine or authentic.

While most research on forgiveness focuses on the offended party's experience, relatively little attention has been paid to the complexity of the interpersonal process—it remains largely unexplored, especially the interactions around transgressions. In particular, little is known about the communication of forgiveness between victim and wrongdoer, including differences in verbal and nonverbal communication. For example, does making a private decision to forgive affect the victim's thoughts, feelings, motivations, or behaviors? And if so, can offenders detect the changes if a decision is made but not communicated explicitly? Likewise, are the behaviors of wrongdoers or their judgment toward the victim or themselves affected when sensing that their victim experiences forgiveness but is reluctant to say so? Finally, we know little about the responsibility wrongdoers have in initiating and contributing to the interpersonal process of forgiveness.

Likelihood of Forgiveness The multifaceted nature of forgiveness is also apparent in such motivational indicators or predictors of interpersonal forgiving in close relationships as cited earlier: personality, quality of relationship, nature of offense, and social behavior. We know that forgiveness is less likely with people who are selfish or apathetic, and more likely when someone's personality is selfless and empathetic. It also is less likely with relational qualities where one party gains much and invests little, and more likely where there is little to gain and heavy investment. Then too, forgiveness is less likely where the transgression is discovered through a third party and includes a serious offense, and more likely when revealed by a partner and includes a trivial offense. Finally, it is less likely in terms of social behavior when the offense is intentional or malicious, and more likely when it is unintentional or harmless.[13]

2. Forgiveness Is a Process.

Just as there is consensus in the research literature about how to define forgiveness, so also is there agreement that forgiveness is a process (or the result of a process). More than steps, stages, phases, levels, techniques, or skills, forgiveness is a process. The experience of forgiveness normally is not a static series of steps to follow. Nor is it often a linear set of stages through which to pass. It is usually more than a predictable sequence of phases to go through. It doesn't operate only on a matrix of fixed layers or levels. And it involves more than mere technique or specific skills.

Forgiveness is usually an intentional and voluntary process involving a change in emotions and attitudes toward an offender. It often results in a decrease of retaliation, estrangement, and negative emotions toward an offender. As we have seen previously, it may also include replacing negative emotions toward an offender with positive emotions such as compassion and benevolence.

While we can learn to forgive, there is no one-size-fits-all formula for forgiveness. The pathway to forgiveness is a complex journey that everyone approaches differently, depending on previous experience and role models.

Normally, forgiveness is a dynamic, emergent, synergistic process. It helps to view forgiveness as a multidimensional, systemic, ever-changing way of relating. Rather than a rigid, step-like sequence to follow, forgiveness is a flexible set of processes with feedback and feed-forward loops.[14] As cited earlier, Enright and his colleagues describe a process model of forgiveness divided into four phases:

- An *uncovering phase* where people get in touch with their pain, explore the injustice they've experienced, and realize that previous ways of coping may not be effective or serving their purpose.
- A *decision phase* where people explore what forgiveness is and what is involved in the process of forgiveness before committing to actually forgiving—even when they do not feel forgiving at the time.
- A *work phase* where people accept and absorb one's pain and the offender's pain rather than pass it on to others or back to the offender.
- A *deepening or outcome phase* where people realize that forgiveness is a gift given to the offender, healing is experienced, and overall health improved—psychologically, emotionally, mentally, spiritually, and relationally.

The practice of forgiveness is complicated by differences in the way people experience forgiveness. For instance, they may skip back and forth, and go back and rework previous parts of the processes. Although forgiveness is a choice, not a duty, even after deciding to forgive, it usually takes time and unfolds at its own pace. Forced or rushed, it can result in false forgiveness. Moreover, not all anger is counterproductive. Frequently, anger is a positive, life-affirming demand to change hurtful behavior.[15] Even though forgiveness and justice can occur together, forgiveness and reconciliation often occur separately. To satisfy our demands for justice, however, and for our own well-being, we may choose not to reconcile or decide to wait until an apology is offered, wrongdoing admitted, change demonstrated, or reparations completed.

While we can learn to forgive, people learn in different ways and time frames. Education, training, therapy, and counseling are all options to help us learn how to forgive someone, especially people who hurt us deeply.[16] Such help can have a variety of results, including an increase of self-esteem, hope, and well-being, and a decrease in anger, resentment, depression, and anxiety. Much research in the young science of forgiveness shows a link between forgiving and improved mental, physical, psychological, spiritual, and relational health. The practice of forgiveness has many other potential and varying benefits as well. We know that after forgiving, people can experience healing, be more at peace, be more productive at work, be better able to handle relationships, be better able to make decisions about career and relationship issues, become models of forgiveness for other people to follow, and gain control over addictions and substance abuse. In short, properly understood, embraced, and practiced, forgiveness can be good even if experienced differently.

Although forgiveness can be good, it doesn't mean that unforgiveness is bad. The costs of uncritical forgiveness lead clinicians and scientists to study possible limits of forgiveness and potential benefits of unforgiveness. We've learned that it is not always wise to give up resentment, anger, even hate and vengeance, at least not hastily or irrationally. Sometimes premature forgiveness results in losing self-respect, a weakening self-defense, and threatening social order. Domestic abuse is one such instance. Hasty forgiveness or overlooking wrongdoing can lead to a cycle of violence. Victim safety and protection from further violence are needed before attention can turn to forgiveness. Freedom from fear, humiliation, manipulation, control, and danger is of immediate concern. Likewise, unless abusers are held accountable for their violent behavior, there's little reason for them to stop and little deterrence to repetitive abuse. There are no excuses for domestic abuse. Free passes for violent behavior embolden abusers to continue their abuse, and apparent immunity from prosecution weakens respect for law and order.

As with handling conflict and using power, forgiveness offers both challenge and opportunity. Neither inherently good nor bad, what matters is how we understand and practice the process of forgiveness. Forgiveness may not be instantaneous, although there may be times when we can forgive and move on, not letting the other have control over us or infect us over and over again. And at times it will be wise to withhold forgiveness or refuse to forgive until conditions that threaten self-respect, self-defense, and law and order are faced and addressed. The proper granting of forgiveness and reduction of unforgiveness have promise to transform relationships that are stuck, at risk, or broken into ones that move forward, are life-giving, and have been repaired.

3. Our Reactions to Wrongdoing in the Processes of Forgiveness and Reconciliation Matter.

Often we approach forgiveness by focusing on how victims ought to react to wrongdoing as if responsibility for forgiveness rests primarily or solely on them. But why is forgiveness mainly the responsibility of the victim or person wronged? Why doesn't the onus of forgiving fall equally, if not primarily, on the wrongdoer? In any event, both parties are involved in the practice of

Table 4.2. Reactions to Wrongdoing (The Process of Forgiveness)

REACTIONS	WRONGDOER—FORGIVEE	VICTIM—FORGIVER
Emotions	Guilt & shame	Vengeance & hostility
	Sadness & remorse	Hurt & sadness
	Anger & defensiveness	Righteous indignation
	Concern for victim	Distress & anxiety
Thoughts	Deny & excuse actions	Confusion about event
	Think victim overreacts	Repeatedly replay event
	Blame victim	Blame perpetrator
Behaviors	Wrongdoing	Restrain vengeance
	Neglect victim	Avoid perpetrator
	Confess wrongdoing	Hold a grudge
	Apologize sincerely	Forgo vengeance
	Make amends	Demand atonement or reparation
	Ask for forgiveness	Offer forgiveness
	Receive forgiveness	Extend forgiveness
	Repair relationship	Reconcile relationship
	Don't repeat wrongdoing	Rebuild trust

forgiveness—we are, after all, talking about relationships between people. So, what are normal negative and positive reactions to wrongdoing in the *process of forgiveness?* Examine the normal emotional, cognitive, and behavioral *reactions to wrongdoing* for both the wrongdoer or forgivee, and the victim or forgiver found in table 4.2.

Process of Forgiveness

Victims' reactions to wrongdoing are influenced by several factors, including personal tendencies, the nature of wrongdoing, and the nature of their relationship to the wrongdoer. Empirical literature finds that victims tend to be harsher, more vengeful, and more hostile if they have negative reactions such as low empathy, low tolerance for misbehavior, high self-restraint, and external motivation. Conversely, victims' powerful impulse toward vengeance is tempered and greater forgiveness occurs when they tend to have such positive reactions as empathy, insight and understanding, agreeableness, and tolerance of misbehavior. Victims also experience greater anxiety, avoidance, hostility, and desire for vengeance in response to more severe wrongdoing that devalues the relationship or is perceived as deliberate and controllable. Reactions also tend to be stronger immediately following wrongdoing than at a later time. Finally, reactions are less negative in highly committed relationships.[17]

Empirical literature on wrongdoers' reactions to wrongdoing reveals that they experience guilt and remorse when they commit wrongdoing by behaving selfishly or violating relational obligations such as neglecting their victim. As forgiveness researchers Caryl Rusbult, Peggy Hannon, Shevaun Stocker, and Eli Finkel point out:

> Typically, feelings of guilt induce patterns of perpetrator affect, cognition, and behavior that are conducive to promoting victim forgiveness. For example, perpetrator guilt is associated with displays of sadness and remorse, thoughts centering on concern for the victim, and inclinations toward confession, apology, and amends.[18]

The path to forgiveness is often made difficult when victims and wrongdoers do not perceive wrongdoing the same way. On the one hand, victims experience greater distress, and see wrongdoer behavior as more arbitrary, incomprehensible, and gratuitous. They also believe the wrongdoer is more responsible than themselves and describe wrongdoing as more severe. And they believe greater damage is done to the relationship. On the other hand, while wrongdoers typically experience greater guilt, they also tend to view victims' reactions as somewhat excessive and out of proportion to the nature of their wrongdoing. Likewise, when victims do not take extenuating circumstances into account, wrongdoers tend to become defensive and deflect blame to justify their wrongdoing. They also are reluctant to offer amends in proportion to what their victims demand or feel entitled to. Such consequences of perceiving wrongdoing differently can, indeed, make the path to forgiveness a difficult and challenging one to navigate.

As noted earlier, reactions tend to be stronger immediately following wrongdoing than at a later time. Research on forgiveness in ongoing relationships has examined how far victims progress toward forgiveness over time in terms of the degree of initial restraint (e.g., control the impulse to lash out when hurt), ongoing forbearance (e.g., reduce the frequency of hostile accusations), and extended (or complete) forgiveness. Social science research indicates that gut-level impulses tend to be hostile and vengeful immediately following the perception of wrongdoing. These impulses progress or temper over time according to *severity of wrongdoing, empathy,* and *commitment level.*

Forgiveness actually begins within seconds, not hours or days, following an experience of wrongdoing with restraint of vengeful, retaliatory reactions based on severity of wrongdoing but not from empathy or level of commitment. Forbearance or extended restraint in terms of patient leniency or long-suffering tolerance follows in the minutes and hours after perceived wrongdoing according to the degree of restraint and level of commitment rather than the severity of wrongdoing or empathy. And *extended forgiveness* or complete forgiveness over time spans the hours following perceived wrongdoing to several days or even months, according to empathy and commitment level rather than from severity of wrongdoing or degree of restraint and forbearance.

As is evident in table 4.2, an important behavior in the process of forgiveness that increases the degree of victim forgiveness over time is for the wrongdoer to make amends by accepting responsibility for their wrongdoing, offering sincere apology, and providing genuine atonement. In particular, discussing the incident in a concerned and apologetic manner can help the victim initially restrain vengeance and hostility and begin to feel empathy or to identify extenuating circumstances. Likewise, providing partial repayment or amends can result in a cooling-off period. Similarly, rather than respond to a victim's righteous indignation with anger and defensiveness, a wrongdoer's heartfelt apology can lead a victim to extend restraint and forebear vengeful acts and hostile behavior. Feelings of guilt and shame often motivate a wrongdoer to make such amends as apology, confession, and change of behavior. Furthermore, heartfelt amends acknowledge the existence of a debt that the wrongdoer wishes to repay, making it easier for a victim to move toward renewed trust and providing assurance that the wrongdoing won't be repeated. As mentioned earlier, the whole process of forgiveness occurs more quickly in relationships that previously had a high level of trust and commitment. In short, as wrongdoers seek to "cancel" the negative consequences of their actions and communicate in a positive manner, victims experience an increasing freedom that makes it less risky or humiliating to extend a healing hand of forgiveness.

Victims and wrongdoers may or may not seek reconciliation, relational repair, or an ongoing relationship following wrongdoer amends and victim forgiveness. Even when complete forgiveness is experienced, one or both partners may find that they continue to carefully monitor one another's actions, interact unnaturally or awkwardly, or feel ambivalent about their relationships. They may also find it difficult to recover sufficient levels of trust and commitment to reconcile with one another, repair their relationship, or reestablish a healthy relationship. To the extent that the relationship is worth it, efforts to reconcile and repair the relationship may be worth it as well.

Process of Reconciliation

In contrast to our rather extensive knowledge about the process of forgiveness, little is known about the process of reconciliation. Thus, by far, most interventions are geared to help people change their internal experiences of forgiveness while few interventions have been devised to promote reconciliation. The field is too young and funding too meager to determine which intervention factors promote forgiveness. For example, are there different interventions and patterns of behavior between people with vengeful personalities and those who merely hold grudges?

As best we know, it appears that the same type of wrongdoer and victim behaviors that lead to forgiveness reestablish ongoing relational well-being. In particular, reconciliation, relational repair, and ongoing relational health are enhanced by such wrongdoer behaviors as apology, amends, and promise not to repeat wrongdoing. These results are likewise enhanced by victim restraint, forbearance, and extended forgiveness—especially empathetic listening to the wrongdoer's perception of wrongdoing and its consequences, and by accepting their apology, amends, and promises. Such conciliatory behaviors can reduce uncertainty, calm anxiety, increase intimacy, deal with stress, and reduce the likelihood of repeated wrongdoing. It also can be helpful to reach agreements about reasonable debt repayment and to put into place healthier ways of relating to one another, including specifying consequences of future wrongdoing. These behaviors and agreements are the building blocks of sustained, coordinated investment toward the goal of complete reconciliation and relational repair that restores mutual trust and commitment.

We have now examined normal negative and positive reactions to wrongdoing in the processes of forgiveness and reconciliation. Hopefully, we now have greater awareness about the complexity and multifaceted nature of our experience of forgiveness. We also know what behaviors lead to forgiveness, reconciliation, and restoration of relational health. But how does our newfound understanding about these processes help us improve our practices of forgiveness and reconciliation in everyday relationships? Consider the following typical scenario.

Frankie and Dannie Scenario

As they walk out the door for a drive to a family Thanksgiving dinner, two people who live together have this conversation:

Frankie: Do you want me to back out the Jeep so we can take the car today?

Dannie: Sure, that's a good idea. I'll get the car.

Frankie: (Backs out the Jeep and starts to get into the car.) You want me to drive?

Dannie: Well, yeah, at least you'd finally be doing something today.

Frankie: Oh, aren't you in a bad mood? (Gets in the passenger seat and slams the door shut.)

Dannie: (Stomps on the gas pedal and drives off.) Well, I put a lot of work into preparing the dessert to take to your parents' house and all you did this morning was sit there reading the paper and watching your football game on TV.

Frankie: What did you expect me to do?

Dannie: For starters, you could have gotten your vacuuming done.

Frankie: Maybe so, but I can do that anytime.

Dannie: No, the floors are really dirty and needed vacuuming days ago.

Frankie: Hey, get off my case and just pay attention to your driving.

Dannie: I have a right to feel resentful for your failure to do your household chores. I've about had it with you today. I'm going to pull the car over and you're going to get out right now. (Pulls over and stops the car.) Get out of the car!

Frankie: You've got to be kidding. You're overreacting and acting like a spoiled brat.

Dannie: Then you can just drive the rest of the way.

Frankie: Fine. Get over here and I'll drive.

Dannie: (Exchanges places and refuses to talk the rest of the way.)

Frankie: (Breaks the silence upon arrival at parents' house) Okay, I'm sorry for my part in the row we had earlier. I do appreciate the work you put into making the dessert. I'm sorry for failing to notice and hope you can forgive me.

Dannie: Thanks for saying so. I guess things did get out of control there for a while and perhaps I did overreact just a little. I'm sorry for that. I accept your apology and forgive you for not appreciating my work.

Frankie: I'm glad. Thank you too for admitting that you may have overreacted.

Dannie: You're welcome. Now, about the vacuuming . . . ?

Frankie: Oh, yes, about that. I'm sorry I've neglected my vacuuming chore and promise to get it done when we get home tomorrow.

Dannie: Sounds good. I feel better about things now. Let's go in and say hello to the folks.

Frankie: I'm glad we've worked things out, too. It's good we don't have these rows very often.

What wrongdoing occurred in this scenario? From Dannie's perspective, Frankie fails to say "thank you" for the time and effort it took to prepare a dessert. Dannie feels hurt and blames Frankie for failing to be appreciative. Dannie also is resentful that Frankie has not done the vacuuming. From Frankie's perspective, there is confusion about what Dannie expects; after all, the vacuuming will get done eventually. Frankie also feels Dannie over-reacts by pulling the car over and demanding that Frankie get out. Frankie feels angry and defensive, and blames Dannie for childish behavior. Dannie restrains hostility and vengeance, although demands that Frankie drive the rest of the way. Frankie avoids Dannie, and Dannie neglects Frankie as they refuse to speak to one another and travel in silence the rest of the way to their Thanksgiving dinner.

As they arrive for dinner, the couple seeks to repair their relationship before getting out of the car. Frankie confesses wrongdoing and apologizes for failing to notice and appreciate the effort Dannie expended in making the dessert. Forgoing further hostility, Dannie accepts Frankie's apology although demands that Frankie make reparation by promising to get the vacuuming done. With Frankie's agreement, the relationship seems repaired and reconciled. Notice, too, Frankie's observation that even though this will not be their last such row, such episodes do not happen frequently enough to threaten the overall health of their relationship. With sufficient trust re-established, Dannie and Frankie are ready to greet their family as if nothing happened and to have a pleasant Thanksgiving Day dinner.

This conversation demonstrates several other aspects of the practices of forgiveness and reconciliation. Notice that as the conversation evolves, a new controversy emerges: Dannie resents having to make dessert while Frankie watches TV rather than doing the vacuuming. Initially, Frankie resents Dannie's bringing up the vacuuming issue and changes the subject by accusing Dannie of overreacting. This scenario also demonstrates the appropriateness of the wrongdoer accepting blame, admitting guilt, and asking for forgiveness. Also present is a desire and commitment to repair the relationship, to reconcile with one another, and to reestablish relational health. As forgiveness is extended, healing and a renewal of trust seem to happen quickly. Finally, the conflicts that occur are well handled and effective listening skills are employed.

It is also apparent that not all negative and positive reactions to wrong-doing will occur in every scenario. In this scenario, while guilt is present, shame, sadness, and remorse are not. Likewise, while anger and defensiveness are present, righteous indignation is not. While confession is present, holding a grudge is not. Whereas forgiveness is not offered, it is requested, extended, and received. Nonetheless, the processes of forgiveness and reconciliation followed in this instance seem sufficient to repair and restore the relationship between Dannie and Frankie. In other instances, there will be a mixture of different reactions as these processes and practices unfold. Emotions, thoughts, and behaviors will vary, as will the pace of the process and the prospects for renewed trust and commitment. Finally, the use of effective conflict management and listening skills will vary from instance to instance and have an important bearing on the success of reconciliation, relational repair, and ongoing relational health.

The relatively typical turmoil between Frankie and Dannie, while intense, erupts quickly, is short-lived, and eventually resolves quite simply in mere minutes. Turmoil over wrongdoing can also build slowly, be long-lasting, and face complicated and painstaking resolution, especially among family members.

Common experiences calling for forgiveness and reconciliation in families include turmoil over marital dissatisfaction, infidelity, abuse, and divorce. They are not, however, the only such problems. Families also encounter these problems:

- Unequal treatment of siblings
- Failure to protect children from harm
- Hurt feelings from divorce and remarriage
- Irresponsible or dishonest use of money
- Addiction or mental illness
- Unequal household tasks
- Repeated broken commitments
- Prolonged absences
- Disagreement regarding care of ill or elderly relatives
- Funeral and estate settlement disputes
- Disapproval of a spouse or romantic partner, especially in interracial or same-sex relationships

Unfortunately, little research has been done on how people who are related to one another practice forgiveness and reconciliation. We do know families vary in how they process and practice forgiveness and reconciliation. Some families are comfortable with direct communication about wrongdoing and explicit granting of forgiveness while others find less direct ways of communicating and expressing forgiveness. We also know that families with a good record of forgiving and reconciling with one another are more cohesive, stable, and committed to one another. Members of such families also have greater emotional and physical well-being and healthier levels of family functioning. Finally, much of what we have already learned about the processes and practices of forgiveness and reconciliation is applicable among family members—though turmoil over wrongdoing may mean these processes are much more complicated and these practices much more challenging than between couples or individuals.[19]

When we think of people who are related to one another, we often think of relatives or extended family members such as parents, grandparents, siblings, spouses, partners, children, and in-laws. But there also are people related to us in our congregational families such as our pastors, lay leaders, members, and mission partners. Both types of families experience turmoil, hurtful behavior, careless communication, broken trust, and fractured relationships—and the need to experience forgiveness, healing from hurt, careful communication, reconciliation, repair of broken relationships, and a restoration of relational health.

The experience of Frankie and Dannie gave us a look at the processes and practices of forgiveness and reconciliation among roommates, spouses, or domestic partners. Let us now examine a typical example of turmoil among people in a congregational family, including wrongdoing and these same processes and practices.

Congregational Turmoil Scenario

A one-hundred-member congregation is situated on five acres in an increasingly low-income, multicultural neighborhood. The congregation is eager to reach out to its neighborhood. Longtime members still hope for a return to the glory days of the 1950s and '60s when it was a five-hundred-member congregation.

As the outreach ministry team considers how best to use all the congregation's resources to serve people in need, it wonders if there might be a better use for a sizable portion of their land than as a place for neighbors to walk their dogs. They are mindful of increasing complaints by the building-and-grounds people about how long it takes to mow a field used only once or twice during the year for an ice-cream social or rummage sale. Outreach team members are excited about developing this largely unused portion of its land for much-needed low-income housing in the congregation's community.

Council members are receptive to this ministry opportunity, but immediately run into resistance from a small number of longtime members who feel their dream of congregational expansion slipping away. After holding several informal congregational meetings to brief members on land sale options and to respond to member fears and concerns, the congregation's leaders present a land sale recommendation to the congregation and ask for a vote of approval. Opposition from disgruntled members mounts as the vote draws near.

As chair of the congregational meeting, the pastor makes sure everyone understands the motion, lays out the pros and cons of the proposed action, and calls for discussion. After initial comments of support and opposition to the motion, the pastor asks if anyone has anything to add that has not already been voiced. Seeing none, the pastor calls for a vote, and a clear majority supports the land sale.

Immediately after the vote, the opposition leader is furious, not so much about the decision per se as about the decision-making process: a perception that specifics about the land sale and its implications were insufficient to warrant a vote, and that the pastor railroaded the vote and hopes to get a salary raise from proceeds of the land sale. Over the next few weeks the conflict festers, communication breaks down, anger intensifies, hurt lingers, and mistrust builds until the opposition leader resigns from the council and quits singing in the choir. Attempts by the pastor to reestablish communication are rebuffed with comments such as, "I'm too angry to talk about things now," "I need some time to let things simmer down," and "I'm confused and conflicted about whether I ever want to be active in the congregation again." Eventually, the disaffected member stops coming to worship and cuts off all communication with the congregation.

This scenario illustrates all-too-common turmoil and its aftermath in our families both inside and outside the congregation. Here is a turmoil that builds over time, becomes explosive, is long-lasting, and has an uncertain future. Such turmoil can linger long-term and even result in centuries-old church schisms and in families where some members never talk to one another again. So, how can we move on from such turmoil in ways that result in relational repair and restoration?

Relational Repair and Restoration A cooling-off period over weeks or months may or may not prepare conflicted parties to reconcile their differences and relationships. If the opposition leader's behavior reflects a pattern of disgruntlement that becomes toxic to congregational health, going separate ways may be best for both the now-inactive member and the congregation. However, how might both parties explore reconciliation if they desire to do so?

Once one or both parties decide they would like to reestablish contact, they will need to signal their desire to do so. This may happen indirectly with periodic return to worship services or through grapevine communication. It may also happen more directly with an invitation to have lunch together or with a "How are you doing?" phone call, text, or e-mail.

If their initial contact is positive and results in a renewal of "chitchat" communication, they may then begin to explore each other's perception of the turmoil, either face to face or in writing. For instance, the pastor might send an e-mail apologizing for leading the meeting in a way that led to frustration and hurt for some in the congregation and express a desire to get together and listen to one another's perception of wrongdoing. Likewise, anger at the pastor may become so unbearable that the opposition leader decides to invite the pastor for dinner and conversation in hopes of repairing the relationship.

Such conversation requires careful communication that checks each other's perception about the primary issue that divides them, clarifies what they'd each like to see happen in their relationship, and explores options to begin rebuilding a healthy relationship. In so doing, the parties may learn each other's reactions to perceived wrongdoing, determine what it takes to mend their relationship, and begin a process of forgiveness and reconciliation such as found in table 4.2 that leads to healing of hurt, repair of broken relationships, and restoration of relational health. When turmoil builds over time, boils over, lingers, and faces an uncertain future such as we have just examined, full reconciliation, recovery of trust, and renewed commitment may take weeks, months, or even years.

This completes our exploration of the many ways our reactions to wrongdoing in the processes of forgiveness and reconciliation matter. We now turn to guidelines dealing with a cultural and theological framework for understanding the process of forgiveness as well as practical skills and behaviors for making the process of forgiveness work.

4. Cultural Context Matters.

Cultural context affects how people understand and practice forgiveness. For example, there are important differences in the way people in individual-oriented and group-oriented cultural traditions approach forgiveness and unforgiveness. In particular, as evident in table 4.3, a comparison of eight factors reveals significant differences in how collectivistic and individualistic worldviews influence people's experience of forgiveness.

When people are dependent on one another, it makes sense that the goal of forgiveness is to restore social harmony and that third-party mediators or cultural healers such as shamans, priests, and clergy negotiate conflict and forgiveness through communal rituals and ceremonies. By contrast, when individuals relate to one another by personal choice, it is not surprising that

Table 4.3. Comparison of Cultural Contexts (In Relation to Forgiveness)

FACTORS	COLLECTIVISTIC WORLDVIEW	INDIVIDUALISTIC WORLDVIEW
View of self	Interdependent & socially	Independent & self-defined
View of relationships	defined	Contractual & personal choice
View of power	Communal & social duty	Demanded
Primary face concern	NegotiatedOther-face & self-	Self-face
Reconciliation	face	Sharply distinct from
Self-forgivenes	Closely related to forgiveness	forgiveness
Goal of forgiveness	Lowly valued & implausible	Highly valued & assumed
Tools of forgiveness	Social harmony & well-being	Personal benefit & well-being
	Mediators, rituals &	Therapy, self-help & coping
	ceremonies	skills

Source: Adapted from Steven J. Sandage and Ian Williamson, "Forgiveness in Cultural Context," in *Handbook of Forgiveness*, Everett L. Worthington Jr., ed. (New York: Routledge, 2005), 44–45.

personal benefit is the goal of forgiveness and that professional therapy, self-help resources, and individual coping skills are utilized. Likewise, self-forgiveness makes little sense in collectivistic cultures where relationships are central and power is negotiated whereas it fits an individualistic emphasis on self-determination and freedom from communal authority. Then, too, in collectivistic cultural traditions an offense or loss of face may happen to several people and require group involvement in face-saving and forgiveness, whereas individualistic saving self-face might happen to heal a loss of self-esteem. Finally, in order to preserve personal boundaries, forgiveness and reconciliation are understandably distinct or autonomous in individualistic traditions whereas they are closely related or synonymous in collectivistic-oriented cultures. It is important, then, to recognize and account for various ways people from different cultural contexts understand and practice forgiveness.

5. Forgiveness Is Counterintuitive and Not a Common or Popular Behavior to Practice.

In the gospel narratives, we find Jesus nailed to a cross, suffering the worst imaginable torture. He hangs there an innocent man, for he is found guilty of no crime. And in this most fragile and awful of human conditions, how does Jesus face his final conflict? He says to God about those crucifying him, "Forgive them; for they do not know what they are doing" (Luke 23:34).

Rather than self-righteously maintaining his innocence, as would be understandable, he forgives. Rather than feel defensive, as he had every right to do, he forgives. Rather than display vengeance as he had the power to do, he forgives. Perhaps this culminating behavior of our Lord is the ultimate, culminating way for us to handle breakdowns in our relationships.

Unfortunately, this practice of forgiveness is not a common or popular way to handle breakdowns in our relationships. In reality, it is counterintuitive. From a human point of view, it makes no sense. When someone hurts us, instinctively we hold a grudge. When offended, we want to strike back. When we feel we are right, we do not budge. The experience of the brothers who hated one another at Father Chacour's congregation in Ibillin, recounted in chapter 3, demonstrates how carrying vindictiveness is like taking poison to kill our enemies.[20] But how are we to follow Jesus' way of forgiveness?

One of the ways many congregations practice forgiveness is in their Prayer of Confession during worship. Following the model of Jesus, what might such a prayer look like? Here is an example[21]:

Leader: Merciful God, from the cross Jesus spoke to you, saying, "Forgive them"; but we have said of others, "They do not deserve our forgiveness."

People: **Lord, have mercy.**

Leader: Jesus spoke to you, saying, "Forgive them"; but we have said of others, "We can never forgive them for what they have done."

People: **Christ, have mercy.**

Leader: Jesus spoke to you, saying, "Forgive them," but we have said of others, "Forgiveness is too good for them."

People: **Lord, have mercy.**

Leader: Jesus spoke to you, saying, "Forgive them," but we have said of others, "They have done it too many times."

People: **Lord, have mercy.**

Leader: Jesus spoke to you, saying, "Forgive them"; but we have said to others, "They must learn their lesson."

People: **Christ, have mercy.**

Leader: Jesus spoke to you, saying, "Forgive them"; but we say of others, "Justice demands punishment, not forgiveness."

People: **Lord, have mercy.**

(Pause for silent reflection and confession.)

This prayer is striking in its all-too-uncommon naming of specific, concrete, and actual ways we withhold forgiveness. While Jesus' and the Ibillin congregation's practice of forgiveness are models to follow, why are they so difficult to replicate? Because there's more to forgiveness than "just do it!" Seldom do we deserve to be forgiven. Few like owning up to wrongdoing. Talk can be cheap and apologies insincere. Injury to relationships can seem beyond repair. Our capacity to forgive can be woefully inadequate. Here's our quandary: *To forgive, or not to forgive?* It is a baffling question and a puzzling dilemma. So, what are we overlooking? What's the missing link? Theologically, it is called *grace*—to which we turn in our next guideline.

6. Forgiveness Requires Grace—Neither Overlooking Sin Nor Sidestepping Justice.

We've just seen how forgiveness makes no sense from a human point of view. When hurt, we are told, strike back. When belittled, sneer in return. When ignored, turn away. When offended or abused, demand justice. When violated, retaliate. Sure, Jesus can forgive—after all, he is God in human form. And therein lies our key. We need help beyond ourselves to make things right. *Only God can make it okay not to be okay.* Whether it's divine love, atonement for sin, substitutionary death, unmerited favor, or sacrificial offering, we need help beyond ourselves in order for forgiveness to be authentic—to be more than playing games. Otherwise we're being soft on sin, on the one hand, or making justice cheap, on the other hand.

We're all beggars—at risk, vulnerable, and needy—when it comes to forgiveness. As mysterious or miraculous, unmerited or astonishing as it may be, somehow God welcomes all, beggars though we may be, and offers the Way to find bread. And if we are so treated, then who are we to withhold such treatment from one another? In short, as the great civil rights activist and pragmatic politician—former lawyer, guerrilla leader, convicted terrorist, prisoner, president, and Nobel laureate—Nelson Mandela taught us all: *forgiveness is a gift.*

Questions remain, however. First, isn't Jesus being soft on sinners when he invites the adulterous woman's accusers to cast the first stone—if anyone is without sin? We may resent someone else being let off the hook—until we are in need of forgiveness ourselves. So, does this mean that Jesus is soft on sinners? *We'd better hope so!*

Second, isn't Jesus being permissive and condoning of sinful behavior? Not really. After all, doesn't he invite the woman to turn her life around and to go and sin no more? Apparently her life wasn't going too well the way she was living it. So, she is free to find a fresh start and begin living the right way. Yes, Jesus is soft on wrongdoers, but no, he does not overlook wrongdoing. Indeed, accountability for wrongdoing is still required and must not be overlooked.

By way of illustration, let's consider again situations where family peace and justice are threatened by domestic abuse. As stated before, there is no excuse for domestic violence. This is a zero-tolerance social issue. Society must work to prevent such abuse, and, when it is committed, to make sure corrective action is taken to stop the abuse, to offer choices for victim safety, and to work with perpetrators so that family peace and justice are restored. Protection orders may be necessary, arrests made, and court appearances required to neither permit nor condone domestic abuse. Incarceration also may be necessary to prevent repetitive violent behavior, and to see if restorative justice can lead to a return to peaceful domestic relationships.

Third, how is Jesus in a position to forgive? Jesus faces this question after he says to a paralytic man, "Son, your sins are forgiven." Jesus answers with this logic: "Which is easier, to say to the paralytic, 'Your sins are forgiven,' or to say, 'Stand up and take your mat and walk'?" At this response, people were amazed and in awe of Jesus. Luke even adds that people had seen strange things that day.[22] It may still seem strange to us today—but Jesus' logic seems as astonishing and persuasive today as it did two thousand years ago.

Fourth, doesn't forgiveness sidestep or cheapen justice? Certainly, it can seem so from our point of view. Shouldn't people pay for their sins? But what might it look like from God's perspective? Perhaps we will have to wait and see how we all fare in our day of final reckoning and judgment. We ought all to hope for mercy and forgiveness, or else how will it ever be okay not to be okay? Fortunately, in this life, as Singaporean pastor Joseph Prince reminds us, "Knowing that you are completely forgiven destroys the power of sin in your life."

Jesus directly addresses this issue, as reported by gospel writer John, wherein Jesus speaks of God as "Abba"—that is, "Papa"—thereby revealing a relationship of intimacy and equality:

> Indeed, just as Abba God raises the dead and gives them life,
> so the Only Begotten gives life to anyone at will.
> For Abba God judges no one,
> having entrusted all judgment to the Only Begotten,
> so that all may honor the Only Begotten
> as they honor Abba God.
> Whoever doesn't honor the Only Begotten
> dishonors the One who sent the Only Begotten—
> Abba God.
> The truth of the matter is,

whoever listens to my words
and believes in the One who sent me
has eternal life
and isn't brought to judgment,
having passed from death to life. . . .
I can do nothing by myself;
I can only judge as I am told to judge.
And my judging is just,
because my aim is to do not my own will,
but the will of the One who sent me.[23]

Finally, isn't there more to forgiveness than grace alone? Where, for example, do confession, repentance, conversion, and reconciliation fit into the process of forgiveness? It is to these questions that we now turn.

7. Forgiveness, Confession, Repentance, Conversion, and Reconciliation Are Related.

As we have seen previously, while no relationship is perfect, few relationships are expendable. Seldom can we terminate a relationship even though they are broken and repair seems impossible. How, then, are relationships to heal and thrive when sinful behavior threatens relational health?

The process of healing broken relationships and restoring relational health contains four theological dynamics that accompany forgiveness: *confession*—responsibility for wrongdoing is accepted; *repentance*—a change of behavior is taken; *conversion*—a reaching out for the strength of God and the accepting love of significant others is present; and *reconciliation*—repair and restoration of relationships is complete.

Normally, restoration of a relationship is an integral part of the interpersonal process of forgiveness. However, there are instances where forgiveness may occur without reconciliation and reconciliation may occur without forgiveness. For example, as noted by Catherine Philpot, "Forgiveness can be a one sided process, whereas reconciliation is a mutual process of increasing acceptance."[24]

Perhaps no greater public demonstration of the power of forgiveness is the work of South Africa's Truth and Reconciliation Commission following their days of apartheid. Desmond Tutu, a pivotal leader in this process, counsels: "Without forgiveness, there's no future." All four dynamics are present in this heroic, though imperfect, attempt to mend and heal a nation from the evils of apartheid. *Confession* of wrongdoing is required—truth must be told. *Repentance* is required—a change of mind and heart must be evident. *Conversion* is required—a desire for the gift of forgiveness must be expressed.

Finally, *reconciliation* is required—the repair and restoration of relationships must be sought.[25]

The power of forgiveness to break the cycle of violence and bring peace is also apparent in research regarding the propensity to forgive a severe offense in three religious communities in Lebanon: Catholics, Maronites, and Orthodox. Forgiveness researchers Fabiola Azar, Etienne Mullet, and Genevieve Vinsonneau find that "lasting peace cannot be brought about between different communities who have fought each other for many centuries if the cycle of violence (the aggression-revenge cycle) is not broken at some time. This cycle can be broken if the members of the different parties decide to do so and decide not only to negotiate but also to forgive."[26]

8. Forgiveness, Trust, and Faith Go Together.

Earlier we examined examples of reactions to wrongdoing that adversely affect relational health, including violation and destruction of trust. Rebuilding trust when it has been breached requires forgiveness for healing and restoration. As we discovered in chapter 3, the relationship between trust and forgiveness is complicated. Often the experience of trust and the practice of forgiveness occur neither quickly nor spontaneously. John F. Kennedy once remarked, "Forgive your enemies, but never forget their names." It often takes time—sometimes a long period of time—to repair trust and restore broken relationships. It is why Van de Ven and Ring suggest that healing begins with forgiveness.[27] Indeed, the practice of forgiveness gives birth or rebirth to the experience of trust.

Moreover, we've already seen that God is always involved with faith and forgiveness in the Bible. For example, in Mark 1:14 we learn that Jesus came to Galilee proclaiming the good news of God, and saying, "The time is fulfilled, and the kingdom of God has come near; repent, and believe in the good news." It is our belief in the gospel that provides the power to practice forgiveness. As we have seen, our gift of forgiveness to others comes from God's gift of forgiveness to us. God's gift of forgiveness enables us to be okay when we're not okay, and our belief in this good news empowers us to treat others similarly—to believe in and treat them as okay when the way they've treated us is really not okay at all.

9. Care Enough to Forgive and to Be Forgiven.

Forgiveness requires a commitment to dialogue. Robert Frost observed, "To be social is to be forgiving." Someone must care enough about the relationship to take the first step or to initiate the process of forgiveness. And the other party must care enough about the relationship to be forgiven. In short, forgiveness must be sought, offered, and accepted.

The benefit of forgiving is captured well by Elbert Hubbard: "The ineffable joy of forgiving and being forgiven forms an ecstasy that might well arouse the envy of the gods."　William Arthur Ward adds this twist: "Forgiveness is a funny thing. It warms the heart and cools the sting." Few things in life are as overwhelming as being forgiven even before we know we need to be forgiven. Sometimes, if not often, we get to trigger such euphoria in others.

Such rewarding results and outcomes of forgiveness may include the following:

- Healing of relationships
- Restoring relational warmth or intimacy
- Improving mental and physical health
- Lowering of stress
- Stopping blame
- Regaining a sense of control
- Lessening of anger
- Reconciling victims and offenders
- Restoring hope for peace among people and nations.

While beneficial, the practice of forgiveness is not for the faint of heart. Mahatma Gandhi was right when he said, "The weak can never forgive. Forgiveness is an attribute of the strong." Forgiveness requires energy, imagination, intelligence, love, grace, empathy, humility, and compassion. We have already learned these lessons about the complex dynamics and challenging demands of forgiveness: that it is unconditional—it is offered regardless of response; that it is offered for the well-being of the relationship; that it requires breaking free of old habits and feelings; that it does not take place instantaneously; and that one party usually instigates the process and becomes the prime mover in restoring the relationship.

Yes, the practice of forgiveness can require strenuous effort and hard work. But if we care enough to forgive and be forgiven, then we will eagerly commit ourselves to the dialogue that initiates, embraces, and completes such immeasurably rewarding and beneficial work.

10. Forgiveness Doesn't Always Mean Forgetting.
John F. Kennedy once observed: "When you forgive, you in no way change the past—but you sure do change the future." The practice of forgiveness at times involves deep hurt and long-term healing. The consequences of broken

relationships may leave permanent scars, long-lasting impact, and painful reminders of awful, even evil behavior. Forgiveness may be partial, incomplete, or unfinished. Perhaps most insidious of all, overtures of forgiveness may be refused or spurned. And, regrettably, death may intervene before forgiveness is complete. In such cases, how are we to prevent such consequences from causing ongoing pain and suffering?

Sometimes it is impossible to forget about such consequences, to overlook such behavior, or to put to rest unrequited offers of forgiveness. It does not mean, however, that we must allow such consequences, behaviors, or resistance to paralyze us on our path forward. We may need to decide to put full resolution on hold, to forgive and not reconcile, to allow forgiveness sufficient time for completion, or to move on when we have done all we can do to finish the process of forgiveness.

Forgive and forget? Not necessarily so. Forgive and move forward? Perhaps necessarily so. Otherwise, we allow ourselves to get stuck, to be vulnerable to recurring abusive behavior, or to permit painful memories to haunt us. We may so face reality that we are able to move forward without letting others' behavior control our response in negative, immobilizing, dysfunctional ways.

11. A Forgiving Spirit Leads Us to Be Patient with One Another, Ourselves, and God.

An important way to strengthen our capacity to forgive is to cultivate a spirit of forgiveness that leads us to be patient with one another, our self, and God.

It helps to remember that no one is perfect. All of us are at times guilty of wrongdoing. Sometimes, we are the one in need of forgiveness, and sometimes we are the one doing the forgiving. Thomas Fuller has it right when he comments, "Those who cannot forgive others break the bridge over which they themselves must pass for everyone has need to be forgiven." It is why we say during the Lord's Prayer, "Forgive us our sins as we forgive those who sin against us." Sometimes, it will be easy to forgive and/or be forgiven, and sometimes the practice of forgiveness is difficult for both forgiver and forgivee, requiring considerable patience with one another. Sometimes the one we need to forgive is ourselves—not an easy task for many of us.

Self-forgiveness is necessary when we acknowledge wrongdoing and accept responsibility for such behavior. It requires considerable patience and understanding. The shame and guilt we experience for wrongdoing to others or for shortcomings in ourselves are especially difficult emotions with which to deal. Self-forgiveness involves a release of resentment toward ourselves for wrongdoing and an attitude of compassion, generosity, and love toward ourselves. We become less inclined to punish ourselves or to engage in self-destructive behaviors and more inclined to treat ourselves with patience and kindness. These acts are similar to forgiving others in that they unfold over time, involve objective wrong, are freely given rather than being a requirement or entitlement, and are distinct from forgetting, excusing, exonerating, justifying, condoning, pardoning, or reconciling. And these acts are different from forgiving in that while forgiving others is unconditional, self-forgiveness may depend on the condition that we make reparation or change our behavior in the future. Likewise, forgiving others may or may not require reconciliation with wrongdoers whereas reconciliation with one's self is a requirement for self-forgiveness. Finally, consequences of not forgiving one's self may be more severe than consequences of not forgiving others. For instance, we can avoid an offender but we cannot escape an unforgiving self, unless, of course, we are in denial or deceive ourselves.

These two emotions—shame and guilt—are both curses with costs and blessings with benefits. They are beneficial when they *alert* us that we've violated personal, social, and moral standards; *inhibit* us from yielding to temptations; and *motivate* us to handle them constructively and healthily. Unresolved feelings of shame and guilt can be debilitating and interfere with the quality of our lives and relationships. Deep, chronic, distressing feelings may be out of proportion to the severity of our wrongdoing and require self-forgiveness and reparations to resolve them constructively.

It is important to distinguish between true self-forgiveness and false or pseudo-self-forgiveness. True self-forgiveness requires that we acknowledge our wrongdoing and accept responsibility, whereas pseudo-self-forgiveness lets us off the hook by brushing off, excusing, minimizing, or blaming others for our offense and its consequences. Significant anguish and pangs of conscience such as regret, remorse, and embarrassment are necessary for true self-forgiveness, whereas pseudo-self-forgiveness bypasses acknowledgment of harmful consequences, acceptance of responsibility, and significant angst.

It is also important to distinguish between feelings of *shame* and feelings of *guilt*. These are two very different emotions, and we experience and respond to them differently. Shame, on the one hand, involves a painful humiliation that "I am a bad person" and includes a sense of worthlessness or powerlessness. Unfortunately, such painful and debilitating feelings do not motivate constructive changes. Instead, we resort to defensive tactics to hide or escape shameful feelings and to deny responsibility. We may also try to shift blame to make others responsible for the damage we've caused. Guilt, on the other hand, involves a specific behavior that "I did a bad thing" and includes a sense of tension, remorse, and regret over the bad thing done—responses that typically motivate such reparative actions as confessing, apologizing, or repairing the damage done.

Differences in feeling shame and guilt have different implications for self-forgiveness. Because a bad behavior is much easier to change than a bad self, people prone to feeling guilt are in a good position to seek and receive forgiveness from others and to forgive themselves. However, people prone to feelings of shame face a much more daunting challenge, one further complicated by often being more likely to repeat their wrongdoing and by often being less likely to attempt reparation.

Besides helping us be patient with others and ourselves, a forgiving spirit also leads us to be patient in our relationship with God. Anger toward God seems to be a common human experience. Frequent or unresolved anger toward God can lead to emotional distress that negatively affects our physical, psychological, and spiritual well-being. Besides impairing our health, our belief in God's existence may wane. Most people resolve or decrease their anger toward God over time, although it is not clear why. Surely, a forgiving spirit can help us be patient in our exasperations with God.

Indeed, a forgiving spirit leads us to be patient with one another, with ourselves, and with God. Wrongdoing that requires forgiveness to heal and to restore relational health can leave us angry, hurting, and confused. In the words of Alice Duer Miller, "Genuine forgiveness does not deny anger but faces it head-on." In such cases, as well as in normal circumstances, it often takes careful, perceptive, timely listening to forgive one another—to understand the relational dynamics, to decide how to handle relational fracture, to empathize with one another's experience, and to appreciate one another's presence. Patient listening also helps us deal with our feelings of shame and guilt, to discern how best to forgive ourselves, and to handle our anger toward God. Turn to chapter 1 and find practical guidelines to increase your understanding about listening and to enhance your listening skills.

Finally, a patient, forgiving spirit also is required to use a sensible conflict management process that *faces our differences* and *keeps us together*. It can contribute mightily to so *handle our differences* that "all of you be in agreement and that there be no divisions among you, but that you be united in the same mind and the same purpose" (I Corinthians 1:10b). Turn to chapter 1 and find practical guidelines for handling conflict.

12. Forgiveness Leads to Justice and Peace.

"The practice of forgiveness is our most important contribution to the healing of the world." So says Marianne Williamson. Forgiveness and justice can and should coexist. In fact, forgiveness weds truth and justice to produce peace. We can see these dynamics at work in the way Jesus adeptly handles the rift between the adulterous woman and her unscrupulous accusers. As we saw earlier, Jesus transforms the conflict by raising the issue about who among them is without sin. He says to let the person without sin cast the first stone. Jesus slows down the whole proceedings and buys time to discover a fresh, imaginative, creative option. He separates the parties and offers the crowd a life-saving alternative to repent of their actions—they may turn around and walk away. Jesus then restores the woman's dignity by asking her where are her accusers. Seeing none, Jesus sets her free from condemnation to turn around and start a new life. Truth is served—her sin as well as those of her accusers are exposed. Justice is served—all face the consequences of their sin. Blaming no one else for their predicaments, all parties face the truth and consequences of their sinful selves, experience an offer of forgiveness, end their bitterness, and turn around and start a new life. All are invited to follow the right path—to go and sin no more. In short, Jesus' forgiving spirit and actions restore peace in this situation by wedding truth and justice.

Having said all this, there is a paradoxical side to forgiveness in relation to restorative justice. Much depends on what the victim needs or wants. If the goal is to restore victim safety and security, then forgiveness may well be irrelevant. Paradoxically, if the goal is to facilitate victim healing, then forgiveness can be one way to reduce anger and increase empathy. If healing also includes victim safety, then forgiveness may be a secondary concern and stay in the background until a victim requests help with forgiveness. Otherwise, efforts to facilitate forgiveness may be unhelpful, offensive, and compound unsafe feelings. And in no cases must forgiveness be used to excuse an offender or to forget or trivialize an offense. Such coercive efforts further victimize the victim. When victims do desire forgiveness, most likely they will need an apology and seek remorse from their offender. They will also need a safe place for dialogue to occur, particularly in dealing with such experiences as parental neglect, sexual abuse, or domestic violence.[28]

Summary and Conclusion

Forgiveness is a multifaceted process both complicated to understand and challenging to practice. There is not one but several definitions of forgiveness depending on different types of forgiveness and relationships.

The pathway to forgiveness is a complex journey that people experience in different ways and time frames, depending on previous experience and role models. Forgiveness is neither inherently good nor bad, so we must learn when to grant forgiveness, to withhold forgiveness, and to reduce unforgiveness in order to move forward from broken relationships toward healing and repair.

In the processes of forgiveness and reconciliation our emotional, mental, and behavioral reactions to wrongdoing matter for both wrongdoers and victims of wrongdoing. We saw how wrongdoing adversely affects relational health and that rebuilding trust requires forgiveness for healing and restoration. Relational repair and restoration may take time to unfold even when both parties decide that is their desired outcome.

Cultural factors affect our understanding and practice of forgiveness. Individual-oriented and group-oriented cultural traditions approach forgiveness and unforgiveness differently.

Unfortunately, the practice of forgiveness modeled by Jesus is neither a common nor popular way to handle breakdowns in relationships. It is counterintuitive and makes no sense from a human point of view. Forgiveness is a gift—soft on sin without being permissive or condoning wrongful behavior. Grace is required so that we neither overlook sin nor sidestep justice.

The process of healing broken relationships and restoring relational health includes theological dynamics that accompany forgiveness, including confession, repentance, conversion, and reconciliation. When we care enough to forgive and be forgiven we will put forth the necessary effort and work required to receive the rewards and benefits of forgiveness.

It is no surprise that forgiveness doesn't always mean forgetting. Sometimes hurt is deep and healing long-term. We may need to forgive and move forward so as not to permit ourselves to get stuck or allow painful memories to haunt us. We can move forward without letting others' behavior control our response or immobilize our lives.

A forgiving spirit leads us to be patient with ourselves, others, and God and often requires patient listening and sensible handling of conflict. And we've seen how forgiveness joins truth and justice to create peace—depending on what victims need or want from their offenders.

These guidelines for practicing forgiveness can lead us to be more effective in how we relate to one another, thereby creating healthier relationships.

Practical Applications

1. Which definition(s) of forgiveness make the most sense to you? Why so?
2. Which positive and negative emotional, mental, and behavioral reactions to wrongdoing are most typical for you both as a wrongdoer and a victim of wrongdoing during the processes of forgiveness and reconciliation? (Use table 4.2 as a resource.)

3. In your experience, which cultural factors affect how people understand and practice forgiveness? (Use table 4.3 as a resource.)

4. How does your congregation practice forgiveness during worship? Create a prayer of confession based on the way Jesus models forgiveness.

5. How does forgiveness neither overlook sin nor sidestep justice?

6. What are personal, congregational, or societal examples of the way confession, repentance, conversion, or reconciliation are related to forgiveness? How about the way forgiveness, trust, and faith go together?

7. Prepare a case study that includes a breakdown in communication during an argument with a close friend or family member, or turmoil in your congregation. Briefly re-create the conversation or sequence of events. Then trace the processes of forgiveness and/or reconciliation as they unfold over time, assess the outcome noting both what went well and what could have led to a better outcome, and summarize what you learn.

8. What evidence have you seen that the practice of forgiveness requires strenuous effort and hard work? To what extent has forgiveness meant forgetting in your experience? How about forgiving and moving forward?

9. Try to think of instances where a forgiving spirit led you to be patient with others, yourself, or God. How have shame and guilt been costly and/or beneficial in your experience? In what ways have listening and conflict-management skills been useful?

10. What are some instances where forgiveness joined trust and justice to create peace?

For Further Study

Augsburger, David. *Caring Enough to Forgive—Caring Enough to Not Forgive* (Scottdale, PA: Herald, 1981).

Azar, Fabiola, Etienne Mullet, and Genevieve Vinsonneau. "The Propensity to Forgive: Findings from Lebanon," *Journal of Peace Research* 36, no. 2 (1999), 169–81.

Enright, Robert D., and Richard P. Fitzgibbons. *Helping Clients Forgive: An Empirical Guide for Resolving Anger and Restoring Hope* (Washington, DC: American Psychological Association, 2000).

Enright, Robert D., and Joanna North, eds. *Exploring Forgiveness* (Madison: University of Wisconsin, 1998).

McCullough, Michael E., K. Chris Rachal, Steven J. Sandagae, Everett L. Worthington Jr., Susan Wade Brown, and Terry L. Hight. "Interpersonal Forgiving in Close

Relationships. II. Theoretical Elaboration and Measurement." *Journal of Personality and Social Psychology* 75, no. 6 (1998), 1586–1603.

McCullough, Michael E., Kenneth I. Pargament, and Carl E. Thoresen, eds. *Forgiveness: Theory, Research, and Practice* (New York: Guilford, 2000).

Palmer, Earl. *The Blessing of Aaron and the Character of God.* DVD (Arroyo Grande, CA: Essential Media Services).

Worthington, Everett L., Jr., ed. *Handbook of Forgiveness* (New York: Routledge, 2005).

~

CHAPTER FIVE

Using Power

- *"He did what? Again? Personnel committees must deal with way too many power-related issues among congregational leaders."*
- *"Pastors and lay leaders behave in some of the stupidest ways."*
- *"I don't want to work with her anymore. She's a control freak."*
- *"When our board president pushes her agenda, I don't know what to say."*
- *"I feel intimidated when our pastor goes off on one of his rants."*

All-Too-Common Scenario

While serving on her Presbytery's Committee on Ministry, my wife coined a term that describes why so much committee time and energy is spent picking up the pieces of shattered lives: "stupid pastor syndrome" (SPS). Laypersons are not immune to such behavior, either. At the root of many dumb and inappropriate things clergy and lay leaders do is their abuse of power and their violation of ethical standards. They can be like crocodiles, lying in wait to pounce on an unsuspecting victim, throwing their weight around and using their sharp teeth to make vicious attacks in attempts to threaten, overpower, control, subdue, silence, even destroy.

In order to create healthier ways of relating to one another, leaders and members of our congregations can learn to use their power and influence in appropriate, ethical ways. Pastors and lay leaders alike need help in recognizing when they have misused their power, crossed boundaries, and abused people and congregations. They also need the wisdom to deal with the dysfunction, abuse, and destruction they can cause. Likewise, congregational leaders need help to recognize and deal with the abuse and misuse of power by parishioners and organizational systems.

Much of this abuse is preventable. More intervention is needed. Much healing, reconciliation, and redemption may be necessary. But where are the members and leaders of our congregations to learn appropriate, ethical behavior for their practice of ministry?

Supervised practice of ministry experiences and clinical pastoral education placements that include training in the appropriate use of power and in clergy ethics for our seminarians are good places to begin. Many church judicatories now require pastors to complete periodic training in clergy misconduct.[1] Yet the pervasiveness of SPS suggests additional training is required. Current seminary practical ministry coursework and continuing education workshops for congregational leaders normally approach the study of ethics from philosophical, social, political, or religious perspectives. What's often missing is the study of ethical responsibility in human communication from a relational perspective.

Since our goal is to help people create healthier ways of relating to one another, the guidelines in this chapter will help people be more effective in how they use power. In short, to improve the quality of communication in our congregations and everyday lives, these guidelines will promote healthier ways of relating to one another by learning how to influence one another wisely, properly, and ethically.

Ten guidelines for using power are presented in this chapter on these topics:

- Misuse of power
- Relational ethics
- Persuasive communication
- Peacemaking
- Controlling others' lives
- Broken relationships
- Privilege
- Gender differences
- Multicultural communication
- Prophets

These practical, sensible guidelines can go a long way toward helping people create healthier ways of relating to one another in their congregational life and ministry, in their personal and social lives, in their encounters with strangers and neighbors, and in their global communities.

Guidelines for Using Power

1. Misuse of Power Creates Relational Havoc.

We get a glimpse of the biblical view of power from the Apostle Peter's first letter to those having oversight of congregations in Asia Minor. He offers this pastoral exhortation: "Do not lord it over those in your charge, but be examples to the flock" (I Peter 5:3). Power may be understood as the ability to influence. As such, it is neutral and depends on how it is used. American novelist William Gaddis puts it this way: "Power doesn't corrupt people, people corrupt power." As with conflict and trust, power may be used positively to empower or serve others. It may also be used negatively to control or dominate others. Welsh politician Aneurin Bevan notes, "The purpose of getting power is to be able to give it away."

We have already seen that pastors and laypersons do the stupidest things when they use their ability to influence unwisely, improperly, and unethically. Such misuse of power all too often causes relational havoc and destruction. Consider this example.

Let's say that a member of the congregation asks to talk to the pastor following the death of a family member. All goes well during the initial visit until it comes time for the parishioner to leave. During their departing handshake, they suddenly find themselves attracted to one another and the leave-taking becomes awkward and uneasy. Since they are both single, they are uncertain about how their next visit will go. The pastor remembers being taught in seminary and in clergy misconduct workshops that role-relationship boundaries exist between pastor and parishioner, ones that put the pastor in a powerful position of influence—especially since the parishioner is emotionally vulnerable in this instance. The pastor is tempted to take advantage of this power differential and cross the boundary by turning the counseling relationship into a romantic one. And the distraught parishioner is tempted to seduce the pastor into doing more than offer advice. Will the pastor exercise the role of pastoral influence and boundary-keeping wisely, properly, and ethically, or not? And will the parishioner exercise the role of counselee and boundary-keeping wisely, properly, and ethically, or not?

Mindful that pastors and laypeople can do the stupidest things, there is considerable uncertainty about what will happen at the next counseling appointment. How ought the relationship between pastor and parishioner move forward? What relational ethics should guide relational behavior in this instance? Our next guideline will help us deal with this quandary.

2. Relational Ethics Guide Relational Behavior.

How ought the pastor behave? How should the parishioner act? What should they talk about? And what type of relationship ought they to build? The field of ethics deals with just such questions of "oughts" and "shoulds," with what is "proper" and "improper," "good" and "bad," "moral" and "immoral," "appropriate" and "inappropriate." It helps us to determine whether the way we influence one another is right or wrong. And with respect to our use of power, Martin Luther King Jr. gets it right when he says, "I am not interested in power for power's sake, but I'm interested in power that is moral, that is right and that is good." There are, of course, different ways to define and interpret right and wrong. Nonetheless, as philosopher S. Jack Odell comments, "Ethical principles are necessary preconditions for the existence of a social community. Without ethical principles it would be impossible for human beings to live in harmony and without fear, despair, hopelessness, anxiety, apprehension, and uncertainty."[2]

We will now turn our attention to communication ethics in general, and relational ethics in particular. Then we will consider such practical applications of communication ethics as our misuse of language and communication power, transcultural communication ethics, and the ethics of cyberspace.

Communication Ethics

Communication scholar Stella Ting-Toomey defines ethics as "a set of standards that upholds the community's expectation concerning 'right' and 'wrong' conduct."[3] Another communication studies scholar, Dennis Mumby, suggests, "From a communication perspective, 'acting ethically' is a dynamic practice that requires an ongoing awareness of the everyday operation of power, and a willingness to engage 'the other' in a manner that is both responsive to his/her/their difference and that opens up the possibility for self-transformation."[4]

More specifically, explains Mumby, "The study of ethics is centrally concerned with the ways in which one engages with 'the other'; to what extent is the other treated as an object to be strategically manipulated or as a human who fully engages and interrogates our own sense of self."[5] Consequently, he contends, power must be examined "in terms of how it impacts—either positively or negatively—the possibilities for realizing human beings' life chances. Power and human agency (either individual or collective) is ethical to the extent that it creates possibilities for the greater realization of human community and well-being; it is unethical to the degree that it forecloses life possibilities, or else arbitrarily privileges the realization of some life-chances over others."[6] British statesman Benjamin Disraeli puts it this way: "Power has only one duty—to secure the social welfare of the People."

In offering a vision of applied ethics for communication studies, professor of philosophy and communication Josina M. Makau speaks of the power of communication this way:

> It is through communication that the human heart expresses love, compassion, and care. Communication offers comfort, heals spiritual and emotional wounds, and fosters community building across divides. Each day, communicative acts raise consciousness, shine a light on acts of moral courage, disrupt the forces of corruption, greed, ignorance and tyranny, and create conditions for peaceful, just resolution of conflict. Across the globe, responsible story tellers, parents, community activists, educators, political leaders, artists, scholars and others illuminate, inspire, encourage, and otherwise empower through responsible use of communication's powers.[7]

Central to communication ethics, then, is Mumby's question: "Do communication practices work to serve narrow interests and construct politically expedient divisions and differences, or do they work to produce understanding, connection, and a sense of the possibilities that inhere in the human communication condition?"[8] Put succinctly, *human flourishing* is central to the practice of communication ethics.

Relational Ethics

To guide relational behavior in our everyday use of power, we need to discover an ethical system based on *relational ethics*.[9] Let's examine such a system.

In *Practicing Relational Ethics in Organizations*, Danish organizational psychology consultants Gitte Haslebo and Maja Loua Haslebo base their social constructionist perspective on the ethical value of "goodness." They believe we construct our view of reality through language and communication. Relational moral responsibility and the process of dialogue are central principles. As people construct shared meaning they generate mutually beneficial actions to build a desirable future for everyone. People choose to obligate themselves to moral responsibility to which others are entitled. Power is viewed as making one's voice heard and respecting views of others. Haslebo and Haslebo prefer "modern power" that is productive, coalition driven, shared, and people centered to "traditional power" that is repressive, top down, coercive, and institution centered. Their relational ethical system is guided by five moral obligations and entitlements or "compass points"[10]:

- Context—social responsibility
- Relationship—dialogic obligations
- Discourse—shared responsibility for positioning
- Power—the obligation to interact as morally responsible agents
- Appreciation—inquiry of value to the work community

While this social constructionist perspective offers a fresh approach to relational ethics, we are left with the task of identifying and developing the requisite communication skills and behaviors for practicing relational ethics. What we need is an approach to relational ethics that integrates theory and practice. Let us consider an approach based on the central theme of this book: creating healthier relationships.

Let's create a system of communication ethics based on *relational health*. Earlier, in chapter 3, we saw that these four qualities are at the heart of relational health: openness, acceptance, warmth, and support.[11] Sets of communication skills and practices may be identified and integrated to create guidelines for each of our four qualities or principles of relational health. Here, then, are the goals, principles, and guidelines for a system of relational communication ethics:

Goals: Relational health and satisfaction
Principles: Openness, acceptance, growth, and warmth
Guidelines for Openness: Sharing, risking, and assertiveness
Guidelines for Acceptance: Listening, trusting, and empathy
Guidelines for Growth: Supporting, empowering, and curiosity
Guidelines for Warmth: Caring, connecting, and mutuality

Notice that this system of relational ethics identifies specific communication skills and behaviors we've already encountered for building relationships, leading meetings, experiencing trust, and practicing forgiveness—or will encounter later in this chapter.

The practice of relational communication ethics requires flexibility and adaptability in guideline usage depending on relational *type* (strangers, acquaintances, friends, good friends, or intimates), *context* (private, confidential, public, interpersonal, group, organizational, transcultural, and cyberspace), *role* (personal, professional, social, formal, or informal), and *purpose* (inform to learn, persuade to decide, entertain to appreciate, care to help).

Let us now see how our new system of practical relational ethics gives direction for our quandary. What is a right, proper, or ethical way for the pastor and parishioner to behave at their next counseling appointment?

Let's frame our quandary this way: What relational principles and guidelines will foster a healthy relationship between parishioner and pastor? What communication skills will create a proper level of openness, acceptance, growth, and warmth in this situation?

First, the pastor and parishioner need clarity of relational type, context, role, and purpose. They need to define their relationship as acquaintances (or intimates), meeting in a confidential public (or private) context, with a professional (or personal) role-relationship, for the purpose of caring (or entertainment). Their quandary is whether it is right or wrong to redefine their relationship as intimates, meeting in private, in a personal role-relationship, for the purpose of enjoyment. In order to do so, the pastor and parishioner can use the communication guidelines or skills to foster the openness, acceptance, growth, and warmth to create a healthy relationship.

Here is a conversation between our parishioner (Sam) and pastor (Kit) at their next counseling appointment to see if our new system of relational ethics can be used to steer a course between behaving wisely and ethically to foster a healthy relationship rather than acting stupidly and unethically to create an unhealthy one.

Kit: Hi Sam, please come in and have a seat. Would you like something to drink?

Sam: Good morning, pastor. Thank you for seeing me again. And, yes, a cup of coffee sounds great.

Kit: How are you and your family coping with the loss of your mother?

Sam: I think our feelings vary from sadness and loss to anger and regret.

Kit: It sounds as though you're coping with your mother's dying and death quite well, then. Is that how you see it?

Sam: Well, I think we're all struggling. Some of us are doing better than others.

Kit: How are you doing?

Sam: Pretty well, all things considered. I'm a bit confused by our relationship, though.

Kit: Before going there, perhaps we ought to talk about the funeral arrangements.

Sam: Okay. Why don't you come over and meet with our family today or tomorrow?

Kit: That sounds like a good plan. I could come over sometime tomorrow morning.

Sam: That should work for us. I'll check with my family members and let you know when we can get everyone together.

Kit: Now, about us.

Sam: Yes. What about us?

Kit: Until now, we've had a professional relationship—pastor to parishioner. I think we've kept that boundary well until we said goodbye at our last counseling appointment.

Sam: I agree—on both counts. That does help explain my confusion, then.

Kit: It is true that we are both single and looking for a deeper, satisfying, healthy relationship. I'm not sure that it's a good idea for us to allow our relationship to move from a professional one to a personal one. I am attracted to you, but I think it is not a good idea to pursue a closer relationship while I'm your pastor. Such special relationships between pastor and parishioner are not easily understood or accepted by others in the congregation. Perhaps things would be different under different circumstances.

Sam: Well, I am attracted to you, and would be interested in a dating relationship. But I agree that there are boundary issues that we should respect. Is there a way out of our relational quandary?

Kit: Perhaps there is. Would you consider going to another congregation—at least for the time being?

Sam: Oh. I hadn't thought about that option. How would I explain leaving our congregation when I'm so heavily involved right now?

Kit: Yes, that is a complicating factor. Gets kind of messy, doesn't it?

Sam: Well, let me think about things a little more. Maybe we can come up with something. How about if we meet for coffee next week and continue our conversation?

Kit: As much as I'd like to do so, I don't think that's a good idea at this time. Let me think about things, too. Why don't we talk about things sometime after your mom's memorial service? Let's make an appointment to see how you are doing in a week or two. Maybe by then we can come up with a creative option that respects our pastor-parishioner boundaries and permits us to pursue a closer relationship—one that is healthy and satisfying for both of us.

Sam: If we can't find a way through our quandary by that time, maybe we can see a counselor or even talk with the bishop.

Kit: I might be open to that, if it becomes necessary. I like the idea of proceeding cautiously and creatively.

Sam: I do, too. Sounds like a mutually agreeable plan—and the right way to go!

It is apparent from the conversation between parishioner Sam and pastor Kit that their goal is to find a path to relational health and satisfaction by talking openly about redefining their relationship. They are *open* in their communication by sharing honestly, by risking being misunderstood or not taken seriously, and by asserting rather than avoiding or manipulating their thoughts and feelings. *Acceptance* of one another's thoughts and feelings also is present through perceptive listening, trusting one another to work at redefining their relationship, and empathizing with one another about their relational quandary. Moreover, rather than deny or become defensive about the awkwardness of their evolving relationship, they find a way to *grow* their relationship by being supportive, empowering, and inventive. And they find a way to acknowledge their newfound *warmth* and affection through genuine care, authentic connection, and decision-making mutuality without crossing the boundary from professional propriety to personal intimacy. Their journey is not complete, but they chart an ethical course to relational health and satisfaction that is promising and hopeful.

We now turn our attention to practical applications of communication ethics, including misuse of language and communication power, transcultural communication ethics, and ethics of cyberspace.

Misuse of Language and Communication Power

Language can be used to denigrate, degrade, objectify, dehumanize, and suppress people in order to exclude them from being treated with normal moral and ethical decency. Although the following terms may rarely, if ever, be heard from the pulpit, such names, labels, and stereotypes as "coon," "gook," "savage," "chick," "faggot," "cockroaches," "parasites," and "extremists" have been used to justify harmful behavior, blame victims, show superiority, deny human rights, and legitimize genocide. Use of racist, sexist, and homophobic language as well as hate speech, pornography, and obscene music lyrics are other ways people misuse their communication power to defame, demean, dehumanize, control, and attack people because of their race, religion, ethnicity, sex, gender, or sexual preference. In short, "communication that dehumanizes views others, not as persons inherently worthy of minimal respect as humans, but as things or objects to be manipulated for the communicator's pleasure or selfish gain."[12]

Communication and peace studies scholar Stanley Deetz believes genuine conversation can be blocked or distorted by unethical behavior that attempts to control or dominate discussion and decision-making. This misuse of power includes such unethical communication practices as[13]:

- Freezing the conversation—labeling that limits free and open examination of ideas
- Disqualification—preventing equal opportunity to speak
- Naturalization—silencing discussion by claiming one view is "the way it is" or "self-evident"
- Neutralization—treating one viewpoint as the only possible one and hiding underlying reasoning
- Topic avoidance—excluding certain topics and preventing variety of viewpoints
- Subjectification of experience—suppressing free expression and difference of opinion
- Meaning denial—making a comment and then denying doing so

Deetz suggests three ethical ways to use our communication power to remove such blockages and to reopen conversation, including *critical reflection* that examines what is taken for granted, *rhetorical sensitivity* that resists premature closure of discussion and decision-making, and *strategic disruption* that challenges vested interests that block consensus.[14]

An example of such unethical communication practices is the assertion, "This is just the way I am," or "That's just a matter of opinion." These statements silence or close conversation instead of opening up a topic for further discussion. Similarly, comments such as, "You're just saying that because you are angry," are meant to exclude someone's viewpoint, disqualify their opinion, and prevent development of mutual understanding. Moreover, citing facts without providing selection criteria or without disclosing sources can disguise information or block examination of someone's credibility.

Requests for supporting evidence, acknowledgment of people's emotional states, challenges to closed-minded thinking, and posing alternative perspectives are ways to remove blockages from discussion and to further genuine conversation.

Transcultural Communication Ethics

Thus far we have considered ethical guidelines for people with similar worldviews. But what might ethics on a global scale look like? Are there generic ethical guidelines that allow people from diverse backgrounds to communicate ethically? The New Ethic website proposes "a new ethic for the information age, acceptable to all humans regardless of religion, ethnicity, or sex, based on good will, cooperation, and equality and the avoidance of domination, deceit, and exploitation."[15]

Recognizing that ethical standards vary within and between cultures, communication scholars Richard Johannesen, Kathleen Valde, and Karen Whedbee in *Ethics in Human Communication* offer the following universal standards that they think transcend cultural, ethnic, and socioeconomic differences: humanness, truthfulness, trust, promise keeping, nonviolence, and caring relationships.[16]

Similarly, scholars of communication ethics, philosophy, and religion Clifford Christians and Michael Traber suggest universal ethical values as guides for communication in different cultures, including truth-telling, commitment to justice, freedom in solidarity, and respect for human dignity.[17]

The authors of *The Handbook of Communication Ethics* provide the following core values as grounding or starting points for a vision of applied ethics for communication studies: truthfulness, integrity, courage, humility, care, love, compassion, receptivity, response-ability, responsibility, justice, fairness, kindness, and responsiveness.[18]

Communication and labor studies scholar Dennis Gouran suggests that discussion and decision-making groups use "ethical sensitivity" to guard against making quick, dogmatic, either-or ethical decisions, including concern for impact on others, thorough discussion, accurate use of information, mutual respect, and guarding each other's self-worth.[19] Drawing on insight from small group research, John Gastil and Leah Sprain have developed an ethical checklist that members of small groups can use to guide their group formation, process and procedures, and external relationships.[20] Topics addressed include setting group boundaries, developing group contracts, welcoming new members, clarifying lines of authority, establishing group rules and norms, responding to minority opinions, avoiding groupthink, impacting the wider public, and guarding against depersonalizing or denigrating others.

To guide ethical communication in organizations, communication scholars George Cheney and Phillip Tompkins suggest that communicators practice guardedness or care in assessing information, accessibility or openness to change, nonviolence or avoidance of coercive conformity, and empathy that listens genuinely and welcomes diversity.[21]

Stella Ting-Toomey "encourages the importance of cultivating creative visions and alternative options, and seeking globally inclusive solutions to address diverse ethically wrangling situations."[22] She also urges us to "move beyond polarized either-or thinking and advocates the importance of using human imagination and a creative mindset to come to some constructive resolution."[23] Urging that multiple voices are known and respectively heard, she calls "for the empowerment of the self and others to seek multiple truths, the courage to dialogue side-by-side with culturally unfamiliar others, and the wisdom to make a principled decision."[24]

Finally, the National Communication Association Credo offers a comprehensive set of principles for ethical communication that promotes responsible thinking, decision-making, and relational development across contexts, cultures, channels, and media.[25]

Ethics in Cyberspace

Computers, fiber optics, and satellites create a communication superhighway. High-speed communication, such as the world-wide Internet, weblogs, and social media, links people with information and one another. This comprehensive, immediate, and global digital communication system connects us to computers, tablets, and mobile devices. And it expands our power to communicate through browsing, e-mailing, texting, webcaming, blogging, tweeting, chatting, recording, streaming, conferencing, and networking.

With respect to new ethical challenges created by global information technology and our digital cyberspace universe, Gary Woodward and Robert Denton in *Persuasion and Influence in American Life* acknowledge, "Some of the problems associated with technology can be regulated. However, as is the case with most questions of ethics, issues are very complex. Resolutions are generally the product of human judgment colored by the particular context and norms established through previous experience. The public will continue to encounter ethical implications in the use of technology."[26]

Cyberspace ethical concerns include honesty, dehumanization, deception, privacy, social responsibility, fairness, and accessibility. For example, fair and equal access to global Internet and cyberspace communication by people who are marginalized, devalued, or neglected by society is one such challenge. Facing limitations to Internet access and use due to economic status, gender, ethnicity, and geographic location is an urgent concern. Internet access at public libraries and financial subsidies may become increasingly important to avoid the emergence of what Thomas Cooper identifies as an "information underclass."[27]

Ethical guidelines have been created for computer and weblog use. For instance, the Computer Ethics Institute proposes Ten Commandments of Computer Ethics.[28] Ethical weblog use is complicated because it is unmediated, uncensored, and uncontrolled. Nonetheless, Rebecca Blood suggests the following six ethical standards for responsible weblog creators and users[29]:

- Publish as fact only that which you believe to be true.
- If material exists online, link to it when you reference it.
- Publicly correct any misinformation.
- Disclose any conflict of interest.
- Note questionable and biased sources.
- Write each entry as if it could not be changed; add to, but do not rewrite or delete, any entry.

These standards are especially important in gaining and maintaining your credibility. It requires conscientiousness and hard work to create interesting, varied, and reputable content.

Blood also offers these six online rules of the road to enhance your reputation rather than damage it[30]:

- Do not post when you are angry.
- Always argue the facts, never the personalities.
- Ignore personal attacks or refocus the issue with facts and not in kind.
- Do not hijack conversations.
- State your arguments clearly and cogently and then learn from others' responses.
- Represent other people's positions respectfully and accurately.

These rules are particularly important in creating an online persona and active presence in an online forum, community site, or personal blog. This advice is especially relevant when you address a controversial topic.

3. Persuasive Communication Is Pervasive and Effective—Properly Understood and Practiced.

Earlier, we defined power as the ability to influence. But what is the nature and source of influence? Moreover, what tactics do people use to influence one another? In other words, let's refine our understanding of what we mean by power as influence.

With respect to the *nature of power*, it is helpful to think of influence on a continuum between *domination or forced choice*, e.g., the use of control or coercion through position, constraint, or threat of force, and *liberation or free choice*, e.g., the use of engagement or collaboration through equality, restraint, or persuasion.

With respect to the *source of power*, it is helpful to think of a variety of types of influence. Such sources include force (coercion, deterrence, violence, war), position of privilege (class, race, ethnicity, gender, geography, religion), persuasion (credibility, passion, reason), expertise (knowledge, skills, ability), resource (property, food, water, money), and charisma (enthusiasm, personality, celebrity). Appropriate sources of power may be used according to the communication situation. For instance, in times of civil unrest or strife, coercive or deterrent force may be necessary to prevent or stop loss of life, and to get adversaries to halt violence and hold peace talks.

With respect to *tactics of power*, there is a variety of ways to influence people—to push or prompt people into particular action. While not exhaustive, the list in table 5.1 is suggestive of tactics that often have negative (–), varied (+ –), and positive (+) consequences. Tactics are organized in sets of three according to their likelihood for *domination* or *holding onto power*, *varied use*, and *empowerment* or *sharing power*.

As we saw in chapter 1, people are purposeful in their speaking and listening behavior whether in public, interpersonal, small group, or organizational settings. When we speak to illumine and listen to learn, informative communication is appropriate. Persuasive communication is useful when we speak to convince and listen to decide. Informative and persuasive communication is pervasive and effective—properly understood and practiced.

For instance, in terms of the *nature of power*, it is usually more effective if our communication enables and helps rather than controls and constrains. In order for our *source of power* to be effective, it needs to be wisely employed and appropriately matched to the communication situation. Moreover, we can select *power tactics* according to their effectiveness in accomplishing the appropriate results of our communication behavior. Some tactics will be appropriate and effective in some contexts and less in others. Other tactics will be inappropriate and ineffective in some contexts and more in others. How do we know which power sources and tactics to use in a particular situation? Here is where we need to let our relational ethics guide the choices we make and the pathways we follow in order for our persuasive communication to be appropriate and effective.

Philosopher H. P. Grice's ethics for everyday conversation are useful guidelines.[31] He says that the quality of our contributions should be sufficient to accomplish our communication purposes and not more than required. Our contributions should be truthful and based on adequate evidence. They

Table 5.1.   Tactics of Power (Likelihood for Domination, Varied, or Empowerment)

DOMINATION (holding onto power) −	VARIED (depends on use) + −	EMPOWERMENT (sharing power) +
Control	Oppose	Collaborate
Coerce	Yield	Cooperate
Defy	Justify	Apologize
Aggress	Defer	Assert
Condescend	Complain	Appreciate
Violate	Confront	Serve
Subdue	Defend	Support
Force	Abdicate	Negotiate
Cajole	Bargain	Persuade
Repress	Resist	Liberate
Suppress	Evade	Release
Obfuscate	Vacillate	Reason
Lie	Omit	Reveal
Destroy	Tolerate	Enjoy
Confuse	Inform	Clarify
Ignore	Direct	Discuss
Punish	Threaten	Reward
Manipulate	Divert	Adapt
Put down	Criticize	Affirm
Bully	Restrain	Intervene
Trivialize	Humor	Inspire
Silence	Demand	Protest
Attack	Disengage	Question
Insulate	Enable	Consult
Resist	Delay	Proceed

should be relevant and tailored to the conversational flow. And they should be clear, brief, and orderly rather than intentionally ambiguous and obscure.

Woodward and Denton suggest that ethical persuasive communication is essentially identical to all other ethical communication, and suggest that the following ten values are characteristic of an ethical communicator, particularly for those with a Western worldview[32]:

- Honesty—truthful, open, sincere, and objective
- Integrity—principled values and willing to take a stand
- Caring—empathetic and concerned about others' feelings and circumstances
- Respect—believe in human dignity and value
- Fairness—committed to diversity of opinion and equal justice for all
- Democracy—value liberty, equality, and freedom of expression

- Accountability—responsible for actions and ideas advocated
- Civic virtue—committed to public service and responsible citizenship
- Competence—knowledgeable, intelligent, and capable
- Reliability—dependable, consistent, and loyal

An illustration of appropriate and inappropriate use of power tactics and of ethical and unethical persuasive communication is what we say, and don't say, when trying to convince someone that our idea is better than theirs. A common strategy to advance the persuasiveness of our viewpoint is to promote or intensify the strong points of our argument and downplay or misconstrue its weak points. Our source of power here is *knowledge*—some shared and some withheld. And our reasoning uses the tactics of *evading* and *manipulating* the truthfulness of our position. While a rather common persuasive tactic, it fails the "honesty" test by obfuscating, skirting, or manipulating the truth. Are we willing to sacrifice our integrity—our credibility—in an unethical attempt to short-circuit the truth? Apparently we are. Sometimes, all it takes to guard against using doublespeak and deceptive claims, and thereby advancing the persuasiveness of our reasoning, is to use a qualifier, grant an exception, or specify the limits of our argument. Otherwise, we face the prospect of damaging our credibility, weakening our argument, and failing to accomplish our persuasive purposes. Moreover, our unethical behavior damages our relationship with our communication partners.

Thus far we have focused on the way we seek to persuade others. In everyday life, persuasive messages are pervasive. They dominate our attention. Most of the time we are the one being persuaded rather than the one doing the persuading. Just as important, then, if not more important, is the responsibility we have on the receiving end of the power of persuasion—as critical and responsible consumers of persuasion. In *Persuasion: Reception and Responsibility*, Charles Larson urges receivers of persuasion to "observe yourself being persuaded and how persuasion happens. You will be more critical and therefore more effective in rejecting persuasive messages when appropriate—and in accepting others when that is wise."[33] Similarly, he reaches this conclusion: "You need to become a critical receiver who makes responsible decisions about which product to buy, which candidate to vote for, and which ideas or ideologies to endorse."[34]

Larson also advises both receivers and senders of persuasion "to engage in 'response-ability,' or your ability to wisely and critically respond to the persuasion you encounter and to make wise choices and ethical decisions when you both process and craft persuasion. It would have been good in past times for persuaders and audiences to have response-ability. If they had, many tyrants might not have risen to power, and wars might have been avoided."[35] Thomas Jefferson makes a similar point when he suggests, "Experience hath shewn, that even under the best forms of government those entrusted with power have, in time, and by slow operations, perverted it into tyranny." Unfortunately, as Irish statesman Edmund Burke observes, "The greater the power, the more dangerous the abuse." Or, as American author Edward Abbey notes, "Power is always dangerous. Power attracts the worst and corrupts the best."

Theologian and biblical scholar Walter Wink offers a realistic, balanced, and practical perspective about the nature of power—both individual and institutional powers. He views powers as good, and fallen, and redeemable:

> They are good by virtue of their creation to serve the humanizing purposes of God. They are all fallen, without exception, because they put their own interests above the interests of the whole. And they can be redeemed, because what fell in time can be redeemed in time.[36]

Wink elaborates:

> We must view this schema as both temporal and simultaneous, in sequence and all at once. Temporally: the Powers *were* created, they *are* fallen, and they *shall be* redeemed. This can be asserted as belief in the final triumph of God over the forces of evil. But this schema is also simultaneous: God at one and the same time *upholds* a given political or economic system, since some such system is required to support human life; *condemns* that system insofar as it is destructive of fully human life; and *presses for its transformation* into a more humane order. Conservatives stress the first, revolutionaries the second, reformers the third. The Christian is expected to hold together all three.[37]

Our next guideline examines how to use these good, and fallen, and redeemable powers for peaceful and just purposes, and the following guideline describes how these powers are often misused to control other people's lives.

4. Power Can Be Used for Peaceful and Just Purposes.

French philosopher and scientist Blaise Pascal observes, "Justice and power must be brought together, so that whatever is just may be powerful, and whatever is powerful must be just." And with respect to war and peace and justice, communication scholar Robert Ivie contends, "Fighting wars to obtain a just peace is an all-too-common and seemingly self-sustaining occurrence. Yet, a stable peace cannot be achieved except by peaceful (i.e. nonviolent) means."[38] Moreover, Ronald C. Arnett believes peacemaking is an alternative to violence on an interpersonal as well as international level. As he states in *Dwell in Peace: Applying Nonviolence to Everyday Relationships*:

> One can affirm a basic trust in an alternative to extremes of violence and avoidance, which consists of dialogue inclusive of non-violent peacemaking. The nonviolent peacemaker recognizes the sanctity of life while she works for a dialogical resolution "between" opponents. He is open to the other's view while he announces his own voice clearly and firmly. . . . Perhaps non-violent peacemaking along with human dialogue is a needed alternative in the task of resolving conflict "between" humans.[39]

Arnett suggests that both violence and avoidance are often the result of a basic mistrust that is rooted in the fear of meeting the other in dialogue. How so? Because "violence denies the other's humanity and right to live. Avoidance of conflict does not recognize that life is by nature sometimes conflict generating."[40]

I think Arnett is correct in believing in the power of dialogue to overcome the fear and mistrust between people, thereby creating peaceful and just relationships between people and nations. Dialogue builds relationships. It creates trust, overcomes fears, and bridges the walls that divide us.

Ivie also suggests that "peace-building communication works to predispose polities toward better understanding of, more tolerance toward, and increased cooperation with adversaries so that conflict might be managed constructively. It seeks to bridge political divisions enough to prevent armed conflict while advancing the cause of social justice, collective well-being, and human fulfillment."[41] Turn to chapter 1 for further ways to build relationships, including ways to handle conflict. Experiencing trust and practicing forgiveness also require a commitment to dialogue, as we saw in chapters 3 and 4, respectively.[42]

5. Power Can Be Misused to Control Other People's Lives.

We have already seen examples of stupid pastor (and lay) syndrome. However, some misuse and abuse of power is more than just "stupid." It is mean. It can be demeaning, controlling, fearful, vicious, dangerous, toxic—even evil. As noted earlier in this chapter, these people can be like crocodiles that pounce on an unsuspecting victim, throw their weight around, and use their sharp teeth to make vicious attacks in attempts to threaten, overpower, control, subdue, silence, even destroy. As we saw in chapter 2 regarding dealing with dysfunctional group members, some behaviors are so egregious, demeaning, controlling, and abusive that they must be identified and exorcised. However, negativity and abusive behavior can do much more damage than squashing group interaction. They also can lead to discriminatory, oppressive, fearful, and dangerous situations. Moreover, they crash systems, sap energy, kill joy, hamper work, and undermine relationships.

Here is an all-too-common type of conversation between pastor Melissa and Chester, an outreach ministry team lay leader.

Melissa: How do you think our new Sunday night program is going?

Chester: (combative and demeaning) Not well at all—and it's all your fault.

Melissa: Oh, how so?

Chester: (sneering) You didn't do your job, that's why.

Melissa: As I recall, this new program was your idea. You knew the outreach ministry team had serious reservations about its success. I think you know I've supported this program and tried to make it work.

Chester: (in heated anger) No, you haven't. If you had, it would have worked.

Melissa: It is apparent that we see things differently. I'm sure we will be talking about where we go from here at our next ministry team meeting.

Chester: That's right. I'm sure they'll agree with me.

Understandably, the pastor was shaken by this encounter. Fearful that Chester's abusive behavior was likely to be repeated, Melissa decided not to be alone with him in future conversations.

Lay leader behavior such as Chester's can create a climate of fear and negativity that permeates a congregation's leadership team as a whole. Consider this conversation at the next board meeting:

Melissa: You have all seen the outreach ministry team's review of our new Sunday night program. Are there any questions or comments?

Chester: What the report omits is Pastor Melissa's refusal to support this program. We all know that is why it failed.

Shiho: Our outreach ministry team reviewed Pastor Melissa's role in this program. We concluded that the program was implemented well and worth the effort. Unfortunately, it just isn't an approach that works at this time.

Hanan: That's right. We gave it our best shot, and it is time to move on and try something else.

Chester: Is that the way everyone sees it?

Melissa: Yes, that's an accurate assessment and recommendation.

Chester: (sneeringly) I wasn't talking to you. We all know she's the problem here.

Roberto: This is not the time or place to review Pastor Melissa's work. Furthermore, I think you need to apologize for your demeaning comment, Chester.

Chester: Okay, I'm sorry. I didn't mean anything by my comment.

Roberto: At the risk of losing our friendship, Chester, I don't think you are sorry at all. You meant to hurt Pastor Melissa.

Chester: Is that how you see it? Well then I'm out of here! (Angrily leaves the board meeting.)

At this point, the leadership team has a decision to make about how it will handle Chester's behavior, the emotional intensity of which they describe with such strong words as tirade, temper, vehemence, shocking, scary, threatening, and controlling. Realizing that things have escalated to a breaking point, the denomination's regional ministerial relations chairperson is contacted. After reviewing this and similar previous encounters, and the resultant dysfunctional relational climate among leadership team members, the chairperson reports the following observations and recommendations:

- This traumatic encounter has happened before and is likely to happen again.
- The incident was disruptive to the meeting and damaging to board relationships.
- Chester's comments were attacking, condescending, controlling, and abusive.
- Chester's behavior is inappropriate, regardless of context or underlying factors.
- In workplaces this behavior warrants disciplinary action and likely termination.
- Chester needs assistance to learn how to manage his frustrations and emotions.
- The board must decide if it should take further actions now or in the future.

This encounter between board members is not an isolated incident. Nor is it unusual in congregations. What is unusual is the way the leadership team deals with dysfunctional board member behavior. It acknowledges the problem, and it seeks help when it does not know how to face and handle abusive behavior and the resultant unhealthy relationships among board members. If Chester seeks the help he needs to control his emotions and change his abusive behavior, then he may return to active board leadership at a later time. If not, he will not be allowed to continue as a lay leader of this congregation.

Learning experiences such as this can be eye-opening, healing, and re- demptive for congregational leaders. Unfortunately, such experiences may not always have successful outcomes. Nor may this be the last time such challenges occur. As mentioned in chapter 2, attendance at healthy con- gregation workshops such as those offered by Peter Steinke also can help congregational leaders learn to foster and restore relational health.

Here are several examples of how our board members handled the next challenging encounters.

Whenever Pastor Melissa was away from the congregation on vacation or study leave, a disgruntled board member of the congregation could be overheard speaking negatively of the pastor to visitors. The next time the pastor was away, a council member was alert to negative comments about the pastor and prepared to pull the critical member aside and say, "This criti- cism of our pastor to visitors is inappropriate—you are welcome to remain if you stop making these comments, and you'll need to leave if you persist." Such intervention effectively identifies the critical member's inappropriate behavior and eliminates the power to defame the pastor.

A similar incident happened in the congregation's fellowship hall. One particular nurture ministry team member was adamant that glass coffee cups be used during coffee hour rather than paper ones. When this member rotated off the ministry team, remaining members began using paper cups because no one wanted to wash the glass ones. During the next coffee hour, the former member got out the glass cups and was determined to use them. To address this meddling in ministry team affairs, the new moderator pulled the former member aside and simply said, "We don't do it this way anymore." Caught off guard, the former member put the glass cups away and decided not to help with coffee hour anymore. In reality, the former member's power to control coffee hour protocol was removed, thereby freeing the ministry team to operate in a new way.

6. Power Can Be Used to Restore Broken Relationships.
While power can Be misused to control other people's lives, it can also be used appropriately to restore broken relationships. Consider this scenario.

The board secretary of a congregation makes accusations without apparent foundation and inappropriately challenges the integrity of the pastor at a personnel committee meeting. The board secretary then rebuffs an attempt to arrange a reconciliatory meeting with the pastor. Next, the secretary ignores a request by the congregation's board to resign. Moreover, the secretary refuses to cooperate with a process of reconciliation moderated by a denominational representative. Finally, the board secretary unilaterally circulates confidential information about proceedings to selected members of the congregation.

Here is a case where a lay leader repeatedly fails to honor the practice of love and reconciliation with colleagues in ministry, and similarly fails to uphold the peace of the congregation by refusing to cooperate in a process of healing broken relationships with the board and pastor and by handing out selected confidential information to certain members of the congregation. Having exhausted attempts to curtail inappropriate behavior and to reconcile with offended parties, the congregation's board takes further action. Charges against the board secretary are filed and a disciplinary hearing scheduled to adjudicate the offenses. Testimony substantiates the charges and the secretary is found guilty.

A censure of temporary exclusion from membership in the congregation is imposed until the secretary satisfactorily completes a rehabilitation program that includes a face-to-face apology to the board and pastor; refraining from activities detrimental to the peace and unity of the church and the practice of love and reconciliation with colleagues in ministry; and completion of a counseling program that addresses managing conflict, understanding the necessity for confidentiality, proper use of authority, and learning to control aggressive and hostile behavior.

It is important to realize that the power of disciplinary proceedings and actions is geared not to punish offensive behavior but to stop inappropriate behavior and to restore broken relationships. Power is used for cooperation and restoration rather than for domination or retribution. As Mahatma Gandhi observes, "Power is of two kinds. One is obtained by the fear of punishment and the other by acts of love. Power based on love is a thousand times more effective and permanent than the one derived from fear of punishment."

7. Power and Privilege Are Related.

Understanding Power and Privilege

Privilege is a right, advantage, favor, or benefit some people have and others do not. It may be granted, demanded, authorized, conferred, or entitled. It may be inherent in an individual, group, system, or institution. It may be fair and used appropriately or be unfair and misused. It crosses the fairness or appropriateness line when one class or group of people is favored over another, resulting in unequal or limited access to resources or power that should be available to all.

In most denominations and religious bodies, for example, membership and participation shall not be denied to anyone on the basis of ethnicity, race, gender identity, status, class, sexual orientation, age, disability, educational level, appearance, geography, or theological conviction. White privilege, for instance, is an institutional set of benefits or access to resources and power granted to people classified as white but not to people of color. It creates an unequal racial balance of power in society and its institutions. The acquisition of such favoring, valuing, enriching, and validating can result in a system of domination or control that restricts access to resources, opportunity, and power by one class of people over another when such access should be available to everyone.

Awareness of such acquisition and domination by people of privilege is often a first step in changing or reversing unfair and inappropriate use of power. John T. Warren, professor of communication pedagogy, suggests that "whiteness is slippery," and advises, "Our ongoing struggle is to be well read, well versed, humble and willing to be accountable for things we did not know we were doing. It is about taking a stance of grace in this conversation, being active without assuming we know how it will (or through what efforts it might) end."[43] Such awareness might come through attending a White Privilege conference or from reading consciousness-raising books.[44] One way universities raise awareness is by requiring students to complete a class in some area of cultural, social, political, or economic diversity. Likewise, many businesses and organizations provide cultural proficiency training.

Dealing with Power and Privilege

Changing patterns of unfair privilege and unequal access to power require intentional, concerted, patient, persistent, and committed social action that challenges systems of domination and demands sharing of power and resources that should be equally available to everyone. An especially prevalent example in our society and congregations is ability privilege, about which communication studies scholar Deanna L. Fassett comments:

> While each of us experiences a unique range of abilities, and while each of us attempts to engage others who are different from us in meaningful and respectful ways, we all participate in ableism—in a pedagogy of ability—in

a social system that, by articulating ability as a possession we either own or lack, perpetuates the normalizing and privileging of apparently able-bodied individuals. Interrogating our participation in this process makes possible the praxis, the reflection, and action on the world in order to transform it, that is our responsibility and challenge.[45]

Here is what the president of a major university did to raise awareness and address inequality and privilege on her campus.

University of Washington president Ana Mari Cauce, in a speech introducing a wide-ranging Race and Equality Initiative, said, "This is not someone else's problem. And, while I'm not any more sure of the solutions than anyone else, I do know the best way to get out of a hole is to stop digging. We may not be able to solve racial inequity, and all those other forms of 'isms' everywhere in this country or in the world, but we've got to begin by not being part of the problem. We can only do that by recognizing it and acknowledging that it resides in us."[46]

Cauce goes on to point out, "Racism and all those other 'isms' are inside all of us—passed down over generations, in our cultures and histories, imbibed by new immigrants as they arrive on our shores. But it's often subtle, sometimes out of our own consciousness. That is why we have to actively struggle to get beyond it. We can't just will it or ignore it away. We have to become culturally aware and self-aware." Furthermore, she says, "Let's not forget that the men—and they were men—who wrote that 'all men were created equal,' such a liberating and powerful idea, really meant all men who were white—many owned slaves! Racism was baked into our country's founding, and it remains in the fabric of our country—indeed in every country I know of—and it is there underneath the surface of our daily lives."

And with respect to the power of communication, she says this:

Words don't break bones, but they crush souls. Stereotypes may be all in your head, but they can shape reality. And, they create the conditions that lead others to break bones, or burn crosses, or lead to exclusionary or biased policies and institutional practices that lead to and maintain racial and other forms of inequity and deny real people opportunities. Such policies or practices are often much less obvious, but ultimately more corrosive.

Cauce also cautions, "It's not up to those in the oppressed groups to educate us and enlighten us. And, when we allow them to struggle for equity alone, rather than struggling alongside or serving as allies, we are only increasing their burden—or more precisely, we are giving them our burden to carry."

In his blog post, "Basic Whiteness Lessons from an Old White Guy," communication scholar John Stewart offers an excellent model of how to work at understanding the problem of whiteness and discover ways to remedy the status quo being sharply skewed in the direction of white privilege.[47] Stewart documents how the playing field is tilted in favor of whiteness in such areas as income and wealth, hiring, housing, drug arrests, and in the exercise of federal and state laws and policies on education, home mortgages, law enforcement, and other positions of power. He also points out that equity does not mean equality; rather, equity demands unequal remedies that threaten some people's freedom and justice and fairness requires a transfer from those of us who have more to those who have less. Fortunately, as Gloria Steinem reminds us, "It is more rewarding to watch money change the world than watch it accumulate."

Stewart goes on to demonstrate the importance of curiosity in learning about our own and others' cultures. And he underscores the importance of substituting "response-ability" for guilt by helping remedy problems of systemic racism even though we may have had nothing to do with creating them. Finally, he invites us to read about whiteness, talk about race, attend a workshop or conference, volunteer or participate as an ally in an organization that serves people of color, and work for cultural equity in our own sphere of influence.

Educational ministries in our congregations are excellent places to raise awareness and gain understanding about inequality and unfair privilege in our communities and society. Likewise, our outreach and social ministries are promising avenues for taking actions that address and remedy patterns of unequal access to power and of inequity.

Relating to Difference

Another dimension of power and privilege is how we relate to difference. For example, as Josina Makau points out, "Influxes of newcomers into long-dominant monocultural communities often foster enmity, fear, and xenophobia between newer and older residents. Violence, injustice, exploitation, and in some cases genocide are among the terrible outcomes of these responses."[48] Understanding how we relate to difference, then, is vitally important. For instance, differences viewed as dangerous or to be feared and avoided, as Makau goes on to comment, "significantly compromise fulfillment of communication's potential in today's globally interdependent, technologically interconnected world. Among other things, people encountering difference in these ways find it difficult to build the trust, respect, regard, and mutual understanding required to hear and be heard, to understand and be understood. In these and related ways, relating to difference as something to fear or as an obstacle to overcome compromises abilities to live well together and to collaborate in pursuit of sound decision making."[49] So, how are we to engage difference constructively?

Harlan Cleveland, former U.S. assistant secretary of state, ambassador to NATO, president of the University of Hawaii, and president of the World Academy of Art and Science, gets it right when he comments, "Civilizations will be built by cooperation and compassion, in a social climate in which people in differing groups can deal with each other in ways that respect their cultural differences."[50] He also points out, "Equality is not the product of similarity; it is the cheerful acknowledgment of difference."[51] Moreover, "for the 21st century, this 'cheerful acknowledgment of difference' is the alternative to a global spread of ethnic cleansing and religious rivalry."[52] Cleveland goes on to say, "The required solvent for civilization is *respect for differences*. Or, as one of my World Academy colleagues puts it, we need to learn *how to be different together*."[53]

Imagine that you have just been asked to join your congregation's multicultural ministry team. Your pastor and several members of the congregation see possibilities of reaching out to your increasingly multicultural neighborhood. They have attended several denominational multicultural conferences in recent years and have been slowly introducing ways for your church to become a congregation-of-all-nations. This new ministry initiative is an outgrowth of these efforts.

You are astonished to learn that there are more than one hundred languages spoken by students in a nearby elementary school where six or seven of your parishioners now volunteer as tutors. Your congregation is still predominately Caucasian, but in recent years has had regular visitors from many lands. Recently, council has taken the significant step of deciding to become an intentional multicultural congregation. Currently, you have a Native American council member, as well as members from Indonesia and Cambodia, and several Kenyan families are ready to join the church. Several multicultural potlucks have been well received by the congregation. Even so, some longtime members feel threatened by the changing demographics and fear a loss of familiarity and control. How are our congregations to overcome such fear and reluctance to diversity?

Recognition that one another's perception of the world is partial is a good starting point for engaging our differences. Often, notes Makau, "a humble recognition of our partiality and related commitment to fairness paves the way for open hearted, nondefensive, attentive listening. This enactment of *balanced partiality* in turn enables us to reach across differences in pursuit of mutual understanding."[54] This perspective helps prevent getting locked into a position and avoiding reflection on or reconsideration of our values and assumptions. Makau also suggests that engaging difference constructively involves "listening attentively, opening one's heart to the Other, pursuit of mutual understanding, acknowledging the limits of one's perspective, and responding thoughtfully to views potentially at odds with one's own."[55]

Another way to deal constructively with difference is by practicing curiosity, humility, and empathy. In their essay, "How to Deal with Difficult Difference," John Stewart and Tiye Sherrod recommend that we overcome our typical "fight or flight" mind-set by making these three responses (curiosity, humility, and empathy) our default option when a cultural difference between ourselves and another person creates a difficulty in communication. They point out that the way we use power can make things easier or harder when we make decisions about how we respond to difficult differences. And they say that practicing curiosity, humility, and platinum empathy (treating others the way they would like to be treated) is beneficial in our relationships with other people:

> Since anger is based on fear, when curiosity replaces defensiveness or anger, it puts you in a more powerful position than the person who's yelling and accusing. Similarly, people respect humility because it also demonstrates strength. It takes a self-assured person to hold her cultural identifiers lightly. The same thing's true of platinum empathy. It shows poise and confidence.[56]

No less a figure than former Chicago mayor Richard J. Daley has learned, "Power is dangerous unless you have humility." And underscoring the value of empathy and curiosity, American actress Susan Sarandon comments, "When you start to develop your powers of empathy and imagination, the whole world opens up to you."

Stewart and Sherrod also note how these three response options have the power to promote fruitful conversation:

> Curiosity, humility, and platinum empathy will encourage others to stay engaged with you, to deal with difference rather than let it escalate or sweep it under the rug. So if your experience of difficult difference is around one of the advantaged parts of your cultural identity, this response option can helpfully level the playing field. And if your experience is around one of the targeted parts of your cultural identity, this response option can encourage candid conversation.
>
> The thing to remember is that the three responses go together. Only when you begin by being curious about your own cultural identifiers and those of

others will you be in a position to have a fruitful conversation rather than a hostile one. Only by holding your own cultural identifiers loosely will you be able to understand the other person from their own point of view. And only when you practice platinum empathy will you be in a position to be genuinely curious about the difficult difference.[57]

While these suggestions for relating to difference are useful to you and your congregation seeking to become intentionally multicultural, your congregation's reluctance remains. Let's examine more closely, then, ways to overcome reluctance to welcoming diversity.

Overcoming Reluctance

One reason we may hesitate in welcoming diversity is that diversity can expose our privilege. Social psychologist Christena Cleveland comments with depth and honesty about why she struggles with diversity[58]:

> In our stratified society, it's fairly easy for privileged people like me to turn a blind eye to inequality. As long as I stick to certain neighborhoods and social settings, I am unlikely to meaningfully interact with people who struggle to survive underneath society's oppressive boot. This makes it easy for me to sidestep feeling guilty about my privilege and the relative ease with which I move through life. But racial diversity has a way of bringing racial, economic and other forms of inequality into conscious awareness.

Cleveland continues:

> For this reason, as a person who identifies with some privileged groups (e.g. the upwardly-mobile, the educated, the mentally able, etc.) I sure as heck don't want more diversity in my church. More diversity would expose my privileged life by bringing the inequality "out there" into the very sanctuary pews where I sit. True diversity would require me to stay alert to the reality of inequality. It would demand that I confront my privilege, recognize the ways that I benefit from a society that oppresses my brothers and sisters, repent, and join the fight for justice.
>
> But I'd rather not confront my privilege. I'd like to keep believing that I've "earned everything that I have", that "if people just work hard enough, they'll succeed", that "if people just obey the law, they won't be harassed by the police" and that, frankly, I deserve to be treated better and earn more than others.
>
> Diversity exposes my privilege, my desire to take credit for the social power that I possess and my tendency to justify holding onto the money that passes through my hands.

Cleveland goes on to point out that Jesus loves diversity: "Indeed he was so passionate about creating a diverse family with us that he crossed metaphysical planes, <u>abdicated his privilege</u> [underline in original], morphed into physical form, and spent 30 years on earth *just hanging out with us*—all the while knowing that his pursuit of diversity would ultimately cost him his life."[59]

Another form of reluctance occurs when we have opportunity to acknowledge and use our power of privilege in everyday situations, such as when a group of friends laughs at sexist or racist jokes. As sociologist Allan G. Johnson observes,

> It's just a moment among countless such moments that constitute the fabric of all kinds of oppressive systems. But it's a crucial moment, because the group's seamless response to the joke affirms the normalcy and unproblematic nature of it in a system of privilege. It takes only one person to tear the fabric of collusion and apparent consensus. On some level, each of us knows that we have this potential, and this knowledge can empower us or scare us into silence. We can change the course of the moment with something as simple as visibly not joining in the laughter, or saying "I don't think that's funny." We know how uncomfortable this can make the group feel and how they may ward off their discomfort by dismissing, excluding, or even attacking us as bearers of bad news. Our silence, then, isn't because nothing we do will matter. Our silence is our not *daring* to matter.[60]

As Pakistani teenage activist and Nobel Peace Prize laureate Malala Yousafzai puts it, "When the whole word is silent, even one voice becomes powerful."

Truly, notes Johnson, "like everything else in social life, privilege and oppression exist only through social systems and people's participation in them. People make systems and their consequences happen through paths of least resistance that shape who people are and how they participate."[61]

Paying attention to underlying or root causes of systemic domination is a way to understand and correct power imbalances. By way of illustration, often in protest rallies or demonstrations, results of oppression receive prominent attention while underlying causes are overlooked or ignored. *Seattle Times* staff columnist Jerry Large puts it this way: "Symptoms get our attention, and if we then identify the source of the problems, and fix them, the symptoms go away. Our bodies work that way, and communities do, too."[62] Large continues, "How police treat black, Latino and Native American citizens is a longstanding issue, though one largely invisible to the majority of white Americans until recently, but that isn't the root cause of our troubles.

It's just the most dramatic symptom." Adding perspective, Large goes on to comment:

> Social media and video recordings have made a big difference. Small protests become large protests that attract mainstream media attention, especially when they disrupt life as usual in a community—when they become an irritant. And when some protesters turn violent, coverage and attention soar.
>
> In the absence of information that provides context, many people ask: "Why are they doing this? Why are they burning their community?"
>
> Most reactions I read or heard were all about surface symptoms: police behavior, protest tactics, etc., at least early on. But there are deep problems in the neighborhoods where protests took place, high unemployment, poor schools, dangerous streets and hazardous housing. Some of the neighborhoods where people protested have not fully recovered since they exploded in 1968 after Martin Luther King Jr. was assassinated.

Other root causes can include federal and local government policies, especially housing policies, for producing and maintaining segregation and inequality. Access to good jobs, transportation, housing, education, and other services in the areas where people of limited means live are also beneath-the-surface symptoms.

These suggestions for overcoming reluctance to welcoming diversity can prove useful to your congregation in its efforts to become increasingly multicultural. However, the congregation needs to remember that such cultural transformation takes time and long-term commitment. There are phases in creating bridges rather than walls, or as Ronald Arnett suggests, walls with bridges,[63] in the journey from *sameness*, to *difference*, to *unity*.

At first, many people in your congregation simply do not see the differences between themselves and their multicultural newcomers. This is the "sameness" stage. This lack of awareness may lead to ignoring, denying, or minimizing cultural differences and result in cultural insensitivity and communication incompetence such as arrogant, rude, or defensive behavior. Differences can be threatening and result in fearful loss of familiarity and control.

Once they begin to notice cultural differences, the next phase of transformation is to learn what these differences are. This "difference" phase may lead your multicultural task force to showcase cultural differences at upcoming potluck gatherings. Now people begin to learn about one another's ethnic backgrounds and what it means to belong to diverse groups. Differences become valued rather than threatening. Such positive encounters begin to build a multicultural sense of community as healthy relationships are created between longtime members and newcomers. In this phase, relationships deepen between people who are different from one another.

Next, as differences "unite," diversity becomes the new normal—after all, we're all human beings made in the image of God! There is growing aware-ness of a new commonness built on difference—a "unity amid diversity" phase that we learned about back in chapter 2. In this phase of transforma-tion, people become curious and eager to learn more about differences rather than get stuck in a fear of loss of familiarity and control. They now welcome diversity and support inclusiveness. They learn how to adapt to one another's differences and integrate newcomers fully into the congregation's life and ministry. In this final phase, transformation from monocultural congregation to multicultural congregation-of-all-nations is now complete. There will be setbacks and challenges along the way, so recognition that such transforma-tion takes time and long-term commitment is essential as your congregation cycles back and forth and through the phases of its journey from sameness, to difference, to unity-through-diversity.[64]

8. Gender Differences Affect the Power to Communicate.

Power differences based on gender are communicated verbally and nonver-bally. As communication scholars Deborah Borisoff and Lisa Merrill point out in *The Power to Communicate: Gender Differences as Barriers*, "Cultural stereotypes for men and women, whether communicated through verbal or nonverbal channels, are as much symbols of power or powerlessness as they are models of gender differences."[65] They suggest that since gender-linked traits are learned rather than innate behaviors, stereotypes are also a "fic-tion." They acknowledge that many of us have long-held internalized models of femininity and masculinity. And yet, they say, "linguistic practices—as sources of social power—have also been sources of resistance. Throughout history, there have been women and men who violated societal norms."[66] However, as they go on to comment:

> Resistance exacts a price; women have been labeled "unnatural" and "man-nish" and men "effeminate" when they communicate in a manner which calls into question a strict and mutually exclusive gender dichotomy. At this point in time it has become apparent that a rigid adherence to the sex-role stereo-types is a disadvantage that limits both women and men, although in different ways. We believe that individuals are capable of creating other, less limiting communication models. In order to accomplish this, we first must examine in greater detail the specific verbal and nonverbal behaviors through which our respective stereotypes are manifested.[67]

Limiting negative stereotypic gender images and strategies with which many of us have been reared include women being soft spoken, compliant, self-effacing, emotional, and subjective, and men who listen ineffectively, make categorical assertions, dominate discussion, and show few emotions. These feminine and masculine stereotypes also have nonverbal gender-linked traits or strategies that imply a power differential of dominance and submission. Stereotypic male nonverbal behaviors of dominance include staring, touching, frowning, invading another's space, and pointing. Stereotypic female nonverbal behaviors of submission include averting eye contact, responding to touch, smiling, moving away, and going where directed.

Allan Johnson reminds us that people don't learn these gender differences in styles of talk primarily in same-sex play groups as children or in late-night talks with peers; rather, "they learned them from adults in families, the mass media, and in schools. In other words, they learned them by participating in a society where conversation is a major arena in which male privilege is played out."[68]

We see this dynamic played out in congregational council meetings led by clergywomen whose authority, expertise, and professional commitment are routinely challenged by men, in particular. Unlike their behavior toward male clergy, some male council members argue or question every point, feel free to interrupt, or assume their female pastor does not know what she is talking about. Such behavior is demeaning, controlling, abusive, and wearing. Moreover, her softer voice can be ignored or discounted, a pause to reflect before speaking seen as uncertainty, a casual reply viewed as flippancy, an assertive remark perceived as pushy. To restore respect for her authority in such situations, my wife resorted to wearing a clergy collar. Sadly, such behavior is so exhausting and intolerable that some clergywomen decide to leave the ministry altogether.

In *Communicating Power and Gender*, Deborah Borisoff and James Chesebro suggest, "People are more likely to become more effective communicators if they can condition and train themselves to view the application of sex roles as an opportunity to make choices and develop strategies that can be judged as more or less effective depending upon the people and circumstances encountered."[69]

So, how are we to diminish the power differential of typical, though limiting, gender roles in our verbal and nonverbal communication? Borisoff and Merrill suggest the following strategies to create healthier ways of relating to one another[70]:

- Use correct, standard, culturally appropriate grammar and articulation.
- Learn to speak without hesitation and uncertainty.
- If interrupted, say, "You interrupted me. I haven't finished speaking yet."
- Use open-ended and yes-no questions appropriately.
- Use tag questions, qualifiers, disclaimers, and requests appropriately.
- Use touch comfortably, reciprocally, and unambiguously.
- Smile, nod, and raise eyebrows genuinely and nonjudgmentally.
- Refuse to have your space violated and assert your presence nonverbally.
- Use appropriate eye contact, gestures, and tone-of-voice variation.
- Avoid irrelevant, tangential, impersonal, ambiguous, or incongruous responses.
- Adjust pitch and volume to enhance credibility, capability, intelligence, and maturity.

Another way to overcome limiting negative gender images and traits is to consider androgyny—combining positive masculine, feminine, and gender-neutral traits—as a way to increase the range and effectiveness of sex-role communication strategies. For example, stereotypic masculine traits such as being decisive, determined, assertive, intelligent, and analytical could be combined with stereotypic feminine traits such as being compassionate, outgoing, sensitive, understanding, and warm, and with gender-neutral traits such as being honest, creative, and hardworking. As Borisoff and Chesebro conclude, "An individual is likely to function as a more effective communicator if all of the strategies associated with masculinity and all of the strategies associated with femininity are appraised as needed, thereby any one of which could be employed for its potential effectiveness regardless of whether or not one is a male or female."[71]

9. Power Differences Affect Group Participation in Multicultural Situations.

In chapter 4, we saw that collectivistic-oriented cultures tend to view power as negotiated, whereas individualistic-oriented cultures are more apt to view power as a demand. And in chapter 2, we saw that cultural sensitivity leads to more inclusive group participation and decision-making in a multicultural community. In particular, we learned that some cultures expect everyone to participate in group discussion, while people from other cultures are reticent to speak up. For example, Eric Law believes that group participation in a multicultural setting is highly dependent on how leaders and members perceive where they are on a power continuum. He says:

> Depending on the cultural contexts, a group's expectation from the leadership could be very different. Leading or facilitating a group has to do with power—power to influence others and being aware of the power dynamic among the group members. Therefore, it is very important for a group leader first to determine where he or she is in the power perception continuum. How does it influence the way she behaves and interacts with others? What assumptions and expectations does he bring to the group?
>
> Secondly, when the group leader is in a multicultural situation, there is a need to know where the people are on this power continuum.[72]

Law goes on to describe groups of people at the two ends of this power continuum. Here is the group at one end of the continuum, one approximating a demand-oriented individualistic culture:

> If all participants have a strong sense of their own individual power, then everything learned in white middle-class group processing would be helpful here because everyone believes that he or she is equal to everyone else unless there are "experts" in the room. A good leader is someone who enables the group to do what it needs to accomplish. People are expected to volunteer their thoughts, feelings, and talents. Differences of opinion are debated verbally. A good leader attempts to get consensus from the group. Decisions can be made by compromising. When a consensus or compromise cannot be reached, decisions fall back on voting. Robert's Rules of Order is a prime example of group process based on these assumptions. Voting, when it is not unanimous, presumes that there are winners and losers. Groups with these kinds of assumptions automatically set up a competitive environment.[73]

Law describes such leaders this way:

> An image of a good leader in a white group is a pre-traffic-lights traffic cop who stands on a platform in the middle of an intersection. His or her job is to keep all the self-moving autonomous individuals from colliding with each other. The worst of the leaders in this setting is someone who sits back and lets people fight and escalate the conflict, all in the name of democracy and respect for individual opinion and freedom. Then when things get out of hand, the leader comes in with his or her own agenda and says, "See, I gave you the power to decide and you can't seem to be able to do it. So why don't you let me decide for you?"[74]

And here is Law's description of the group at the other end of the continuum, one approximating a negotiation-oriented collectivistic culture:

> If everyone in the group falls on the other end of the power continuum (that is, they have a fragile sense of their individual power and would not challenge authority), someone will have to take charge and be the authoritative figure. The authoritative figure is usually the designated leader of the group. If no one takes on this role, nothing will get done. A good leader is sensitive to the needs and talents of everyone in the group.[75]

Here is how he describes such leaders:

> An image of a good leader is an octopus who has its tentacles extended in to the different parts of the community. This person has a network of trusted people who give him or her information about what the community wants, who wishes to participate, and who has the gifts to fulfill the tasks. This person spends a lot of time before a meeting to acquire the essential information. At the meeting, the concept of invitation becomes very important because no one will volunteer. The leader has to invite people directly to offer their ideas and services. The leader will have difficulty if there are power struggles between two or more persons who believe they all have authority in the group. The worst of the leaders in this kind of group are those who use their power to push their own agenda because in such a group no one will challenge their authority.[76]

Law invented the process of mutual invitation as a process to give everyone opportunity to participate in group discussion and decision-making in multicultural communication settings. As described in chapter 2, this process of group interaction decentralizes the power dynamic. After the leader invites someone to share, the process takes over as group members take turns giving one another permission to speak.

10. Prophets Are Powerful and Influential.
Prophets play an important role in our individual and collective lives. They challenge the status quo when we go astray. They are influential as conscience-bearers of a community. Their power comes from the moral strength of their message and from the assertiveness of their call to right behavior.

In a world of power, money, violence, religious intolerance, and civil rights violations, their influence is welcomed by some, and not by others. Often their message and call are met with resistance, even brutal resistance, as in the case of some Old Testament prophets, Jesus, Hildegard of Bingen, Sojourner Truth, Dietrich Bonhoeffer, Martin Luther King Jr., Janani Luwum,

Dorothy Day, Oscar Romero, and K. H. Ting.[77] At times we are called to take on the prophetic role of challenging falsehood, asserting equality and equity, and demanding that domination give way to empowerment. As Archbishop Oscar A. Romero puts it, "Each one of you has to be God's microphone. Each one of you has to be a messenger, a prophet."

Old Testament Prophets

Old Testament prophets presented an alternative vision to Pharaoh's system of forcing the people of Israel to produce more and more bricks to build more and more storehouses to hold more and more of his possessions, and, later, to Solomon's system of quotas and production schedules for accumulating wealth and sustaining lavish living. As Walter Brueggemann points out, these Hebrew prophets were poets rather than predictors of the future or social activists per se.[78] They used the power of rhetoric to imagine a new way of living—one characterized by fidelity to God and making the truth about God relevant for their times.[79] Prophets sketch a new way of living not available before their utterances—something never seen or heard before—as do all good artists. Most often speaking as outsiders and over-against the powers that be, it is somewhat surprising that such "poetry from the edges" made it inside the Hebrew Bible.

Here is how Brueggemann describes imaginative poetic visions from Old Testament prophets and their striking relevance for today:

> The prophets lived a culture of acute denial and they had to have rhetorical strategies to try to penetrate the denial. You hear the poetry read, and then you have to sit with it, follow the rhetoric, watch for the images and phrases, and notice the new world that emerges out of that poetry.
>
> The prophetic poets remind people that there is moral accountability and that choices have consequences that cannot be evaded no matter how powerful or wealthy you are. Eventually a society that violates the moral center and turns away from a covenantal relationship with God is going to pay for it.
>
> In the end, the prophets are not preoccupied with judgment or with sadness or with grief or with loss; they are preoccupied with God's resolve to do something new that will be an embodiment of God's Shalom.
>
> In our society, Pharaoh takes the form of the rat race, and the rat race drives us to want more. We will never make enough bricks to satisfy ourselves! It is the great seduction of a consumer economy to think that you always have to have more.
>
> In a time of anxiety like our times there is a great temptation in the church to want to offer certitudes and find answers and closure. The poetic force of the prophets is their imagination keeps refusing certitude by opening up another line of thought and emotion.[80]

Jesus-the-Prophet

Then comes Jesus, an outsider from Galilee, proclaiming another mysterious, revolutionary vision of the Kingdom of God. Here is how Walter Wink describes Jesus-the-prophet:

> The words and deeds of Jesus reveal that he is not a minor reformer but an egalitarian prophet who repudiated the very premises of the Domination System: the right of some to lord it over others by means of power, wealth, shaming, or titles. In his beatitudes, his healings, and his table fellowship with outcasts and sinners, Jesus declared God's special concern for the oppressed.[81]

Like Old Testament prophets imagining a vision of fidelity to God and exposing the truth of oppressive production-oriented systems used by Pharaoh and Solomon to accumulate vast wealth, Wink sketches a similar picture of Jesus' message:

> The gospel of Jesus is founded on economic equity, because economic inequities are the basis of domination. Ranking, status, and classism are largely built on power provided by accumulated wealth.[82]

Breaking with domination means ending the economic exploitation of the many by the few. The rich were not to be given special status. Wink reminds us of Jesus' vision of the Kingdom of God:

> It is rather the poor whom God elects and blesses, the meek and brokenhearted and despised who will inherit God's coming reign on earth. It is the merciful not the mighty, the peacemakers not the warriors, the persecuted not the aristocrats, who will enter into the joy of God (Matt. 5:3–12). In parable after parable, Jesus speaks of the "reigning of God" using images drawn from farming and women's work, not warfare and king's palaces. It is not described as coming from on high down to earth; it rises quietly and imperceptibly out of the land. It is established, not by armies and military might, but by an ineluctable process of growth from below, among the common people. He is, in sum, not looking for a kingdom for himself or anyone else where God imposes the divine will on the world. Rather, he is inaugurating God's domination-free order.[83]

After describing the powerful way Jesus reimagines the religious thinking of his time about such wide-ranging topics as nonviolence, women, purity and holiness, families, law, and sacrifice, Wink concludes:

> Looking back over Jesus' ministry, what emerges with bracing clarity is the *comprehensive* nature of his vision. He was not intent on putting a new patch on an old garment, or new wine in old skins (Mark 2:21–22). He was

not a reformer, bringing alternative, better readings of the law. Nor was he a revolutionary, attempting to replace one oppressive power with another (Mark 12:13–17). He went beyond revolution. His struggle was against the basic presuppositions and structures of oppression—against the Domination System itself. Violent revolution fails because it is not revolutionary enough. It changes the rulers but not the rules, the ends but not the means. Most of the old repressive values and delusional assumptions remain intact. What Jesus envisioned was a world transformed, where both people and Powers are in harmony with the Ultimate and committed to the general welfare—what some prefer to call the "kindom" of God.[84]

Assertive Nonviolence

And how are we to create within the shell of the old society the foundations of God's domination-free order—to begin living as if the Reign of God were already arriving? Wink insists that Jesus introduces what he calls a "third way" to secure human dignity and to change the power equation as an alternative to the ways of passivity and violence, submission and assault, or flight and fight. He advocates assertive nonviolence where "turning the other cheek" is an act of defiance, where impoverished debtors use the system against itself, and where "going the second mile" exposes oppression.

Here is Wink's explanation of Jesus' third way and identification of modern-day followers:

> He articulates, out of the history of his own people's struggles, a way by which evil can be opposed without being mirrored, the oppressor resisted without being emulated, and the enemy neutralized without being destroyed. Those who have lived by Jesus' words—Leo Tolstoy, Mohandas Gandhi, Muriel Lester, Martin Luther King, Jr., Dorothy Day, Cesar Chavez, Hildegard and Jean Goss-Mayr, Mairead (Corrigan) Maguire, Adolfo Perez Esquivel, Daw Aung San Suu Kyi, and countless others less well known—point us to a new way of confronting evil whose potential for personal and social transformation we are only beginning to grasp today.[85]

Ivie believes "nonviolent struggle against injustice requires a deep respect for the humanity of others, a recognition that one's own status is debased—not elevated—by debasing others, and a goal of persuading adversaries rather than destroying opponents; that is of addressing the sources of conflict rather than directing hate and anger toward enemies."[86] Moreover, suggests Ivie, "nonviolent resistance as an approach to positive peace requires a humanizing rhetoric of identification in order to struggle for social justice without triggering the myth of just war—the myth that supposes war is the only practical option for eliminating the threat posed by an enemy who has been reduced to the image of evil savagery."[87] To illustrate his point, Ivie refers to the way Jim Wallis humanized our nation's adversaries in the global war on terrorism through the peacemaking lens of a transnational church:

> As a high-profile peace activist speaking in a prophetic voice to a self-proclaimed Christian people, Wallis invited Americans to acknowledge and heal the darkness that resided within the nation's political soul. Evil, he observed, exists within everyone, and thus it is dangerous to avoid looking inward by projecting darkness outward. He called upon the nation to confront its own sins in a spirit of self-examination and to address the injustices that breed terrorism rather than become the enemy it envisions. His call to choose political healing and reconciliation over close-minded vengeance and redemptive violence transformed narrow national self-interest by adopting a wider worldview of compassion and humility. It was an exercise in reflective perspective-taking and empathizing self-criticism, which was prompted largely by reminding Christian Americans that they were part of an international faith community made up of multiple perceptions of the U.S. response to terrorism and suggesting that the nation reconnect to its respect for humanity by considering the views of other Christians around the world. By adopting the transnational viewpoint of a worldwide church in order to transform a narrow and self-righteous nationalism, Wallis redirected attention to humanizing values and articulated the interdependency of attending ethically to the common good and enhancing pragmatically global security.[88]

Similarly, Archbishop Romero put things into perspective when he said:

> Peace is not the product of terror or fear.
> Peace is not the silence of cemeteries.
> Peace is not the silent result of violent repression.
> Peace is the generous, tranquil contribution of all to the good of all.
> Peace is dynamism.
> Peace is generosity.
> It is right and it is duty.

As noted at the beginning of this guideline, there will be times when we are called to take on prophetic tasks such as challenging falsehood, asserting equality and equity, and demanding that domination give way to empowerment. Like Old Testament prophets, Jesus-the-prophet, and modern-day prophets, our prophetic role may be daunting, even dangerous. Nonetheless, our prophetic work can make a powerful impact in our sphere of influence.

Summary and Conclusion

Effective ways to deal with some of the stupid, even evil, ways power is used and misused in our congregations are presented in this chapter. First, we gained an understanding of communication ethics and ethical systems. We then used the perspective of relational communication ethics to identify principles and skills to deal with typical relational quandaries facing people in our congregations, thereby fostering healthier relationships between leaders and members. We also saw how our misuse of language and communication power creates blockages to genuine conversation; how transcultural communication ethics can be applied to create healthy relationships with people from diverse cultural, ethnic, and socioeconomic backgrounds; and how to deal with new ethical challenges created by global information technology and our digital cyberspace universe.

Next, we learned how to properly understand and practice persuasive communication both as ethical persuaders and as responsible consumers of persuasion. Following Walter Wink's view that powers are good, fallen, and redeemable, we examined how these powers may be used for peaceful purposes, misused to control other people's lives, and used to restore broken relationships.

We then saw how power and privilege are related. In particular, we considered how to change patterns of unfair privilege and unequal access to power by how we address white privilege, relate to differences, and overcome our reluctance to use our power of privilege to expose causes of oppression and correct power imbalances.

We also saw how gender differences affect our power to communicate, and discovered choices and strategies to overcome typical limiting negative gender images and traits. And we saw how group participation in multicultural situations is highly dependent on how leaders and members perceive where they are on a power continuum, whether in a demand-oriented individualistic culture or in a negotiation-oriented collectivistic culture. We also saw how Eric Law's process of mutual invitation gives everyone opportunity to participate in group discussion and decision-making in multicultural communication settings.

Finally, we learned about the important role that prophets play in our individual and collective lives. They challenge the status quo when we go astray, serve as communal conscience-bearers, and use the moral strength of their message to call us to right behavior. At times we are all called to take on the prophetic role of challenging falsehood, asserting equality and equity, and demanding domination give way to empowerment. Examples from Old

Testament prophets, from Jesus-the-prophet, and from modern-day prophets point the way to create God's domination-free order through assertive nonviolence that struggles against injustice and promotes positive peace.

All ten of these guidelines for using power offer ways to help us create healthier ways of relating to one another in our congregations, homes, workplaces, neighborhoods, and wider global communities.

Practical Applications

1. Think of relational quandaries you've encountered in your congregation. How can relational communication ethics guide relational behavior to create healthier ways of relating? Where relevant, notice how misuse of language and communication power creates blockages to genuine conversation, how transcultural communication ethics can create healthier intercultural communication, and how ethical challenges in cyberspace can best be addressed.

2. How can you improve your persuasive communication both as persuader and persuadee?

3. What are examples of good, fallen, and redeemable powers? How might these powers be used for peaceful purposes, be misused to control people's lives, or be used to restore broken relationships?

4. Assess your experience with power and privilege. What steps can you take to change patterns of unfair privilege and inequitable access to power, to improve the ways you relate to differences, and to overcome reluctance to use powers of privilege to expose oppression and to correct power imbalances?

5. How do gender differences affect the power to communicate in your life and in your congregation? What choices and strategies can help you and members of your congregation overcome limiting negative gender images and traits?

6. Where do you fall on the power continuum in multicultural communication situations? How might the process of mutual invitation be useful in giving everyone an opportunity to participate in group discussion and decision-making in intercultural settings?

7. Reflect on the role that prophets play in your congregation and in society. What have you learned from Old Testament prophets, Jesus-the-prophet, and modern-day prophets that you can use when you or your congregation is called to take on a prophetic role?

For Further Study

Arnett, Ronald C. *Dwell in Peace: Applying Nonviolence to Everyday Relationships* (Elgin, IL: Brethren, 1985).

Battalora, Jacqueline. *Birth of a White Nation: The Invention of White People and Its Relevance Today* (Houston: Strategic, 2013).

Blood, Rebecca. *The Weblog Handbook* (Cambridge, MA: Perseus, 2002).

Borisoff, Deborah, and Lisa Merrill. *The Power to Communicate: Gender Differences as Barriers*, 3rd ed. (Prospect Heights, IL: Waveland, 1998).

Brueggemann, Walter. *Embracing the Prophets in Contemporary Culture: Walter Brueggemann on Confronting Today's "Pharaohs."* DVD (Denver: Morehouse Education Resources, 2012).

Cheney, George, Steve May, and Debashish Munshi, eds. *Handbook of Communication Ethics* (New York: Routledge, 2011).

Cleveland, Christena. "3 Reasons Why I Hate Diversity," blog post, February 19, 2015. Available at http://www.christianitytoday.com/edstetzer/2015/february/3 -reasons-why-i-hate-diversity.html.

Haslebo, Gitte, and Maja Loua Haslebo. *Practicing Relational Ethics in Organizations* (Chagrin Falls, OH: Taos Institute, 2012).

Irving, Debby. *Waking Up White, and Finding Myself in the Story of Race* (Chicago: Elephant Room, 2014).

Johannesen, Richard L., Kathleen S. Valde, and Karen E. Whedbee. *Ethics in Human Communication*, 6th ed. (Long Grove, IL: Waveland, 2008).

Johnson, Allan G. *Power, Privilege, and Difference* (New York: McGraw-Hill, 2006).

Larson, Charles U. *Persuasion: Reception and Responsibility*, 13th ed. (Boston: Wadsworth, 2013).

Nakayama, Thomas K., and Rona Tamiko Halualani, eds. *The Handbook of Critical Intercultural Communication* (Hoboken, NJ: Wiley-Blackwell, 2010).

Robertson, C. K. *A Dangerous Dozen: 12 Christians Who Threatened the Status Quo but Taught Us to Live Like Jesus* (Woodstock, VA: Skylight Paths, 2011).

Rothwell, J. Dan. *Telling It Like It Isn't: Language Misuse and Malpractice/What We Can Do About It* (Englewood Cliffs, NJ: Prentice-Hall, 1983).

Singleton, Glenn. *Courageous Conversations About Race: A Field Guide for Achieving Equity in Schools* (Thousand Oaks, CA: Corwin, 2014).

Stewart, John. *Personal Communicating and Racial Equity* (Dubuque, IA: Kendall-Hunt, 2016).

Stewart, John, and Tiye Sherrod. "How to Deal with Difficult Difference," blog post, April 3, 2015. Available at http://www.johnstewart.org/how-to-deal-with-dif ficult-dif/2014/12/5/how-to-deal-with-difficult-difference-john-stewart-tiye-sher .html.

Wink, Walter. *The Powers That Be: Theology for a New Millennium* (Minneapolis: Augsburg Fortress, 1998).

Woodward, Gary C., and Robert E. Denton, Jr. *Persuasion and Influence in American Life*, 7th ed. (Long Grove, IL: Waveland, 2014).

~

Appendix A

Paraphrasing Exercise ("Opinionaire")

Instructions: Use the Opinionaire provided below to practice the skill of paraphrasing. Here is how it works.

1. Ask participants to complete the Opinionaire. Encourage them to push their responses to the extremes as much as possible (e.g., "strongly disfavor" and "strongly favor").

2. In dyads, have participants select a topic on which they most disagree and about which they are willing to express their opinions to their partner.

3. Have one partner express their opinion on the selected topic for several minutes (2 to 3 minutes should suffice) during which time their partner is to listen carefully without interruption.

4. After the speaker is finished, the listener is to paraphrase what they understood their partner to say—to the speaker's satisfaction. Remind participants that phrasing is not simply repeating what they hear word for word, but rather putting into their own words what they understand their partner to say.

5. Repeat steps 3 and 4 with partners reversing their roles.

6. Debrief the experience as a group. Ask participants to describe their experiences and what they learned about the skill of paraphrasing, and then draw conclusions and applications as appropriate.

7. If desired, the process may be repeated on a second topic to put into practice and to imprint what participants learned in the debriefing experience.

Opinionaire

	Strongly Disfavor				Strongly Favor
1. Permit citizenship for illegal immigrants					
2. Provide national health insurance					
3. Decriminalize marijuana use					
4. Pass stricter gun control laws					
5. Increase national defense spending					
6. Sign international global-warming treaties					
7. Permit prayer in public schools					
8. Liberalize prison regulations					
9. Use inclusive language for God					
10. Approve same-gender marriage					
11. Restrict legalization of gambling					
12. Limit abortion rights					
13. Permit clergy to marry same-gender couples					
14. Permit consensual sex for all adults					
15. Dismantle Israeli settlements in Palestine					
16. Permit tent-city sites for the homeless					
17. Restrict residency of sex offenders					
18. Limit damage awards for corporate crime					
19. Increase social-service spending					
20. Increase auto emission standards					

Appendix B

Listening Awareness and Skills Inventory

Instructions: The following ten items describe various listening behaviors. In responding, please consider the way *you typically act* when you are in a listening situation. Circle the number that best represents your listening behavior, using a scale ranging from one (1) to six (6) with one (1) being "Never" or "Not at All" and six (6) being "Always" or "Completely." Work rapidly; your first answer is likely to be the most accurate.

When I'm in a listening situation, I typically:

	Never Not at All				Always Completely	
1. Am open-minded	1	2	3	4	5	6
2. Am interested in others' interests	1	2	3	4	5	6
3. Adapt to others' appearance	1	2	3	4	5	6
4. Avoid making premature judgments	1	2	3	4	5	6
5. Grasp central ideas	1	2	3	4	5	6
6. Eliminate distractions	1	2	3	4	5	6
7. Keep my listening purposes in mind	1	2	3	4	5	6
8. Give sufficient time and effort	1	2	3	4	5	6
9. Know when I misunderstand others	1	2	3	4	5	6
10. Perception check if meaning is unclear	1	2	3	4	5	6

~

Appendix C

Strength Bombardment Exercise

Instructions: Use this activity to improve the awareness and skills of purpose-ful listening: to learn, to decide, to enjoy, and to help. It may also be used to strengthen people's self-concept through the gift of affirmation.[1] Here is how it works:

1. With people who have at least some acquaintance with one another, sit in a circle of 3 to 30 people.
2. Pass out sheets of blank paper and ask participants to jot down several characteristics, traits, abilities, or strengths they especially like, appre-ciate, respect, or admire about each person in the circle. The number of qualities that participants list for each person will, of course, vary depending on their level of acquaintance. If desired, you may also ask participants to jot down a hope, wish, or challenge for each person in the group.
3. Focusing on one person at a time, have group members take turns bombarding that person with the qualities they've written down. Go around the circle, one comment at a time, until no one has any more

---

[1] Much of the feedback that we get throughout our lives is negative. Most of us know all too well what we do poorly. For some reason, most of us do not get a comparable amount of positive feedback to give us a balanced view of ourselves. In short, we do not get sufficient positive feedback to have an accurate self-concept. The Strength Bombardment exercise is beneficial to develop our ability to affirm one another, and to raise our view of ourselves to a more accurate level—to "the you that others see."

strengths to affirm. Move to the next person until everyone experiences the group's "strength bombardment."

4. Pause after each person receives their feedback to allow them to check out a particular comment someone made regarding "the you that others see." This is where purposeful listening is most necessary and beneficial: to understand what they hear, to decide the accuracy and value of what they hear, to enjoy what they hear, and to benefit from the help they receive. Note: don't be surprised if people experience both the "thrill of discovery" and the "agony of attention." I find that most people are greedy for this information, yet have difficulty receiving it. It is not uncommon for people to feel like raising their arm in front of their face to shield themselves from embarrassment while at the same time using their other hand to beckon others to keep the comments flowing.

5. If desirable and if time permits, ask people to add their hope, wish, or challenge for one another, either right after the affirmations are offered or as a separate activity following the strength bombardment exercise.

The amount of time needed for this activity depends on the number of people in the circle. For 6 to 10 participants, allow at least 45 minutes to an hour. For 30 participants, you'll need 2 to 3 hours or longer, perhaps with a break in the middle. While you may be tempted to divide the group into smaller circles to conserve time, you can expect that people would rather get feedback from everyone in the group, even if it means taking more time to do so. Hence, you may need to limit the size of your group to fit your time frame, or to schedule sufficient time for the size of your group in order to complete the exercise in a relaxed, comfortable, unhurried atmosphere.

~

Notes

Chapter 1. Building Relationships

1. Andrew Newberg and Mark Robert Waldman, *Words Can Change Your Brain: 12 Conversation Strategies to Build Trust, Resolve Conflict, and Increase Intimacy* (New York: Plume, 2013), 29.

2. Ibid., 29.

3. See David Augsburger, *Caring Enough to Hear and Be Heard* (Ventura, CA: Regal, 1982), 102–4.

4. John Stewart also discusses relational communication emerging between persons in "A Contribution to Ethical Theory and Praxis," in *Handbook of Communication Ethics*, ed. George Cheney, Steve May, and Debashish Munshi (New York: Routledge, 2011), 19–23. Also discussing the notion of creating space for dialogue between or in between persons so that all voices are heard and people from diverse backgrounds may live well together are Debashish Munshi, Kirsten J. Broadfoot, and Linda Tuhiwai Smith in "Decolonizing Communication Ethics: A Framework for Communicating Otherwise," in *Handbook of Communication Ethics*, 128–29. Likewise, Stella Ting-Toomey underscores the importance of fostering a "third space" between ethnic and cultural groups so that all have equal access to and equal opportunity for discussion, and where no one group monopolizes dialogue and intercultural collaboration in "Intercultural Communication Ethics: Multiple Layered Issues," in *Handbook of Communication Ethics*, 348. In chapter 3 we will see how taking a third-culture approach for bridging cultures leads to finding common ground by creating unity amid diversity.

5. Augsburger, *Caring Enough to Hear and Be Heard*, 6.

6. Ibid., 6–7.

7. In *Together: Communicating Interpersonally*, 6th ed. (New York: Oxford, 2005, 23–54), authors John Stewart, Karen E. Zediker, and Saskia Witteborn suggest that meaning is collaboratively constructed. They also think the most important single communication skill is what they call "nexting"—doing something helpful next or responding fruitfully to what's just happened and taking an additional useful step in the communication process.

8. Jack R. Gibb, "Defensive Communication," *Journal of Communication* 11, no. 3 (September 1961), 141–48.

9. This data is adapted from the commonly cited studies by Albert Mehrabian and Morton Weiner, "Decoding of Inconsistent Communications," *Journal of Personality and Social Psychology* 6, 1 (May 1967), 109–14; and Albert Mehrabian and Susan R. Ferris, "Inference of Attitudes from Nonverbal Communication in Two Channels," *Journal of Consulting Psychology* 31, 3 (June 1967), 248–52. It should be emphasized that this research applies specifically to situations where we are uncertain about how someone feels about us. Also, Judee K. Burgoon, David B. Buller, and W. Gill Woodall argue in *Nonverbal Communication: The Unspoken Dialogue*, 2nd ed. (New York: McGraw-Hill, 1996, 3–4 and 136–37) that this research overestimates the percentage of meaning derived nonverbally and suggest instead that nonverbal cues contribute around two-thirds of the meaning in typical social situations. Perhaps the exact percentages are less important than our awareness that nonverbal cues play a huge role in interpreting what someone means from what we see and hear them say.

10. A comment is in order given today's demand for instant communication and the advent of personal communication devices and social network media. If immediate posting of information is desired, then Facebook or Twitter may be a satisfactory form of communication. If a quick exchange of information is all we require, then text messages may be an adequate way to communicate. Notice that these one-way and two-way forms of communication are limited to words alone. Voicemails and phone conversations have the added advantage of using our tone-of-voice resources. Face-to-face conversation, whether in person or electronic (e.g. via web cam or video conferencing), however, allows us to engage our facial expressions as well as our tone of voice and words. Fortunately, face-to-face communication remains viable where miscommunication is likely, communication breakdowns are predictable, or relationship development is desired. For more information about ways social networking impacts our relationships, see Nicholas A. Christakis and James H. Fowler, *Connected: The Surprising Power of Our Social Networks and How They Shape Our Lives* (New York: Little, Brown, 2009). For more information about the use and power of multisensory and multimedia rhetoric in persuasive communication, see Tex Sample, *Powerful Persuasion: Multimedia Witness in Christian Worship* (Nashville: Abingdon, 2005), 39–52.

11. The *primacy of enthusiasm* dates all the way back to our first speech teachers in the fifth century BC, Corax and Tisias; then to Socrates, Plato, and Aristotle in their teaching of rhetoric in the Greco-Roman world; and it extends all the way to modern-day speech communication teaching, research, and community service.

12. See Harry C. Triandis, "Culture and Conflict," in *Intercultural Communication: A Reader*, 13th ed., Larry A. Samovar, Richard E. Porter, and Edwin R. McDaniel, eds. (Boston: Wadsworth Cengage, 2012), 34–35. Also see Peter A. Anderson, "The Basis of Cultural Differences in Nonverbal Communication," in *Intercultural Communication: A Reader*, 298–99.

13. See Stella Ting-Toomey and Leeva C. Chung, *Understanding Intercultural Communication*, 2nd ed. (New York: Oxford University Press, 2012), 5.

14. Ibid., 30.

15. For more information about these claims, see Martin B. Copenhaver, *Jesus Is the Question: The 307 Questions Asked and the 3 He Answered* (Nashville: Abingdon, 2014).

16. See Florence I. Wolff and Nadine C. Marsnik, *Perceptive Listening*, 2nd ed. (New York: Harcourt Brace Jovanovich, 1993), 3.

17. Ibid., 16.

18. Florence I. Wolff et al., *Perceptive Listening* (New York: Holt, Rinehart and Winston, 1983), 2.

19. Wolff and Marsnik, *Perceptive Listening*, 17.

20. Augsburger, *Caring Enough to Hear and Be Heard*, 167–69.

21. Fred B. Craddock et al., *Preaching the New Common Lectionary, Year A, Advent, Christmas, Epiphany* (Nashville: Abingdon, 1989), 133.

22. Paul makes this point in Romans 14:14ff in reference to the pursuit of what makes for peace and mutual up-building.

23. Roger S. Nicholson makes this same point about both conflict and power being neutral terms in *Temporary Shepherds: A Congregational Handbook for Interim Ministry* (Herndon, VA: Alban Institute, 1998), 40.

24. G. Douglass Lewis, *Resolving Church Conflicts: A Case Study Approach for Local Congregations* (New York: HarperCollins, 1981), 63–64.

25. Ibid., 64.

26. Ibid., 64.

27. Ibid., 65–66.

28. Notice that my three-question conflict management process is similar to Fisher and Ury's principled negotiation method that focuses on the problem, basic interests, and mutually satisfying options. For more information about using their principles of negotiation, see Roger Fisher, William Ury, and Bruce Patton, eds., *Getting to Yes: Negotiating Agreement Without Giving In*, 2nd ed. (New York: Penguin, 1991), 17–80.

29. Fisher and Ury also acknowledge that their principles of negotiating have limitations. For example, what if one side is more powerful than the other? What if one side won't play by the rules? Or what if they resort to dirty tricks? They also offer practical, no-nonsense, tough, and effective approaches to handle these complicating circumstances. These approaches include developing your best alternative to a negotiated agreement, using negotiation jujitsu (self-defense), and taming the hard bargainer. For more information on these approaches, see Fisher, Ury, and Patton, *Getting to Yes*, 97–143.

30. See Ting-Toomey and Chung, *Understanding Intercultural Communication*, 198–202.

31. Ibid., 199.

32. Ibid., 199.

33. Ibid., 201.

34. Ibid., 201.

Chapter 2. Leading Meetings

1. Patrick Lencioni, *Death by Meeting: A Leadership Fable . . . About Solving the Most Painful Problem in Business* (San Francisco: Jossey-Bass, 2004), viii.

2. David Sawyer, *Work of the Church: Getting the Job Done in Boards and Committees* (Valley Forge, PA: Judson, 1986), 55

3. Ralph M. Stogdill, *Handbook of Leadership: A Survey of Theory and Research* (New York: Free Press, 1974), 411–20. In Stogdill's summary and discussion, he points out that leaders should maintain a group's goal, direction, and role structure. For a documentation and synthesis of work done in group communication's fifty-year history, see Lawrence R. Frey, Dennis S. Gouran, and Marshall Scott Poole, eds., *The Handbook of Group Communication Theory & Research* (Thousand Oaks, CA: Sage, 1999). These speech communication scholars divide their overview into six broad areas: foundations of group communication theory and research, individuals and group communication, task and relational group communication, group communication processes, group communication facilitation, and group communication contexts and applications.

4. Others who take this view of leaders as helpers include Celia A. Hahn in *Growing in Authority, Relinquishing Control: A New Approach to Faithful Leadership* (Bethesda, MD: Alban Institute, 1994), who advises leaders to do what is needed to serve their groups rather than attempt to control things (see especially chapters 2 and 6); and Gaylord Noyce in *Church Meetings That Work* (Herndon, VA: Alban Institute, 1994), who recommends that leaders help groups build effective consensus and exercise creative group action (see especially chapter 2).

5. You will find suggestions for facilitating member participation in my Alban publication, *Small Groups in the Church: A Handbook for Creating Community* (Herndon, VA: Alban Institute, 1995), appendix F. For additional ideas, see Noyce, *Church Meetings That Work*, chapter 4. Noyce suggests specific skills to draw everyone into group discussion and particular roles to achieve full-group participation.

6. I am grateful to First Presbyterian Church, Kent, Washington, for use of these resources from its Conversations on the Way ministry.

7. For more information about this approach, see Kirkpatrick, *Small Groups in the Church*, appendices A, B, and C.

8. Clyde Reid, *Groups Alive—Church Alive: The Effective Use of Small Groups in the Local Church* (New York: Harper & Row, 1969), 104.

9. See Kirkpatrick, *Small Groups in the Church*, 83.

10. Eric H. F. Law, *The Wolf Shall Dwell with the Lamb: A Spirituality for Leadership in a Multicultural Community* (St. Louis: Chalice, 1993), 83.

11. See Henry M. Robert III, Daniel H. Honemann, Thomas J. Balch, Daniel E. Seabold, and Shmuel Gerber, *Robert's Rules of Order Newly Revised*, 11th ed. (Philadelphia: Da Capo, 2011).

12. Lencioni, *Death by Meeting*, 221.

13. Ibid., 224.

14. Ibid., 224.

15. Ibid., 226.

16. Ibid., 229.

17. C. Jeff Woods, *We've Never Done It Like This Before: 10 Creative Approaches to the Same Old Church Tasks* (Herndon, VA: Alban Institute, 1994), vii.

18. Ibid., vii.

19. Ibid., viii.

20. Examples of such DVD series include Amy-Jill Levine, *Great Figures of the New Testament* (Teaching Company, 2002) and *What's God Up To?: Bible Stories Through New Eyes* (EcuFilm Classics, 2010); Adam Hamilton, *Christianity and World Religions: Wrestling with Questions People Ask* (Abingdon, 2005), *Christianity's Family Tree: What Other Christians Believe and Why* (Abingdon, 2007), *Seeing Gray in a World of Black and White: Thoughts on Religion, Morality, and Politics* (Abingdon, 2008), and *Enough: Discovering Joy through Simplicity and Generosity* (Abingdon, 2009); Walter Brueggemann, *Psalmist's Cry: Scripts for Embracing Lament* (House Studio, 2010); Shane Claiborne, *Economy of Love* (Relational Tithe, 2012); and Morehead Educational Resources *Embracing* series (Marcus Borg, *What It Means to Be Christian*, 2010; Phyllis Tickle, *Emergence Christianity*, 2011; Walter Brueggemann, *Confronting Today's "Pharaohs,"* 2012; Kathleen Norris, *Discovering What Matters*, 2012; Diana Butler Bass, *Dynamics of Experiential Faith*, 2013; Eboo Paatel, *Interfaith Cooperation*, 2013; Barbara Hawthorne Crafton, *Forgiveness—What It Is and What It Isn't*, 2014; and Richard Rohr, *Legacy of St. Francis*, 2014).

21. Lencioni, *Death by Meeting*, 233, 235.

22. Ibid., 235.

23. Ibid., 250.

24. Ibid., 250–51.

25. Ibid., 253.

Chapter 3. Experiencing Trust

1. Bart Nooteboom, "Forms, Sources and Processes of Trust," in *Handbook of Trust Research*, ed. Reinhard Backmann and Akbar Zaheer (Northampton, MA: Edward Elgar, 2006), 247.

2. See Sanjay Banerjee, Norman E. Bowie, and Carla Pavone, "An Ethical Analysis of the Trust Relationship," in *Handbook of Trust Research*, 308.

3. For more information about fairness norms, Mark Casson and Marina Della Guista identify six types of obligations (customary, promissory, reciprocal, considerate, sympathetic, and altruistic) in "The Economics of Trust," in *Handbook of Trust Research*, 343–45.

4. See Daniel Kahneman, *Thinking, Fast and Slow*, 1st ed. (New York: Farrar, Straus and Giroux, 2011).

5. See Andrew H. Van de Ven and Peter Smith Ring, "Relying on Trust in Cooperative Inter-organizational Relationships," in *Handbook of Trust Research*, 155. Also John G. Bruhn, *Trust and the Health of Organizations* (New York: Kluwer, 2001).

6. Ibid., 145.

7. Ibid., 158.

8. Bruhn, *Trust and the Health of Organizations*, 30.

9. Van de Ven and Ring, *Handbook of Trust Research*, 158.

10. Ibid., 158.

11. This and subsequent quotes are from James H. Forest, *Making Friends of Enemies: Reflections on the Teachings of Jesus* (New York: Crossroad, 1987), 45–46.

12. See Richard Evanoff, "A Communicative Approach to Intercultural Dialogue on Ethics," in *Intercultural Communication: A Reader*, 13th ed., Larry A. Samovar, Richard E. Porter, and Edwin R. McDaniel, eds. (Boston: Wadsworth Cengage, 2012), 479.

13. See Stella Ting-Toomey and Leeva C. Chung, *Understanding Intercultural Communication*, 2nd ed. (New York: Oxford University Press, 2012), 30.

14. Corey Widmer, "The 75% Rule," *Presbyterian Outlook Magazine*, InSights Opinion/Outpost Blog, June 19, 2013.

15. Ibid.

16. Ibid.

17. For more information about this approach, see Wesley J. Wildman and Stephen Chapin Garner, *Found in the Middle! Theology and Ethics for Christians Who Are Both Liberal and Evangelical* (Herndon, VA: Alban Institute, 2009). See also Adam Hamilton, *Seeing Gray in a World of Black and White: Thoughts on Religion, Morality, and Politics* (Nashville: Abingdon, 2008).

18. For more information about mutual invitation, see chapter 2, 44–45, and chapter 5, 149–51.

19. It is worthwhile to note that Roger Fisher, William Ury, and Bruce Patton insist on using objective criteria as one of their principles of negotiation in *Getting to Yes: Negotiating Agreement Without Giving In*, 2nd ed. (New York: Penguin, 1991), 81–94.

20. More will be said about this conflict and the practice of forgiveness in chapter 4.

21. You will find suggestions for sharing your life story or faith journey in my Alban publication, *Small Groups in the Church: A Handbook for Creating Community* (Herndon, VA: Alban Institute, 1995), appendix E, 115–16.

22. For empirical evidence supporting this point, see Thomas Kirkpatrick, "Conceptualizing and Measuring Relationship Satisfaction" (paper presented at the annual convention of the Western Speech Communication Association, Phoenix, Arizona, 1978).

Chapter 4. Practicing Forgiveness

1. I am grateful to Earl Palmer for insights on this passage from his DVD, *Blessing of Aaron and the Character of God* (Arroyo Grande, CA: Essential Media Services, 2001).

2. This observation is made by Everett L. Worthington Jr., "Initial Questions About the Art and Science of Forgiving," in *Handbook of Forgiveness*, Everett L. Worthington Jr., ed. (New York: Routledge, 2005), 1.

3. Ibid., 1.

4. Ibid., 2.

5. For more information about this process and its effectiveness, see Kristina Coop Gordon, Donald H. Baucom, and Douglas K. Snyder, "Forgiveness in Couples: Divorce, Infidelity, and Couples Therapy," in *Handbook of Forgiveness*, 414–15; and Nathaniel G. Wade, Everett L. Worthington Jr., and Julia E. Meyer, "But Do They Work? A Meta-Analysis of Group Interventions to Promote Forgiveness," in *Handbook of Forgiveness*, 431.

6. See Michael E. McCullough and Lindsey M. Root, "Forgiveness as Change," in *Handbook of Forgiveness*, 91–107.

7. These predictors of forgiveness are based on an article by Michael E. McCullough et al., "Interpersonal Forgiving in Close Relationships. II. Theoretical Elaboration and Measurement," *Journal of Personality and Social Psychology* 75, no. 6 (1998), 1586–1603.

8. See Suzanne Freedman, Robert D. Enright, and Jeanette Knutson, "A Progress Report on the Process Model of Forgiveness," in *Handbook of Forgiveness*, 394–95.

9. See Fred Luskin, "Nine Steps to Forgiveness," September 1, 2004. Available at http://greatergood.berkeley.edu/article/item/nine_steps_to_forgiveness.

10. See Robert D. Enright and Richard P. Fitzgibbons, *Helping Clients Forgive: An Empirical Guide for Resolving Anger and Restoring Hope* (Washington, DC: American Psychological Association, 2000), 29.

11. See Michael E. McCullough, Kenneth I. Pargament, and Carl E. Thoresen, "The Psychology of Forgiveness: History, Conceptual Issues, and Overview," in *Forgiveness: Theory, Research, and Practice*, Michael E. McCullough, Kenneth I. Pargament, and Carl E. Thoresen, eds. (New York: Guilford, 2000), 1–6.

12. For more information about these definitions, see Everett L. Worthington Jr., "More Questions About Forgiveness: Research Agenda for 2005–2015," in *Handbook of Forgiveness*, 566.

13. For more information about these four predictors of the likelihood of forgiveness, see the work of McCullough et al. cited in note 7.

14. For more information about this process, see Robert D. Enright, Suzanne Freedman, and Julio Rique, "The Psychology of Interpersonal Forgiveness," in *Exploring Forgiveness*, Robert D. Enright and Joanna North, eds. (Madison: University of Wisconsin, 1998), 52.

15. For a helpful discussion of anger as a demand, see David Augsburger, *Caring Enough to Confront: How to Understand and Express Your Deepest Feelings Towards Others*, 3rd ed. (Ventura, CA: Regal, 2009), 47–53.

16. Recent research shows that a process-based model of forgiveness wherein individual or group interventions involve cognitive, affective, and behavioral education and counseling are more effective than a decision-based model wherein people merely make a cognitive decision to forgive. Moreover, individual interventions were slightly more effective than group education and counseling. For further information about this research, see Freeman, Enright, and Knutson, "A Progress Report on the Process Model of Forgiveness," 397–99.

17. For more information on the findings from empirical research on reactions to wrongdoing reported in this section, and on the forgiveness process and on relational repair reported in subsequent sections, see Caryl E. Rusbult et al., "Forgiveness and Relational Repair," in *Handbook of Forgiveness*, 193–200.

18. Ibid., 193.

19. For more information on these findings, see Cynthia L. Battle and Ivan W. Miller, "Families and Forgiveness," in *Handbook of Forgiveness*, 233–34.

20. I am grateful to Aubrey Fredericks for this insight.

21. This litany of prayer is adapted from *Worship Workbook for the Gospels, Cycle A*, Robert D. Ingram (Lima, OH: CSS, 1995), 285.

22. Versions of this story appear in all three synoptic gospels, including Mark 2:1–12, Matthew 9:1–8, and Luke 5:17–26.

23. John 5:21–24, 30, *The Inclusive Bible*.

24. See "Forgiveness: A Sampling of Research Results," American Psychological Association, 2006, 5. Available at http://apa.org/international/resources/publications/forgiveness.pdf.

25. For further information about the work and results of South Africa's Truth and Reconciliation Commission, see the official website: http://www.justice.gov.za/trc. For analysis and critique, see Christopher Torchia, "Troubled South Africa Debates Impact of White Rule," April 12, 2013, http://news.yahoo.com/troubled-south-africa-debates-impact-white-rule-145730858.html; and "Muddle through Will No Longer Do," *Economist*, June 1, 2013, http://www.economist.com/news/middle-east-and-africa/21578692-slow-growth-and-sliding-currency-are-alarming-symptoms-deeper.

26. See Fabiola Azar, Etienne Mullet, and Genevieve Vinsonneau, "The Propensity to Forgive: Findings from Lebanon," *Journal of Peace Research* 36, no. 2 (1999), 170.

27. See Andrew H. Van de Ven and Peter Smith Ring, "Relying on Trust in Cooperative Inter-organizational Relationships," in *Handbook of Trust Research*, ed. Reinhard Bachmann and Akbar Zaheer (Northampton, MA: Edward Elgar, 2006), 158.

28. For further information about forgiveness and restorative justice, see Marilyn Peterson Armour and Mark S. Umbreit, "The Paradox of Forgiveness in Restorative Justice," in *Handbook of Forgiveness*, 491–503. Also see Peter C. Hill, Julie Juola Exline, and Adam B. Cohen, "The Social Psychology of Justice and Forgiveness in Civil and Organizational Settings," in *Handbook of Forgiveness*, 486–87.

Chapter 5. Using Power

1. See, for example, such resources as Beth Ann Gaede, ed., *When a Congregation Is Betrayed: Responding to Clergy Misconduct* (Herndon, VA: Alban Institute, 2006); Candace R. Benyei, *Understanding Clergy Misconduct in Religious Systems: Scapegoating, Family Secrets, and the Abuse of Power* (Binghamton, NY: Haworth, 1998); and Karen A. McClintock, *Preventing Sexual Abuse in Congregations: A Resource for Leaders* (Herndon, VA: Alban Institute, 2004).

2. S. Jack Odell in John C. Merrill and S. Jack Odell, *Philosophy and Journalism* (New York: Longman, 1983), 95.

3. Stella Ting-Toomey, "Intercultural Communication Ethics: Multiple Layered Issues," in *Handbook of Communication Ethics*, George Cheney, Steve May, and Debashish Munshi, eds. (New York: Routledge, 2011), 336.

4. Dennis Mumby, "Power and Ethics," in *Handbook of Communication Ethics*, 95.

5. Ibid., p. 94.

6. Ibid., p. 95.

7. Josina M. Makau, "Response and Conclusion: A Vision of Applied Ethics for Communication Studies," in *Handbook of Communication Ethics*, 495–96.

8. See Mumby, "Power and Ethics," 95.

9. For information about other systems of ethics in human communication, see Richard L. Johannesen, Kathleen S. Valde, and Karen E. Whedbee, *Ethics in Human Communication*, 6th ed. (Long Grove, IL: Waveland, 2008), 21–97.

10. See Gitte Haslebo and Maja Loua Haslebo, *Practicing Relational Ethics in Organizations* (Chagrin Falls, OH: Taos Institute, 2012), 271–78.

11. In *Small Groups in the Church: A Handbook for Creating Community* (Herndon, VA: Alban, 1995), 5, 27, and 112, you'll find I report these four qualities as openness, acceptance, warmth, and personal growth. The fourth quality, personal growth, is closely related to the quality of support such that I use them interchangeably. What growth and support have in common is the capacity or power to learn and change.

12. Johannesen et al., *Ethics of Human Communication*, 234. For an insightful discussion of the power of multisensory and multimedia rhetoric in persuasive communication, see Tex Sample, *Powerful Persuasion: Multimedia Witness in Christian Worship* (Nashville: Abingdon, 2005), 39–52. Also see J. Dan Rothwell, *Telling It Like It Isn't* (Englewood Cliffs, NJ: Prentice-Hall, 1983); Casey Miller and Kate Swift, *The Handbook of Nonsexist Writing: For Writers, Editors and Speakers*, 2nd ed. (Lincoln, NE: iUniverse.com, 2001); Haig Bosmajian, *The Language of Oppression*

(Washington, DC: Public Affairs, 1974); and Susan Opotow, "Moral Exclusion and Injustice: An Introduction," *Journal of Social Issues* 46 (1990), 1–20.

13. See Stanley Deetz, "Reclaiming the Subject Matter as a Guide to Mutual Understanding: Effectiveness and Ethics in Interpersonal Interaction," *Communication Quarterly* 38, no. 3 (1990), 233–38.

14. Ibid., 239–240.

15. New Ethic: An Independent Ethics Site. Available at http://ethics1.org.

16. See Johannesen et al., *Ethics in Human Communication*, 229.

17. See Clifford G. Christians and Michael Traber, eds., *Communication Ethics and Universal Values* (Thousand Oaks, CA: Sage, 1997), 341. Similar transcultural values and standards are proposed by Rushworth Kidder, *Shared Values for a Troubled World: Conversations with Men and Women of Conscience* (San Francisco: Jossey-Bass, 1994); His Holiness the Dalai Lama, *Ethics for the New Millennium* (New York: Riverhead, 2001); and Sissela Bok, *Common Values* (Columbia: University of Missouri, 2002).

18. See Josina M. Makau, "Response and Conclusion: A Vision of Applied Ethics for Communication Studies," in *Handbook of Communication Ethics*, 500.

19. See Johannesen et al., *Ethics in Human Communication*, 151.

20. For the complete ethical checklist for small groups, see John Gastil and Leah Sprain, "Ethical Challenges in Small Group Communication," in *Handbook of Communication Ethics*, 161.

21. See Cheney et al., *Ethics of Human Communication*, 163–64.

22. Ting-Toomey, "Intercultural Communication Ethics," 348.

23. Ibid., 348.

24. Ibid., 349. Also see Ting-Toomey's guidelines to frame an intercultural stance using comparative social ecological analysis.

25. Approved by the National Communication Association Legislative Council in 1999. Available at http://www.natcom.org/uploadedFiles/About_NCA/Leadership_and_Governance/Public_Policy_Platform/PDF-PolicyPlatform-NCA_Credo_for_Ethical_Communication.pdf.

26. Gary C. Woodward and Robert E. Denton Jr., *Persuasion and Influence in American Life*, 7th ed. (Long Grove, IL: Waveland, 2014), 352.

27. Thomas W. Cooper, "New Technology Inventory: Forty Leading Ethical Issues," *Journal of Mass Media Ethics* 13 (1998), 71–92.

28. Reprinted in M. David Ermann, Mary B. Williams, and Michele S. Shauf, eds., *Computers, Ethics, and Society*, 2nd ed. (New York: Oxford, 1997), 313–14.

29. Rebecca Blood, *The Weblog Handbook: Practical Advice on Creating and Maintain Your Blog* (Cambridge, MA: Perseus, 2002), 117–21. Also see Martin Kuhn, "Interactivity and Prioritizing the Human: A Code of Blogging Ethics," *Journal of Mass Media Ethics* 14 (2007), 18–36. For further information about ethical use of cyberspace, see Cees J. Hamelink, *The Ethics of Cyberspace* (London: Sage, 2001); Ann H. Gunkel and David J. Gunkel, "Virtual Geographies: The New Worlds of Cyberspace," *Critical Studies in Mass Communication* 14, no. 2 (1997), 123–37; and Jana Kramer and Cheris Kramarae, "Gendered Ethics on the Internet," in *Communication*

Ethics in an Age of Diversity, Josina M. Makau and Ronald C. Arnett, eds. (Urbana: University of Illinois, 1997), 226–43.

30. Ibid., 85–87.

31. For a summary of Grice's views, see Johannesen et al., *Ethics in Human Communication*, 139.

32. Woodward and Denton, *Persuasion and Influence in American Life*, 348.

33. Charles U. Larson, *Persuasion: Reception and Responsibility*, 11th ed. (Belmont, CA: Thomson Wadsworth, 2007), 15.

34. Ibid., 263.

35. Charles U. Larson, *Persuasion: Reception and Responsibility*, 13th ed. (Boston: Wadsworth, 2013), 14.

36. Walter Wink, *The Powers That Be: Theology for a New Millennium* (Minneapolis: Augsburg Fortress, 1998), 32.

37. Ibid., 32.

38. Robert L. Ivie, "Hierarchies of Equality: Positive Peace in a Democratic Idiom," in *Handbook of Communication Ethics*, 385.

39. Ronald C. Arnett, *Dwell in Peace: Applying Nonviolence to Everyday Relationships* (Elgin, IL: Brethren, 1985), 140.

40. Ibid., 139–40.

41. See Ivie, "Hierarchies of Equality: Positive Peace in a Democratic Idiom," 377.

42. For additional resources on nonviolent communication, see Marshall B. Rosenberg, *Nonviolent Communication: A Language of Life* (Encinitas, CA: Puddle-Dancer, 2003); and Marshall B. Rosenberg, *Living Nonviolent Communication: Practical Tools to Connect and Communicate Skillfully in Every Situation* (Boulder, CO: Sounds True, 2012).

43. John T. Warren, "It Really Isn't About You: Whiteness and the Dangers of Thinking You Got It," in *The Handbook of Critical Intercultural Communication*, Thomas K. Nakayama and Rona Tamiko Halualani, eds. (Hoboken, NJ: Wiley-Blackwell, 2010), 457.

44. Contact the White Privilege Conference, http://whiteprivilegeconference.com, and read such books as Glenn Singleton, *Courageous Conversations About Race: A Field Guide for Achieving Equity in Schools* (Thousand Oaks, CA: Corwin, 2014). For understanding and addressing white privilege, see Frances E. Kendall, *Understanding White Privilege: Creating Pathways to Authentic Relationships Across Race* (New York: Routledge, 2006); Jacqueline Battalora, *Birth of a White Nation: The Invention of White People and Its Relevance Today* (Houston: Strategic, 2013); and Debby Irving, *Waking Up White, and Finding Myself in the Story of Race* (Chicago: Elephant Room, 2014).

45. See Deanna L. Fassett, "Critical Reflections on a Pedagogy of Ability," in *The Handbook of Critical Intercultural Communication*, 468–69.

46. This quote and subsequent ones are from Ana Mari Cauce, "We the People: Diversity, Equity and Difference at the UW," April 16, 2015, University of Wash-

ington. Available at http://www.washington.edu/president/files/2015/04/diversity-equity-and-difference-speech-transcript.pdf.

47. John Stewart, "Basic Whiteness Lessons from an Old White Guy," blog post, April 3, 2015. Available at http://www.johnstewart.org/basic-whiteness-lessons-from-a/2015/4/3/basic-whiteness-lessons-from-an-old-white-guy.html.

48. Makau, "Response and Conclusion: A Vision of Applied Ethics for Communication Studies," 501.

49. Ibid., 501.

50. Harlan Cleveland, "The Limits to Cultural Diversity," in *Intercultural Communication: A Reader*, 13th ed., Larry A. Samovar, Richard E. Porter, and Edwin R. McDaniel, eds. (Boston: Wadsworth Cengage, 2012), 501.

51. Ibid., 501.

52. Ibid., 501.

53. Ibid., 501.

54. Makau, "Response and Conclusion: A Vision of Applied Ethics for Communication Studies," 502–3. Similarly, Julia T. Wood suggests that engaging differences often enhances commonality through self-reflection, openness to others, both-and orientation, and curiosity in "Diversity in Dialogue: Commonalities and Differences between Friends," in *Communication Ethics in an Age of Diversity*, Josina M. Makau and Ronald C. Arnett, eds. (Urbana: University of Illinois, 1997), 5–26.

55. Makasu, "Response and Conclusion," 504.

56. Stewart and Sherrod, "How to Deal with Difficult Difference." Also see John Stewart, *Personal Communicating and Racial Equity*, Dubuque, IA: Kendall-Hunt, 2016.

57. Ibid.

58. Christena Cleveland, "3 Reasons Why I Hate Diversity," *Christianity Today*, Ed Stetzer Blog, February 19, 2015. Available at http://www.christianitytoday.com/edstetzer/2015/february/3-reasons-why-i-hate-diversity.html.

59. Ibid.

60. Allan G. Johnson, *Power, Privilege, and Difference* (New York: McGraw-Hill, 2006), 133. For further practical suggestions for balancing inclusiveness and diversity by developing cultural sensitivity and proficiency, see Verna A. Myers, *What If I Say the Wrong Thing? 25 Habits for Culturally Effective People* (Chicago: American Bar Association, 2013).

61. Ibid., 90.

62. Jerry Large, "Looking Back to 1968 for Riots' Root Causes," *Seattle Times*, May 7, 2015, section B, 1–2. Available at http://www.seattletimes.com/seattle-news/looking-back-to-1968-for-root-causes-of-riots.

63. See Ronald C. Arnett, "Communication and Community in an Age of Diversity," in *Communication Ethics in an Age of Diversity*, Josina M. Makau and Ronald C. Arnett, eds. (Urbana: University of Illinois, 1997), 45. Arnett presents a more nuanced view that accounts for the tension that exists between inclusion and exclu-

sion, a tension between community and diversity, a tension that he suggests needs to be kept in balance rather than be resolved.

64. For resources on becoming a multicultural congregation, see Charles R. Foster, *Embracing Diversity* (Herndon, VA: Alban Institute, 1997); and Maren C. Tirabassi and Kathy Wonson Eddy, *Gifts of Many Cultures: Worship Resources for the Global Community* (Cleveland: Pilgrim, 1995).

65. Deborah Borisoff and Lisa Merrill, *The Power to Communicate: Gender Differences as Barriers*, 3rd ed. (Prospect Heights, IL: Waveland, 1998), 16.

66. Ibid., 17.

67. Ibid., 17.

68. Johnson, *Power, Privilege, and Difference*, 94.

69. Deborah J. Borisoff and James W. Chesebro, *Communicating Power and Gender* (Long Grove, IL: Waveland, 2011), 41.

70. Ibid., 19–67.

71. Ibid., 64. Also see *Say What You Really Mean! How Women Can Learn to Speak Up* (Lanham, MD: Rowman & Littlefield, 2014), by English professor Debra Johanyak for practical suggestions to enhance clear communication through crafting and delivering direct and effective messages, thereby saving time and getting things done.

72. Eric H. F. Law, *The Wolf Shall Dwell with the Lamb: A Spirituality for Leadership in a Multicultural Community* (St. Louis: Chalice, 1993), 31.

73. Ibid., 31.

74. Ibid., 31–32.

75. Ibid., 32.

76. Ibid., 32.

77. For more information about some of these and other prophetic visionaries, see Charles Kevin Robertson, *A Dangerous Dozen: 12 Christians Who Threatened the Status Quo but Taught Us to Live Like Jesus* (Woodstock, VA: Skylight Paths, 2011).

78. See, for example, the DVD series *Embracing the Prophets in Contemporary Culture: Walter Brueggemann on Confronting Today's "Pharaohs"* (Denver: Morehouse Education Resources, 2012).

79. The power of rhetoric to reshape society and to imagine a new way of living in modern times includes Abraham Lincoln's Gettysburg Address, "Four score and seven years ago our [forebearers] brought forth on this continent, a new nation, conceived in Liberty, and dedicated to the proposition that all [people] are created equal"; and his Emancipation Proclamation that "all persons held as slaves are, and henceforward shall be free." Contemporary examples include the Martin Luther King Jr. speech "I Have a Dream," and John F. Kennedy's "Ich bin ein Berliner" ("I am a Berliner") speech, as well as his enduring proposition, "Ask not what your country can do for you, ask what you can do for your country." Other examples are Franklin D. Roosevelt's counsel, "The only thing we have to fear is fear itself"; Ronald Reagan's challenge, "Mr. Gorbachev, tear down this wall!"; Mother Teresa's wisdom, "Peace begins with a smile"; and Gloria Steinem's witticism, "A woman without a man is like a fish without a bicycle."

80. These descriptions are assembled from Tim Scorer, *Embracing the Prophets in Contemporary Culture Participant's Workbook: Walter Brueggemann Confronting Today's "Pharaohs"* (Denver: Morehouse Education Resources, 2012), 21, 38, 43, 55, and 84.

81. Wink, *The Powers That Be: Theology for a New Millennium*, 65.

82. Ibid., 66.

83. Ibid., 67.

84. Ibid., 81.

85. Ibid., 111.

86. See Ivie, "Hierarchies of Equality: Positive Peace in a Democratic Idiom," 377.

87. Ibid., 377–78.

88. Ibid., 381.

~

Bibliography

Anderson, Peter A. "The Basis of Cultural Differences in Nonverbal Communication." In *Intercultural Communication: A Reader*, 13th ed., edited by Larry A. Samovar, Richard E. Porter, and Edwin R. McDaniel, 293–313. Boston: Wadsworth Cengage, 2012.

Armour, Marilyn Peterson, and Mark S. Umbreit. "The Paradox of Forgiveness in Restorative Justice." In *Handbook of Forgiveness*, edited by Everett L. Worthington Jr., 491–503. New York: Routledge, 2005.

Arnett. Ronald C. "Communication and Community in an Age of Diversity." In *Communication Ethics in an Age of Diversity*, edited by Josina M. Makau and Ronald C. Arnett, 27–47. Urbana: University of Illinois, 1997.

———. *Dwell in Peace: Applying Nonviolence to Everyday Relationships*. Elgin, IL.: Brethren, 1985.

Augsburger, David. *Caring Enough to Confront: How to Understand and Express Your Deepest Feelings Toward Others*, 3rd ed. Ventura, CA: Regal, 2009.

———. *Caring Enough to Forgive—Caring Enough to Not Forgive*. Scottsdale, PA: Herald, 1981.

———. *Caring Enough to Hear and Be Heard*. Ventura, CA: Regal, 1982.

Azar, Fabiola, Etienne Mullet, and Genevieve Vinsonneau. "The Propensity to Forgive: Findings from Lebanon." *Journal of Peace Research* 36, no. 2 (1999), 169–81.

Baab, Lynne M. *The Power of Listening: Building Skills for Mission and Ministry*. Lanham, MD: Rowman & Littlefield, 2014.

Backmann, Reinhard, and Akbar Zaheer. *Handbook of Trust Research*. Northampton, MA: Edward Elgar, 2006.

Banerjee, Sanjay, Norman E. Bowie, and Carla Pavone. "An Ethical Analysis of the Trust Relationship." In *Handbook of Trust Research*, edited by Reinhard Backmann and Akbar Zaheer, 303–17. Northampton, MA: Edward Elgar, 2006.

Battalora, Jacqueline. *Birth of a White Nation: The Invention of White People and Its Relevance Today*. Houston: Strategic, 2013.

Battle, Cynthia L., and Ivan W. Miller. "Families and Forgiveness." In *Handbook of Forgiveness*, edited by Everett L. Worthington Jr., 227–41. New York: Routledge, 2005.

Bellman, Geoffrey M., and Kathleen D. Ryan. *Extraordinary Groups: How Ordinary Teams Achieve Amazing Results*. San Francisco: Jossey-Bass, 2009.

Benyei, Candace R. *Understanding Clergy Misconduct in Religious Systems: Scapegoating, Family Secrets, and the Abuse of Power*. Binghamton, NY: Haworth, 1998.

Blood, Rebecca. *The Weblog Handbook: Practical Advice on Creating and Maintaining Your Blog*. Cambridge, MA: Perseus, 2002.

Bok, Sissela. *Common Values*. Columbia: University of Missouri, 1995.

Borisoff, Deborah J., and James W. Chesebro. *Communicating Power and Gender*. Long Grove, IL: Waveland, 2011.

Borisoff, Deborah, and Lisa Merrill. *The Power to Communicate: Gender Differences as Barriers*, 3rd ed. Prospect Heights, IL: Waveland, 1998.

Bosmajian, Haig. *The Language of Oppression*. Washington, DC: Public Affairs, 1974.

Bruhn, John G. *Trust and the Health of Organizations*. New York: Kluwer, 2001.

Burgoon, Judee K., David B. Buller, and W. Gill Woodall. *Nonverbal Communication: The Unspoken Dialogue*, 2nd ed. New York: McGraw-Hill, 1996.

Casson, Mark, and Marina Della Guista. "The Economics of Trust." In *Handbook of Trust Research*, edited by Reinhard Backmann and Akbar Zaheer, 332–54. Northampton, MA: Edward Elgar, 2006.

Cauce, Ana Mari. "We the People: Diversity, Equity and Difference at the UW." Speech delivered April 16, 2015, at the University of Washington, Seattle, WA. Available at http://www.washington.edu/president/files/2015/04/diversity-equity-and-difference- speech-transcript.pdf.

Cheney, George, Steve May, and Debashish Munshi, eds. *Handbook of Communication Ethics*. New York: Routledge, 2011.

Christakis, Nicholas A., and James H. Fowler. *Connected: The Surprising Power of Our Social Networks and How They Shape Our Lives*. New York: Little, Brown, 2009.

Christians, Clifford D., and Michael Traber, eds. *Communication Ethics and Universal Values*. Thousand Oaks, CA: Sage, 1997.

Cleveland, Harlan. "The Limits to Cultural Diversity." In *Intercultural Communication: A Reader*, 13th edition, edited by Larry A. Samovar, Richard E. Porter, and Edwin R. McDaniel, 498–502. Boston: Wadsworth Cengage, 2012.

Cooper, Thomas W. "New Technology Inventory: Forty Leading Ethical Issues." *Journal of Mass Media Ethics* 13 (1998), 71–92.

Copenhaver, Martin B. *Jesus Is the Question: The 307 Questions Asked and the 3 He Answered*. Nashville: Abingdon, 2014.

Covey, Stephen M. R. *The Speed of Trust: The One Thing That Changes Everything*. New York: Free Press, 2006.

Craddock, Fred E., John H. Hayes, Carl R. Holladay, and Gene M. Tucker. *Preaching the New Common Lectionary, Year A, Advent, Christmas, Epiphany*. Nashville: Abingdon, 1989.

Dalai Lama. *Ethics for the New Millennium*. New York: Riverhead, 2001.

Enright, Robert D., and Richard P. Fitzgibbons. *Helping Clients Forgive: An Empirical Guide for Resolving Anger and Restoring Hope*. Washington, DC: American Psychological Association, 2000.

Enright, Robert D., and Joanna North, eds. *Exploring Forgiveness*. Madison: University of Wisconsin, 1998.

Enright, Robert D., Suzanne Freedman, and Julio Rique. "The Psychology of Interpersonal Forgiveness." In *Exploring Forgiveness*, edited by Robert D. Enright and Joanna North, 46–62. Madison: University of Wisconsin, 1998.

Ermann, M. David, Mary B. Williams, and Michele S. Shauf, eds. *Computers, Ethics, and Society*, 2nd ed. New York: Oxford, 1997.

Evanoff, Richard. "A Communicative Approach to Intercultural Dialogue on Ethics." In *Intercultural Communication: A Reader*, 13th ed., edited by Larry A. Samovar, Richard E. Porter, and Edwin R. McDaniel, 476–79. Boston: Wadsworth Cengage, 2012.

Everist, Norma Cook. *Church Conflict: From Contention to Collaboration*. Nashville: Abingdon, 2004.

Fassett, Deanna L. "Critical Reflections on a Pedagogy of Ability." In *The Handbook of Critical Intercultural Communication*, edited by Thomas K. Nakayama and Rona Tamiko Halualani, 461–71. Hoboken, NJ: Wiley-Blackwell, 2010.

Freedman, Suzanne, Robert D. Enright, and Jeanette Knutson. "A Progress Report on the Process Model of Forgiveness." In *Handbook of Forgiveness*, edited by Everett L. Worthington Jr., 393–406. New York: Routledge, 2005.

Frey, Lawrence R., Dennis S. Gouran, and Marshall Scott Poole, eds. *The Handbook of Group Communication Theory & Research*. Thousand Oaks, CA: Sage, 1999.

Fisher, Roger, William Ury, and Bruce Patton, eds. *Getting to Yes: Negotiating Agreement Without Giving In*, 2nd ed. New York: Penguin, 1991.

Forest, James H. *Making Friends of Enemies: Reflections on the Teachings of Jesus*. New York: Crossroad, 1987.

Foster, Charles R. *Embracing Diversity*. Herndon, VA: Alban Institute, 1997.

Gaede, Beth Ann, ed. *When a Congregation Is Betrayed: Responding to Clergy Misconduct*. Herndon, VA: Alban Institute, 2006.

Galvin, Kathleen. *Listening by Doing: Developing Effective Listening Skills*. Lincolnwood, IL: National, 1985.

Gastil, John, and Leah Sprain. "Ethical Challenges in Small Group Communication." In *Handbook of Communication Ethics*, edited by George Cheney, Steve May, and Debashish Munshi, 148–65. New York: Routledge, 2011.

Gibb, Jack R. "Defensive Communication." *Journal of Communication* 11, no. 3 (September 1961), 141–48.

Goodman, Denise W. *Congregational Fitness: Healthy Practices for Layfolk.* Herndon, VA: Alban Institute, 2000.

Gordon, Kristina Coop, Donald H. Baucom, and Douglas K. Snyder. "Forgiveness in Couples: Divorce, Infidelity, and Couples Therapy." In *Handbook of Forgiveness,* edited by Everett L. Worthington Jr., 407–21. New York: Routledge, 2005.

Gunkel, Ann H., and David J. Gunkel. "Virtual Geographies: The New Worlds of Cyberspace." *Critical Studies in Mass Communication* 14, no. 2 (1997), 123–37.

Hahn, Celia A. *Growing in Authority, Relinquishing Control: A New Approach to Faithful Leadership.* Bethesda, MD: Alban Institute, 1994.

Hamelink, Cees J. *The Ethics of Cyberspace.* London: Sage, 2000.

Hamilton, Adam. *Seeing Gray in a World of Black and White: Thoughts on Religion, Morality, and Politics.* Nashville: Abingdon, 2008.

Haslebo, Gitte, and Maja Loua Haslebo. *Practicing Relational Ethics in Organizations.* Chagrin Falls, OH: Taos Institute, 2012.

Hill, Peter C., Julie Juola Exline, and Adam B. Cohen. "The Social Psychology of Justice and Forgiveness in Civil and Organizational Settings." In *Handbook of Forgiveness,* edited by Everett L. Worthington Jr., 477–90. New York: Routledge, 2005.

Irving, Debby. *Waking Up White, and Finding Myself in the Story of Race.* Chicago: Elephant Room, 2014.

Ivie, Robert L. "Hierarchies of Equality: Positive Peace in a Democratic Idiom." In *Handbook of Communication Ethics,* edited by George Cheney, Steve May, and Debashish Munshi, 374–86. New York: Routledge, 2011.

Johannesen, Richard L., Kathleen S. Valde, and Karen E. Whedbee. *Ethics in Human Communication,* 6th ed. Long Grove, IL: Waveland, 2008.

Johanyak, Debra. *Say What You Really Mean! How Women Can Learn to Speak Up.* Lanham, MD: Rowman & Littlefield, 2014.

Johnson, Allan G. *Power, Privilege, and Difference.* New York: McGraw-Hill, 2006.

Kahneman, Daniel. *Thinking, Fast and Slow.* New York: Farrar, Straus and Giroux, 2011.

Kendall, Frances E. *Understanding White Privilege: Creating Pathways to Authentic Relationships Across Race.* New York: Routledge, 2006.

Kidder, Rushworth. *Shared Values for a Troubled World: Conversations with Men and Women of Conscience.* San Francisco: Jossey-Bass, 1994.

Kirkpatrick, Thomas G. "Conceptualizing and Measuring Relationship Satisfaction." Paper presented at the annual convention of the Western Speech Communication Association, Phoenix, Arizona, 1978.

———. *Small Groups in the Church: A Handbook for Creating Community.* Herndon, VA: Alban Institute, 1995.

Kramer, Jana, and Cheris Kramerae. "Gendered Ethics on the Internet." In *Communication Ethics in an Age of Diversity,* edited by Josina M. Makau and Ronald C. Arnett, 226–43. Urbana: University of Illinois, 1997.

Kuhn, Martin. "Interactivity and Prioritizing the Human: A Code of Blogging Ethics." *Journal of Mass Media Ethics* 14 (2007), 18–36.

Larson, Charles U. *Persuasion: Reception and Responsibility*, 13th ed. Boston: Wadsworth, 2013.

Law, Eric H. F. *The Wolf Shall Dwell with the Lamb: A Spirituality for Leadership in a Multicultural Community*. St. Louis: Chalice, 1993.

Lencioni, Patrick. *Death by Meeting: A Leadership Fable . . . About Solving the Most Painful Problem in Business*. San Francisco: Jossey-Bass, 2004.

Lewis, G. Douglass. *Resolving Church Conflicts: A Case Study Approach for Local Congregations*. New York: HarperCollins, 1981.

Makau, Josina M. "Response and Conclusion: A Vision of Applied Ethics for Communication Studies." In *Handbook of Communication Ethics*, edited by George Cheney, Steve May, and Debashish Munshi, 494–515. New York: Routledge, 2011.

Makau, Josina M., and Ronald C. Arnett, eds. *Communication Ethics in an Age of Diversity*. Urbana: University of Illinois, 1997.

McClintock, Karen A. *Preventing Sexual Abuse in Congregations: A Resource for Leaders*. Herndon, VA: Alban Institute, 2004.

McCullough, Michael E., Kenneth I. Pargament, and Carl E. Thoresen. "The Psychology of Forgiveness: History, Conceptual Issues, and Overview." In *Forgiveness: Theory, Research, and Practice*, edited by Michael E. McCullough, Kenneth I. Pargament, and Carl E. Thoresen, 1–6. New York: Guilford, 2000.

McCullough, Michael E., Kenneth I. Pargament, and Carl E. Thoresen, eds. *Forgiveness: Theory, Research, and Practice*. New York: Guilford, 2000.

McCullough, Michael E., K. Chris Rachal, Steven J. Sandage, Everett L. Worthington Jr., Susan Wade Brown, and Terry L. Hight. "Interpersonal Forgiving in Close Relationships. II. Theoretical Elaboration and Measurement." *Journal of Personality and Social Psychology* 75, no. 6 (1998), 1586–1603.

McCullough, Michael E., and Lindsey M. Root. "Forgiveness as Change." In *Handbook of Forgiveness*, edited by Everett L. Worthington Jr., 91–107. New York: Routledge, 2005.

Merrill, John C., and S. Jack Odell. *Philosophy and Journalism*. New York: Longman, 1983.

Miller, Casey, and Kate Swift. *The Handbook of Nonsexist Writing: For Writers, Editors and Speakers*, 2nd ed. Lincoln, NE: iUniverse.com, 2001.

Mumby, Dennis. "Power and Ethics." In *Handbook of Communication Ethics*, edited by George Cheney, Steve May, and Debashish Munshi, 84–98. New York: Routledge, 2011.

Munshi, Debashish, Kirsten J. Broadfoot, and Linda Tuhiwai Smith. "Decolonizing Communication Ethics: A Framework for Communicating Otherwise." In *Handbook of Communication Ethics*, edited by George Cheney, Steve May, and Debashish Munshi, 128–29. New York: Routledge, 2011.

Myers, Verna A. *What If I Say the Wrong Thing? 25 Habits for Culturally Effective People*. Chicago: American Bar Association, 2013.

Newberg, Mark, and Mark Robert Waldman. *Words Can Change Your Brain: 12 Conversation Strategies to Build Trust, Resolve Conflict, and Increase Intimacy.* New York: Plume, 2013.

Nicholson, Roger S. *Temporary Shepherds: A Congregational Handbook for Interim Ministry.* Herndon, VA: Alban Institute, 1998.

Nooteboom, Bart. "Forms, Sources and Processes of Trust." In *Handbook of Trust Research,* edited by Reinhard Backmann and Akbar Zaheer, 247–63. Northampton, MA: Edward Elgar, 2006.

Noyce, Gaylord. *Church Meetings That Work.* Herndon, VA: Alban Institute, 1994.

Odell, S. Jack. "Morality: Journalism and Ethics." In *Philosophy and Journalism,* edited by John C. Merrill and S. Jack Odell, 76–106. New York: Longman, 1983.

Opotow, Susan. "Moral Exclusion and Injustice: An Introduction." *Journal of Social Issues* 46, no. 1 (1990), 1–20.

Reid, Clyde. *Groups Alive—Church Alive: The Effective Use of Small Groups in the Local Church.* New York: Harper & Row, 1969.

Robert III, Henry M., Daniel H. Honemann, Thomas J. Balch, Daniel E. Seabold, and Shmuel Gerber. *Robert's Rules of Order Newly Revised,* 11th ed. Philadelphia: Da Capo, 2011.

Robertson, Charles Kevin. *A Dangerous Dozen: 12 Christians Who Threatened the Status Quo but Taught Us to Live Like Jesus.* Woodstock, VA: Skylight Paths, 2011.

Rosenberg, Marshall B. *Living Nonviolent Communication: Practical Tools to Connect and Communicate Skillfully in Every Situation.* Boulder, CO: Sounds True, 2012.

———. *Nonviolent Communication: A Language of Life.* Encinitas, CA: PuddleDancer, 2003.

Rothwell, J. Dan. *Telling It Like It Isn't: Language Misuse and Malpractice/What We Can Do About It.* Englewood Cliffs, NJ: Prentice-Hall, 1983.

Rusbult, Caryle E., Peggy A. Hannon, Shevaun L. Stocker, and Eli J. Finkel. "Forgiveness and Relational Repair." In *Handbook of Forgiveness,* edited by Everett L. Worthington Jr., 185–205. New York: Routledge, 2005.

Samovar, Larry A., Richard E. Porter, and Edwin R. McDaniel, eds. *Intercultural Communication: A Reader,* 13th ed. Boston: Wadsworth Cengage, 2012.

Sample, Tex. *Powerful Persuasion: Multimedia Witness in Christian Worship.* Nashville: Abingdon, 2005.

Sandage, Steven J., and Ian Williamson. "Forgiveness in Cultural Context." In *Handbook of Forgiveness,* edited by Everett L. Worthington Jr., 41–55. New York: Routledge, 2005.

Sawyer, David. *Work of the Church: Getting Jobs Done in Boards and Committees.* Valley Forge, PA: Judson, 1986.

Scheidel, Thomas M., and Laura Crowell. *Discussing and Deciding: A Desk Book for Group Leaders and Members.* New York: Macmillan, 1979.

Scorer, Tim. *Embracing the Prophets in Contemporary Culture Participant's Workbook: Walter Brueggemann Confronting Today's "Pharaohs."* Denver: Morehouse Education Resources, 2012.

Singleton, Glenn. *Courageous Conversations About Race: A Field Guide for Achieving Equity in Schools*. Thousand Oaks, CA: Corwin, 2014.

Stewart, John. "A Contribution to Ethical Theory and Praxis." In *Handbook of Communication Ethics*, edited by George Cheney, Steve May, and Debashish Munshi, 19–23. New York: Routledge, 2011.

———. *Personal Communicating and Racial Equity*. Dubuque, IA: Kendall-Hunt, 2016.

———, ed. *Bridges Not Walls: A Book About Interpersonal Communication*, 11th ed. New York: McGraw-Hill, 2012.

Stewart, John, Karen E. Zediker, and Saskia Witteborn. *Together: Communicating Interpersonally*, 6th ed. New York: Oxford, 2005.

Stogdill, Ralph M. *Handbook of Leadership: A Survey of Theory and Research*. New York: Free Press, 1974.

Ting-Toomey, Stella. "Intercultural Communication Ethics: Multiple Layered Issues." In *Handbook of Communication Ethics*, edited by George Cheney, Steve May, and Debashish Munshi, 335–52. New York: Routledge, 2011.

Ting-Toomey, Stella, and Leeva C. Chung. *Understanding Intercultural Communication*, 2nd ed. New York: Oxford University, 2012.

Tirabassi, Maren C., and Kathy Wonson Eddy. *Gifts of Many Cultures: Worship Resources for the Global Community*. Cleveland: Pilgrim, 1995.

Triandis, Harry C. "Culture and Conflict." In *Intercultural Communication: A Reader*, 13th ed., edited by Larry A. Samovar, Richard E. Porter, and Edwin R. McDaniel, 34–45. Boston: Wadsworth Cengage, 2012.

Ury, William. *The Power of a Positive No: How to Say No and Still Get to Yes*. New York: Bantam Dell, 2007.

Van de Ven, Andrew H., and Peter Smith Ring. "Relying on Trust in Cooperative Inter-organizational Relationships." In *Handbook of Trust Research*, edited by Reinhard Bachmann and Akbar Zaheer, 144–64. Northampton, MA: Edward Elgar, 2006.

Wade, Nathaniel G., Everett L. Worthington Jr., and Julia E. Meyer. "But Do They Work? A Meta-Analysis of Group Interventions to Promote Forgiveness." In *Handbook of Forgiveness*, edited by Everett L. Worthington Jr., 423–39. New York: Routledge, 2005.

Warren, John T. "It Really Isn't About You: Whiteness and the Dangers of Thinking You Got It." In *The Handbook of Critical Intercultural Communication*, edited by Thomas K. Nakayama and Rona Tamiko Halualani, 446–60. Hoboken, NJ: Wiley-Blackwell, 2010.

Wildman, Wesley J., and Stephen Chapin Garner. *Found in the Middle! Theology and Ethics for Christians Who Are Both Liberal and Evangelical*. Herndon, VA: Alban Institute, 2009.

Wilmot, William W., and Joyce L. Hocker. *Interpersonal Conflict*, 7th ed. New York: McGraw-Hill, 2007.

Wink, Walter. *The Powers That Be: Theology for a New Millennium*. Minneapolis: Augsburg Fortress, 1998.

Wolff, Florence I., and Nadine C. Marsnik. *Perceptive Listening, 2nd ed.* New York: Harcourt Brace Jovanovich, 1993.

Wolff, Florence I., Nadine C. Marsnik, William S. Tacy, and Ralph G. Nichols. *Perceptive Listening.* New York: Holt, Rinehart and Winston, 1983.

Wood, Julia T. "Diversity in Dialogue: Commonalities and Differences between Friends." In *Communication Ethics in an Age of Diversity,* edited by Josina M. Makau and Ronald C. Arnett, 5–26. Urbana: University of Illinois, 1997.

Woods, C. Jeff. *We've Never Done It Like This Before: 10 Creative Approaches to the Same Old Church Tasks.* Herndon, VA: Alban Institute, 1994.

Woodward, Gary C., and Robert E. Denton Jr. *Persuasion and Influence in American Life,* 7th ed. Long Grove, IL: Waveland, 2014.

Worthington, Everett L., Jr. "Initial Questions About the Art and Science of Forgiving." In *Handbook of Forgiveness,* edited by Everett L. Worthington Jr., 1–13. New York: Routledge, 2005.

———. "More Questions About Forgiveness: Research Agenda for 2005–2015." In *Handbook of Forgiveness,* edited by Everett L. Worthington Jr., 557–73. New York: Routledge, 2005.

———, ed. *Handbook of Forgiveness.* New York: Routledge, 2005.

Index

187

132; defined, 120; on a global
scale, 127, 155; guidelines, 10, 127,
129; implications, 128; influences,
118–19; issues, 61, 128; practices,
68, 120–22, 126; principles, 120;
responsibility, 118; sensitivity, 127;
standards, 117, 127, 129; study of,
118, 120–21, 127; systems, 121, 156,
173n9
Evanoff, Richard, 73

faith journey, 36, 72, 77, 170n21
Fassett, Deanna L., 139
Ferris, Susan R., 166n9
Finkel, Eli, 93
Fisher, Roger, 167nn28–29, 170n19
Fitzgibbons, Robert D., 86
flexible and adaptable leaders, 38–39,
52
Forest, Jim, 70
forgive and forget, 81, 84, 109
forgiveness: accepting, 88, 108; act
of, 69; apology and, 69, 71, 87–88,
90, 93–97, 111, 138; approach
to, 86, 91, 101, 113; ask for, 70,
88, 92; is authentic, 69, 79, 88,
104; benefits of, 91, 113; capacity
for, 104, 109; is a choice, 84–85,
90; communication of, 88, 98;
components, 84; condemnation and,
81–82; condoning, 85–86, 104–5,
110–11; confession and, 70–71, 84,
87, 90, 93–94, 97, 103, 106, 113–14;
conversion and, 106, 113–14; cost
of, 91; is counterintuitive, 102;
daughter of trust, 69; decision, 83,
90; definition of, 83, 85–87, 89, 112–
13; demands of, 108; development
of, 85; divine, 87; effects of, 83,
86, 108; experience of, 10, 86–90,
94–95, 98–99, 101, 112; face-saving
and, 102; faith and, 107, 114; false,
81, 90, 110, 114; formula for, 81,

89; gift of, 83–84, 90, 104, 106–7,
113; goal of, 101–2; grace and, 83,
104, 106, 108, 113, 129; granting
of, 86, 91, 98, 112; guilt and, 88,
92–94, 109–11, 114; healing hand
of, 94; justice and, 90, 104, 111,
113–14, 173n28; learn to, 84, 89–90;
likelihood of, 85, 89; limits of, 91;
making amends, 84, 90, 94–95;
means of, 83; mercy and, 105; model
of, 85, 89, 91, 112, 114, 172n16;
is multifaceted, 82, 84–85, 89–90,
112; need of, 70, 82, 86, 99, 104,
108–9; offered, 69, 71, 88, 92, 108,
112; of others, 83; outcomes of, 108;
pardon and, 82–84, 86, 106, 110;
peace and, 70, 107, 111, 113–14;
power of, 70, 106–7; practice of, x–
xi, 70–71, 82–85, 90–92, 95, 97–99,
101–4, 107–9, 113–14, 134, 170n20;
predictors, 85, 89, 171n7, 171n13;
premature, 81, 84, 91; process of,
70–71, 79, 82, 86–87, 89–92, 94–95,
98–99, 101, 106–7, 109, 113–14,
172n17; reconciliation and, 90–91,
95, 97–99, 101–2, 106–7, 113–14;
in relationships, 83, 85–89, 91–95,
97–113, 137–38, 156–57; in religion,
83–84; remorse and, 92–93, 97, 110,
112; repentance and, 70, 83–84,
106, 113–14; request for, 70, 87–88,
112; research, 83–84, 88, 90–91, 93,
107; responsibility for, 91; restitution
and, 82–84, 88; self-forgiveness,
86–87, 102, 109–11; shame and, 88,
92–94, 97, 109–11, 114; sin and, 81,
105, 113–14; takes time, 90, 107;
is a transforming process, 69, 71,
83; trust and, 68, 70, 107, 113–14;
types of, 86–87, 112; way of, 103;
withheld, 70, 91, 103, 112
forgiving spirit, 109, 111–14
Fowler, James H., 166n10

~

About the Author

Thomas G. Kirkpatrick is an educator, trainer, writer, and consultant with specialties in interpersonal communication, small group ministries, and conflict management. He is the author of the Alban publication *Small Groups in the Church: A Handbook for Creating Community*. He has been an adjunct professor at the University of Dubuque Theological Seminary, pastor of Westminster United Presbyterian Church, Galena, Illinois, and associate pastor of Little Church on the Prairie Presbyterian Church, Lakewood, Washington. Previously, he was associate professor of speech communication at Whitworth University in Spokane, Washington. He has also served as a campus minister and a program director of camps and conferences. He received his MA and PhD from the University of Washington, D.Min. from San Francisco Theological Seminary, M.Div. from Fuller Theological Seminary, and B.Mus.Ed. from the University of Oregon. His lives with his wife, also a PCUSA minister, in Maple Valley, Washington, and his four children live in Portland, Oregon; Albany, Oregon; Viroqua, Wisconsin; and Snohomish, Washington.

You can reach him at his website, www.tomkirkpatrick.org.